WRITING

for Design
Professionals

SECOND EDITION

WRITING
for Design Professionals

A Guide to Writing Successful Proposals, Letters, Brochures, Portfolios, Reports, Presentations, and Job Applications for Architects, Engineers, and Interior Designers

SECOND EDITION

Stephen A. Kliment

W. W. NORTON & COMPANY

NEW YORK • LONDON

For information about permission to reproduce selections from this book, write to Permissions, W. W. Norton & Company, Inc., 500 Fifth Avenue, New York, NY 10110

Composition and book design by Gilda Hannah
Manufacturing by Hamilton Printing
Production Manger: Leeann Graham

Library of Congress Cataloging-in-Publication Data

Kliment, Stephen A.
Writing for design professionals : a guide to writing successful proposals, letters, brochures, portfolios, reports, presentations, and job applications for architects, engineers, and interior designers / Stephen A. Kliment.–2nd ed.
p. cm.
Includes bibliographical references and index.
ISBN 0-393-73185-5
1. Architectural services marketing – United States. 2. Engineering services marketing – United States. 3. Design services – United States – Marketing.
I. Title.

NA1996.K57 2006
720'.68'8 – dc22   2005054360

W. W. Norton & Company, Inc., 500 Fifth Avenue, New York, N.Y. 10110
www.wwnorton.com

W. W. Norton & Company Ltd., Castle House, 75/76 Wells St., London W1T 3QT

0 9 8 7 6 5 4 3 2 1

For Felicia
Sine qua non

Contents

Acknowledgments

Many people contributed to the birth of this book, knowingly or innocently.

Former deans William Mitchell at the School of Architecture and Planning at Massachusetts Institute of Technology and John Meunier at the School of Architecture, Arizona State University, gave me useful insights into the arcane mores of academic writing and advancement.

Much practical wisdom about the underlying business objectives of writing for design professionals came from Brad Perkins, the late Norman Kurtz, Gene Kohn, Peter Bohlin, Will Bruder, Bill Rawn, Sandi Pei, Chuck Thomsen, the late Arthur Rosenblatt, and many others whose paths have crossed mine over the years.

For enlightening me on the subtleties of writing to global markets, I'm indebted to Leslie Robertson, Herb McLaughlin, and two of Herb's colleagues who have directed his firm's Asian work—Lena Ning Zhang and Ken Minohara.

I also thank the following individuals: the late Tony de Alteriis for sharing with me two mordant letters to the editor of the London *Times* on e-mail etiquette; Rick Bell, Richard Fitzgerald, and Marga Rose Hancock, key chapter executives in the American Institute of Architects, for their practical insights into the workings of a vital profession; Catherine Teegarden, former coordinator for the New York City–based Architecture-in-the-Schools program, who arranged for me to reproduce in chapter 1 examples of clear, unspoiled writing by grade school students; Richard Blowes and Marian Seamans of the Town of Southampton, New York, for making available RfP documents on the town's projected community recreation center.

Special appreciation is due to Dean Ranalli and my colleagues at the School of Architecture, Urban Design and Landscape Architecture at the City College of New York for their support of my work in teaching verbal skills to the students. I further thank former dean Cynthia Weese at the School of Architecture, Washington University, St. Louis, and Assistant Dean William Saunders at the Graduate School of Design, Harvard University, for encouraging me in my teaching verbal skills at their schools.

Indeed, I owe a special debt to my students and former students at those places, as well as to my former editorial colleagues at *Architectural Record*. They contributed to my education more than they can ever realize.

Daughters Pamela and Jennifer are commended for helping me keep in perspective the once explosive issue of gender-conscious language.

I thank Stephanie Mannino, a former editorial colleague at *Principal's Report*, for demonstrating that, in writing, less is often more.

Gordon Bunshaft and Pietro Belluschi separately provided the spur for my embarking on journalism as a career.

Jean Labatut, Don Egbert, Jean Lajarrige, and Bill Caudill have been my mentors at crucial times. They instilled in me standards of clarity in design and writing for which I continue to strive.

I'm indebted to Pat Lambert for skillfully photographing the artwork in the color section.

Finally, this book would not have taken shape without the encouragement and vision of my editors at W. W. Norton, Nancy Green and Andrea Costella.

New York
October 2005

Foreword
by Hugh Hardy, FAIA

Here it is, a Baedeker for the written word. You will find in this volume a guide to all forms of verbal expression—whether printed or electronic—appropriate to the designer's practice. As everyone in the profession knows, words and images are inextricably linked. No matter how compelling their designs, architects and designers are expected to present themselves and their work using words, and all clients express their needs verbally. All the steps that lead to a built environment or a stunning graphic or a well-planned landscape, from concept through realization, require the skillful use of words. Although some professionals use the written language to obscure their intent, believing mystery can increase their allure, such foolishness is quickly dispelled by this volume's terse admonitions: "Keep it Simple," "Be Specific," and "Shun Jargon."

Just as the sensitive designer uses varied visual vocabularies to solve diverse design problems, adept authors choose the forms of written expression that best suit their needs. For instance, proposals require a sensibility different from that employed for brochures. All the relevant styles of text can be found in these pages. In some cases, examples of verbose and opaque communication are contrasted with concise prose that shows how simply ideas can be conveyed. In others, sample letters and documents demonstrate how to write clearly.

Kliment's emphasis upon the reader's need to understand and the professional's need to avoid "designer babble" is typical of the book's calm authority. While some may delight in verbal pyrotechnics, this volume's merit lies in its insistence upon reaching the public, not showing off to one's colleagues. Clear communication and business success are interrelated, and taking these pages to heart cannot help but advance a designer's economic prowess.

Of course a book about writing must itself be exemplary in its use of language, and this volume is a model of lucid prose. Laced with humor, it gently challenges the reader to respect and to delight in the supple language we share. In the pages that follow, good writing becomes not only desirable but also attainable by everyone. This is a splendid and lively primer, an indispensable companion for any professional.

Why Writing Matters: An Introduction

"Let no corrupt communication proceed out of your mouth, but that which is good to the use of edifying, that it may minister grace unto the hearers." (Ephesians 4:29)

In the eight years since the first edition of this book, much has changed in the design professions. There's rigorous activity to use less energy to build and operate structures; innovative procedures to deliver projects; the virtually dominant use of computer technology for marketing and presentations, for developing better construction contract documents, and for improved communication between owners and design team members; increasingly global markets; outsourcing to overseas vendors for some services; and, thanks again to electronic technology, greater freedom in designing and building irregular space and form.

Among the greatest changes, and still on the rise, is the impact of those phenomena on writing and communication. Some of this is welcome, some of it disturbing. On the positive side, I see a general tightening of writing style in conducting the day-to-day marketing and project management business of the firm. The tightened business writing style has been driven in no small way by the nature of on-line communication, whose format thrives on brevity and succinctness.

On the dispiriting side is an embarrassing rise in the verbal obfuscation meted out by designers, critics, academics, and writers as they seek to share their thoughts with colleagues, students, and the general public. This upsurge in obfuscation is harder to explain. It is perhaps due to the geometric expansion in the volume of new high-profile building types such as museums, concert halls, central libraries, and certain campus structures, with many more writers compelled to fashion original commentaries that too often are marked by obscure, invented vocabularies and arcane phraseology.

Yet in many ways the fundamentals of good writing have changed little over the years. A nineteenth-century guide to writing cited in Alan Robbins's 1997 *New York Times* column offered seven ideals of good letter writing. Letters had to be clear, correct, complete, courteous, concise, conversational, and considerate. Not a bad set of principles, when you apply them to today's great host of communication media.

Writing (and speaking) well matters greatly to every design professional and student, as well as to clients, consultants, suppliers of building products,

Many help-wanted advertisements demand some level of communication skills.

and contractors. You write because you want action. You write to a client prospect because you want an interview, or to submit credentials, or to respond to a request for proposals (RfP). You write to current or past clients to be remembered when new projects appear, or to be recommended to other prospects. You communicate with team associates and consultants to keep current projects on track. You contact the media to get your work published, or to have an editor use you as a resource. You connect with your peers or competitors for an alliance, association, or joint venture, or because they serve on selection committees.

As a student, you write well to obtain good grades, or to get a thesis or dissertation accepted. As a faculty member, good writing helps you with promotion or tenure. As a professional, you often must communicate with citizens' groups to get across facts about a project so the project can proceed. You confer, in writing or verbally, with your employees because it's important to have happy campers.

Take a swift look at the help-wanted pages of any newspaper or professional on-line bulletin. Notice the high ratio of jobs that demand some level of communication skills; most of the time employers actually spell it out—e.g., "candidate must possess communication skills."

Effective writing is an unerring career advancer. Review the great range of end products that call for expertise in writing:

Article
Blog
Brochure/portfolio/fact sheets
Design award submittal
E-mail
In-house memorandum
Job application/resume
Job correspondence
Lecture
Marketing correspondence
Newsletter
Presentation
Press release
Promotional or advertising copy
Proposal
Report
Speech
Student assignment
Text on display panel
Web site

Writing categories may also be divided by objective:

Marketing: Proposals. Correspondence. Design award submittals and exhibit boards. Client newsletters. Spoken and multimedia presentations. Press releases. Brochures and portfolios. Standard Form330. Promotional copy. Personal job applications. Text and labels on display boards.

Project-related: Client, project team, and in-house correspondence. Research, feasibility, and planning reports.

Academic Advancement: Faculty reports. Writing for learned journals. Applications for promotion or tenure. Student—Course assignments. Theses and dissertations. Job applications. Design criticism.

Publicity: Approaching the media and getting published. Building descriptions. Technical or practice articles.

Product literature: Direct mail copy. Advertising copy and on-line banners.

Keep in mind several points as you read and use this book.

The medium does have an impact on the message, as the following chapters point out. I keep a quill, an ancient fountain pen, and my old Lettera 22 typewriter next to my word processor. They remind me that the character of the medium helps determine whether the message is (or can afford to be) extensive or succinct, more (or less) legible, in color, illustrated, easily saved, deliberately stored without reading, or promptly discarded.

Remember your audience. The principles I spell out in these chapters are central and necessary, and you can apply them with comfort to anything you write—provided you remember your audience. When addressing a scholarly colloquium on the finer points of stylistic iconography of late–Middle Age cathedral gargoyles, you can risk a higher level of jargon than when speaking to a school architect selection committee that may include a veterinarian, a service station manager, a company CFO, and a head of household. Even when submitting your credentials or delivering a two-inch report to the facilities chief at IBM or to a contracting officer at GSA—all people with, one assumes, a professional background—keep in mind that final decisions typically are made higher up, by top executives and administrators to whom your jargon may be gobbledygook.

I have known architects who claim that part of their charisma is the knack of conveying a bit of mystery about their line of work when speaking to a selection committee or at a community meeting. They are not the only professionals to use this technique. Doctors, lawyers, generals, ministers, even barbers and car salespeople, have been known to invoke this "I know best" ruse. It is not a good technique. We live in the age of the Internet, the Freedom of Information Act, and intense public scrutiny. Frankness, clarity, and honesty are expected of those with special skills and responsibilities.

Remember who *you* are. This book is not designed to spawn a generation of writers whose every letter, memo, or pronouncement is identical in style to everyone else's. One of the qualities that those who hire you look for is uniqueness and personality, and you cannot project uniqueness unless you define your image and that of your organization. Personality will ultimately creep into your writing. Such attributes as hip, formal, cool, folksy, conservative, and kooky will—and certainly should—show through in what you write. I know of one architectural firm that was designing a college facility for a country the head of whose royal house was taking an active part in the project's progress. The firm, known for the informality of its contacts with the world around it, routinely addressed all its prospects and clients with a simple salutation—"Heather:" or "Kevin:", no "Dear." How, then, to address His Majesty? No problem. "King:" The good relationship survived. Another example of such an informal approach appears in chapter 2, pages 38–40.

This book's focus is on the written word, on-line communication, and, to some degree, speech. While multimedia presentations, including animation, are closely connected with written text, the topic's intricacy takes it beyond the scope of the book. Refer to one of the excellent works included in the Resources.

The instructional method I have used in this book consists of narrative text supplemented by examples. Examples are often in the form of real-life scenarios, such as a marketing situation or a school writing assignment, followed by a sample response, and rounded out by comments. Names of firms used in the scenarios are fictitious, except when otherwise stated. Because the design professions are made up overwhelmingly of small firms, many of the examples are geared to modest-sized practices.

Writing should work for you and not against you. For that to happen, certain forms of style, grammar, and syntax (defined as "the due arrangement of word forms to show their mutual relations in the sentence") are known to communicate well, whereas other forms are known to fail. In my years of work at architectural and other design firms, as well as with students, I have come to recognize the difference.

Know your receiver. The nation's most successful firms got there in large part because they deliberately research their clients, then address them in ways that engage the client's personality and temperament. And the best firms carry this off without diluting their own integrity.

Always define to yourself in advance exactly the point or points you want to make, and why. This is a foolproof method to successful communication. Do this, and the rest will flow easily through your fingers into your keyboard and out to your audience.

Finally, be aware that corporate and public clients are consistently appalled by the turgid quality of writing delivered by designers who want to do business with them. So are discriminating deans at the professional design schools, who worry about the level of writing they see among students and especially among faculty, whom students often wrongly look up to as models of clear writing. And the general public continues to wonder why designers, when they write and talk, do not make more sense.

This book is your chance to reverse course, and do yourself some good.

Principles of Writing for Impact 1

The eight principles of good writing that comprise this chapter are designed more as a guide to good writing than as a formula approach. The chapter covers faults that may obscure your meaning, breach the tenets of political correctness, or yield to the temptation to be clever or elegant but not clear.

Every age has its values and its standards. This is as true for writing as it is for sports, nutrition, ethics, and design. The nineteenth-century guide to letter writing cited in the Introduction stated that letters had to be clear, correct, complete, courteous, concise, conversational, and considerate. These are still excellent guides and, given the evolution of writing technology, far-sighted. You can apply them today not only to letters but also to all the other end products of a designer's and student's day-to-day output. Especially "courteous." Courtesy, in the old-fashioned sense of elaborate greeting and sumptuous valediction—the French until recently favored the delectable ending "please accept the assurance of my most distinguished sentiments"—is today more curt, especially in the case of e-mail, as we shall see in chapter 11.

The aim of the eight principles is to serve as an alert for bad sentence forms that obscure your meaning, for word choices that don't fit the level of understanding of your receiver, for human touches that will enhance understanding, and, last but not least, to highlight the advantage of writers who know precisely what they want to say. William Zinsser in *On Writing Well* wrote that it is impossible for a muddy thinker to write clear English.

1. Write as You Would Talk

Many people talk with comfort but freeze when compelled to write. There's an odd but widely held perception that writing is different from speech, that a certain formality is required that differentiates writing from speech. As an editor, I had a letter from an author some years ago who, having told me in one-syllable phrases by phone that his article would be late, followed it up with a letter that included this: "the eventuality of [the article] getting to you in time is problematical." Another writer, urging architects to aspire to greater public respect, wrote that "architects must increase their upward migration capabilities." The perception that writing is somehow different from talking is more at the root of pompous, hard-to-grasp language than nearly any other cause.

Read this example from actual project correspondence.

> Implementation of the schematic design phase will be initiated as soon as proper authorization is received.

No professional would talk this way to another professional. You have to read it twice before the sun of meaning pokes through the clouds. The project manager is merely writing—after perhaps having raised the subject verbally—to say that work will go ahead as soon as a written okay arrives.

Try fixing the sentence, then compare it with a suggested solution. Don't, however, go to the lengths of that brilliant verbal stylist, the late architect William Caudill: "Say 'frog'; we'll jump."

> We'll begin schematic design as soon as you authorize us.

2. Keep Sentences Short

Great eighteenth-century writers often rolled out page-long sentences. It was an era when readers had time to plow through such prose. It was hard to write and authors honed it to a fine skill. Today's design professionals are not in the business of emulating the multipage literary stream-of-consciousness excursions of a James Joyce. The goal today is to keep sentences short. It's easier to make a point clearly if you try not to exceed eighteen words per sentence (this sentence has seventeen words). Avoid cramming in too many ideas—one idea per sentence is plenty.

Read the following example from a proposal.

> Our multi-disciplinary team offers not only capabilities in space programming, site planning, architectural design, structural, mechanical, and electrical engineering, but also provides services in the areas of financial feasibility studies and environmental assessment, as well as in the administration of the construction contract and in the development of post-occupancy monitoring systems, all of which are critical elements in the successful implementation of a viable construction program.

Here the meaning is hidden in a jungle of verbiage. Try to pinpoint the ideas, and make each one into a separate sentence. One solution:

> Our team offers services in several categories:
> - Space programming, site planning, architectural design including construction contract administration, as well as structural, mechanical, and electrical engineering.
> - Financial feasibility studies and environmental assessments.
> - Construction contract administration and development of post-occupancy monitoring systems.

3. Shun Jargon or "Designer-Babble"

Do not confuse jargon with technical terminology. Every profession has its terminology, a kind of shorthand that allows its members to talk with one another without defining every word. Designer-babble is different. Not only does it use technical terms with audiences that do not understand them; it invents words and phrases that confuse the public and may cause even hip professionals to run to the lexicon or throw up their hands in despair. As David Chappell said, jargon "tends to be the last resort of those with nothing much to say."

Acceptable are technical terms such as "decibel," "BTU," "CAD," "lumens," or "pediment." Each describes an object, standard, or condition that could not be stated differently without a long description.

On the other hand, terms such as "space modality," projects that are "either investigative or accommodative," "iconicity," and "contrapuntal juxtaposition" are at best a pernicious effort to invent new terms in hope that they will enter the common language, or are at worst a futile self-indulgence by their inventor.

For examples of unavoidable technical or design terms, see the following list:

BIM (Building Information Model)	floorplate	plenum
blobs, folds, boxes	honeycombing	purlin
brownfield	Howe truss	register (as an hvac component)
BTU	hypocaust	reverberation time
caisson	isometric, axonometric	seismic code
camber	joist	shear
CAD	layer (as in CAD)	shim
capital	linenfold	slump
CMU	lintel	spandrel (historical, contemporary meanings)
corbel	lumens	
decibel	mimbar	
egg-and-dart	mitigation	Vierendeel truss
elevation	module	VOC
emissivity	mullion	voussoir, keyston
English, Flemish, Dutch bond	narthex	web, flange
	oculus	withe
entourage	parging	
FAR	parti	
	pediment	

Now read the following sentence from a building critique.

Colliding volumes provided a convincing contemporary interpretation of spatial transparency, as extrapolated by an axiomatic juxtaposition of superficial tension.

A thought appears to be fighting to break through, but the rest is conjecture. Perhaps the author had in mind the notion that two intersecting building parts were glass-faced so you could see through them (that's the first part of the sentence). The second part is anyone's guess, but it possibly carried the idea that when next to each other, the same two buildings had a bigger impact than when alone. But who can tell?

Here are some other examples of designer-babble. Chapter 7 contains suggested solutions to three examples.

> They are articulating their experiential experience. (refers to a house client)
>
> Justifying [the result] by their contrapuntal juxtaposition. (description of a design)
>
> Projects are either investigative or accommodative. (profile of a firm)
>
> To maintain its cultural, social, and moral value in the face of the media, architecture can no longer rely on its imagery and iconicity alone . . . (excerpt from text accompanying an architect's submittal to a major international competition)
>
> Activating axiomatic topologies of non-nomadic tribal elements . . . have been interpreted within the archaeological context of the site . . . (comment by design award judge)

4. Be Specific

On-line communication and the precision of the computer have little tolerance for the loose and the imprecise. An on-line search can be prolonged indefinitely by not being specific enough. But the need for precision isn't limited to the on-line message; it is a key ingredient of clear communication in any medium. Don't write "bring to reality" when you mean "build"; say "partition," not "divider element"; when discussing a building's security system, someone who might break in is an "intruder," not an "unauthorized level of access person." Avoid inexact space wasters such as "interesting," "impressive," "basically," and "situation"—as in "interview situation." They are filler words and, unless defined, add nothing to your message. Note that use of a vague term where a specific one would work better often stems from vagueness of thought, and in such cases if the thought can be sharpened the words will come.

Consider the following sentence from a proposal introduction.

> The self-contained instructional space—a splendid teaching medium for a specific objective—is simply inadequate for other tasks.

Work on the term "self-contained instructional space," then compare your answer with a solution, below.

> The enclosed classroom, suited to certain types of instruction, simply won't work for other tasks.

5. Keep It Simple

Along with being specific you need to keep your writing simple. Today's client has neither the time nor the patience to wade through seas of murky prose. Whenever construction carries on after strikes by the electrician and sheet metal trades, don't write the client that "circumstances now allow for an effectuation of a resumption of construction." Or why take up space with "optimum" when "best" will do? Here are some other dos and don'ts.

  Don't use:
optimum, initiate, implement, aspirations, maximum, utilize
  Do use:
best, start, carry out, hopes, most, use

> Reluctance to engage expert consultants is often considered under contemporary management practices to be an inefficient utilization of resources.

Fix the above example from a marketing letter. See how your own wording compares with this solution.

> It pays to use consultants.

Or, in a lighter vein,

> "If you have a dog, why bark?"

On occasion, local groups of design professionals agree to write and circulate to clients—especially inexperienced clients—guides to various aspects of the design and construction process. In 1996 the Boston Society of Architects and DPIC, a liability insurance group, prepared a lucid series of such booklets. Topics included fast-track scheduling, value engineering, and the handling of Requests for Information (RfIs) during construction. See the following good excerpt from these documents.

WHAT EVERY OWNER NEEDS TO KNOW ABOUT RFIS

When a contractor has a question about the plans or specifications for a project, a Request for Information (RfI) is submitted to the architect or engineer who created the document. The design professional reviews the RfI and responds to the contractor with the requested additional information or a clarification. The RfI process is a normal and necessary element of the construction phase of a project. It allows the design professional to fine-tune the construction documents by providing answers to reasonable questions from the contractor. When used by competent and well-meaning parties for its intended purpose, the procedure works very well.

ABUSE OF THE PROCESS
The abuse or excessive use of RfIs is another story. Increasingly, some contractors generate unnecessary RfIs at the drop of a hard hat, often when a simple review of the construction documents and other available data would reveal the required information. A contractor who uses the RfI process in this man-

ner is really attempting to unfairly shift its responsibility for thorough document review to the architect or engineer.

Unnecessary Rfls can result from a variety of factors. By far, the most ominous is the contractor who intentionally abuses the Rfl process in order to pave the way for claims for extras and delays.

If the contractor is in a severe time or money squeeze, he or she may look to the Rfl process for financial salvation. The desperate contractor may attempt to build a case for extras and delays by issuing urgent Rfls for every reason he or she can invent. By the end of the project, the total number of Rfls (legitimate and otherwise) may reach into the hundreds or even thousands.

In so doing, the contractor buries the design professional in paper and forces him or her into "unacceptably" long response times. (The infamous Denver Airport project, for instance, reportedly had over 12,000 Rfls filed—many of which were later deemed unnecessary.) This then gives the contractor the pretext to later sue the owner for delays and extras, citing the designer as the cause of the problem. The Germans have a word for it: *papierkrieg*. It means "paper war," or the art of obfuscation by bureaucracy. That's exactly what happens when the use of Rfls is allowed to get out of hand.

I often look back at material written by myself and members of my family in grade school and wonder at the frank, uncomplicated expression of thoughts. So, when I was invited some years ago to view an exhibit of written work and sketches by a group of third-grade children, I hurried over. The show was put on under New York City's architecture-in-the-schools program, sponsored by the New York Chapter of the American Institute of Architects and the New York Foundation for Architecture. I looked to see whether perhaps the next generation knows something that we have managed to unlearn.

I wasn't disappointed. Look at the illustration opposite, sample results of an assignment in which the teacher asked the children to describe a building and what architects do. Note the student's simplicity of language and ability to convey a flood of meaning in very few words.

6. Use the Active Form

The men and women who teach creative writing in our colleges strongly advocate active verb forms to grab and retain the reader's interest. "Jack loves Jane" sparkles; the passive form "Jane is loved by Jack" is dull. The same good advice holds true when design professionals and students write. Apply this advice consistently, and you'll greatly sharpen your impact, as you can see in these before and after examples.

> It is intended that AutoCAD 2005, Form Z-4.0, and 3D StudioMax will be utilized and files plotted to devices using Windows NT Print Manager drivers. *(from a proposal)*

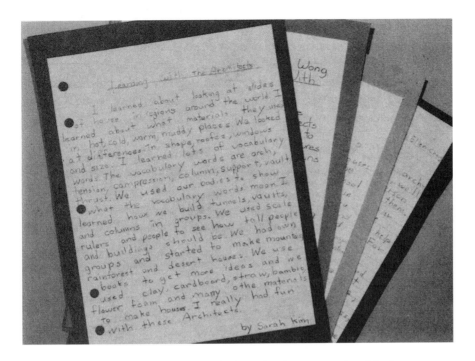

Try turning this sentence around, then check your result with the new version.

> We intend to use AutoCAD 2005, Form Z-4.0, and 3D StudioMax and to plot files to devices using Windows NT Print Manager drivers.

7. Don't Forget People

We are a people-devoted culture. The general media have boosted sales for years by casting their stories around an individual. *People* magazine made an instant hit by focusing its entire contents on people. The professional design media are now taking their cue from this universal human trait, and more and more of their articles, even cover stories, dwell on the personality and performance of designers and their colleagues.

If you intend to capture the interest of a selection committee or a powerful patron, you need to mix in with your writing a generous measure of human references. Clients are more likely to identify with a message if it is styled with people involved, rather than as a dry-as-dust task by an anonymous presence. Avoid this example from a proposal.

> Past costs and schedules on comparative projects are analyzed in order to achieve viable final cost estimates and realistic completion dates.

Try the following instead.

> Jane Smith and her staff analyze past projects to arrive at realistic final cost estimates for your project. Our present management support

staff, lead by George Lopez, review previous job schedules to come up with a feasible schedule for our clients.

8. Know What You Want to Say

An unfailing technique for clear writing is to decide first what you want to say. What is your basic message? Write it down in a single sentence (see some examples below). Test the sentence on colleagues. Break it into its several parts. List them as a progression of points. Is the progression logical? Will the link from one item to the next be clear to the reader or listener? Then start to write.

TYPICAL BASIC SENTENCES

Town's fitness center is designed as community magnet for citizens and
visitors.
4000-student high school is made friendlier by division into eight "houses."
Partner's long-term musical experience enhances firm's qualifications to
design drama school.
Computerized animation lets you judge the landscape design at various
phases of plant growth.

Gender Neutral Language

As recently as the 1960s, anyone who read a report or a pile of project correspondence would have been forgiven for thinking that the design professions consisted entirely of men. Yet more and more women were graduating from the professional design schools, working as designers and becoming principals in firms and faculty and deans in the schools, staffing or heading client facilities organizations, working on construction in the field, and serving as members of selection committees.

The written record showed little evidence of this, however. The language was still peppered with references to *he, his, him, draftsman, workman*. Designers, partners, school board members, hospital administrators, construction workers, and contractors still were referred to routinely as though such jobs were solely in the province of men.

In due course, the consciousness finally broke through that language has to reflect reality, and the reality was that women in growing numbers were working in the design and building industry as active players.

The path to gender-neutral language was anything but smooth, however. Some of the media rapidly established writing guidelines that reflected the new reality; others ignored the problem. In recent years several directions emerged:

Ignore the situation and cover yourself with a statement along the lines of "For simplicity's sake we will use male terminology, with the understanding that this also encompasses females." That is clearly a cop-out.

Every time you are faced with a situation where the possessive form *he/his/him* arises, write *he/she, his/her, him/her* (or even *s/he, her/him*, etc.). This shows good intention, but it is clumsy. Some writers (and speakers) to this day try to compensate for past sins by using the term *she* on all occasions, but this is no better than using *he*. This problem wasn't always so. Some years ago, then-Princeton University provost and later Harvard president Dr. Neil Rudenstine, an English scholar, told me that in Saxon days there was a word that meant *he or she*—an all-gender singular form of the personal pronoun. It atrophied and died. What a pity!

Work around the problem in ways shown below. Opt for a vocabulary that does away with gender-specific references: for instance, make a list of words that through long usage have acquired a male-only or female-only implication, then replace them with words that are gender-neutral.

manpower	*use* workers, human resources
mankind	*use* humanity
manmade	*use* built, synthetic, manufactured
man-sized	*use* large, husky
man-hours	*use* staff hours, hours
manhole	*use* access hole
councilman	*use* council member
fireman	*use* firefighter
eight-man board	*use* eight-member board
salesman	*use* sales representative
cameraman	*use* camera operator
workman	*use* laborer, carpenter, etc.
draftsman	*use* drafting staff (less good: drafter)

(A common point of contention is use of the word "chair" to describe a chairman or chairwoman. I am always embarrassed to hear a person introduced or referred to as a piece of furniture. One is either a chairman or a chairwoman. If you don't know, use "chairperson." My apartment building has a female doorman. Should we call her a "door"?)

Often, gender language carries with it a note of condescension, which you should avoid or rephrase when writing.

career girl	*use* architect, designer, engineer
male nurse	*use* nurse
policewoman	*use* police officer
the fair sex	*use* women
lady of the house	*use* head of household

At times, when use of the singular throws up hurdles, you can draw on a virtue of English grammar that allows you to use the plural. Look at these examples:

> The designer sometimes takes his work home with him.
> *Try:* Designers sometimes take work home.

> The designer should then turn on her computer.
> *Try:* Designers should then turn on their computers.

Every employee must turn in his time-card.
Try: All employees must turn in their time-cards.
Or better still: Every employee must turn in a time-card.

Avoid becoming paranoid over the issue of gender. Indications are that writers in the new generation aren't as skittish as those who grew up a generation ago. Potentially elegant sentences have been butchered on the altar of gender-neutral prose. We read of congresspersons (better: "members of Congress"). Twenty years ago a judge reportedly denied a change of name to a Ms. Cooperman (to Cooperperson) on the grounds that it set a precedent that might lead to a Jackson changing the name to Jackchild, Manning to Peopling, and Carmen to Carpersons.

Partners in design firms and agencies should set a clear policy in the matter of gender-neutral writing. Check first if there is a problem by reviewing samples of recent correspondence, project reports, and brochures. If revisions are in order, develop, circulate, and enforce a simple document based on the foregoing suggestions.

When to Break Rules

When writing, do not let rules or guidelines get in the way of spontaneous expression. If a snappy word, turn of phrase, or rearrangement of material strikes your fancy and in your view adds to the strength or sparkle of your message, trust your intuition and go for it. Mozart was able to rise above the constraints of classical form; why shouldn't you?

For an example of this, see the marketing letter, pages 38–40.

Think of the principles and suggestions in this chapter as guidelines, not as rules. The intent is to trigger in your mind an attitude, not to suggest practices as dogma. With practice, these guidelines will become second nature.

Marketing Correspondence 2

The two principal types of writing—marketing and project—have much in common but also differ in major respects. Both seek to influence an audience; each does it differently. Project writing transmits useful information or instructions; marketing writing sells something—a personal service, a firm's services, a request for a meeting or for data.

Marketing writing follows its own drummer. The next four chapters examine the range of marketing communication most likely to come up in the design firm's day-to-day practice. This chapter tackles marketing correspondence. Chapter 3 covers the brochure and the portfolio. The focus of chapter 4 is on the Request for Proposals (RfP) and how to respond appropriately. Chapter 5 deals with newsletters and other marketing tools.

Marketing correspondence is most commonly triggered by the lure of a commission. Either you are the prime design professional or you are looking to be a consultant to a prime design professional. There are other scenarios. You work in Charlotte and you write to a firm in Chicago suggesting an association on a pending job where you have the home connections and Chicago has the specialized expertise. Or you hear of a project that is to be design-build, and you propose to the designated general contractor and/or owner that you be on the team. Or you want to approach a developer of office buildings with your space planning and interior design services.

The marketing arena, even in a thriving economy, is not designer-friendly. Long lists and short lists of designers are becoming increasingly crowded; designers are being asked to provide more information and pre-agreement services than in anyone's living memory. Firms have to invest growing sums in marketing. (The median today is 7–8% of net billings, including marketing staff costs and direct marketing expenses, according to the 2003 AIA Firm Survey Report *The Business of Architecture*. Staff labor costs typically outnumber marketing expenses by a ratio of 2 to 1.) Yet downward pressures on fees do not always guarantee that these up-front dollars are recouped as profits. Hence, the marketing strategy that precedes the actual writing of the marketing materials is critical.

What actually happens? Your firm, informed of a prospective commission, typically goes through an internal process. The partners meet. A tentative project team is identified, and past firm work, friends in the marketplace, the Web, and other sources are enlisted to size up client and prospects. Is it a real project? Is it funded or likely to be funded in time for design and construction to happen? What is the client's track record in honoring commitments and paying bills? Are competitors out there with an unbeatable lead in the type of work; are they "wired"?

Smaller firms go through this planning process faster than larger firms. On the other hand, smaller firms also tend to spend time and money chasing projects with slim prospects, when they could be massing their efforts on work with more promise or more in line with their experience.

You decide to go for the project. The first item on the agenda is to compose a terrific letter that will bowl over the owner with your skills as a designer, manager, and personality. How do you compose such a letter?

The Marketing Letter

The marketing letter is your first contact. It should not be confused with a cover letter to a proposal. The proposal comes later.

The marketing letter that gets results is best organized in the following parts.

Prospect's name, address: Formerly everything was spelled out, and conservative firms still do so. But in the interest of saving time and space, most firms abbreviate Street (St.), Boulevard (Blvd.), Suite (Ste.). But always use the two-letter state designation (TN, OR).

Salutation: A few firms omit this, but the current usage is still to use Dear, followed by Mr., Mrs., or Ms., or first name if appropriate. The practice, now dwindling, has been to differentiate between women who are married (Mrs.) and those who either are married or single (Ms). Follow the recipient's preferences—if in doubt, use Ms. (The French have solved this puzzle with their usual elegance, using Me. to replace Mme. and Mlle.) If you don't know, use "Dear Heather Wade"—an excellent choice, especially when you're not sure of the gender (Chris, Robin, Leslie, etc.). When writing not to an individual but to a group of mixed gender, *Ladies and Gentlemen* will do—it's surely an improvement over the standoffish *To whom it may concern*. Even better is to use a collective address term such as *Members of the selection board*. Those with a taste for the homespun have been known to use *Folks*. This term is best saved for clients with whom you already have an informal relationship, or cases where you know that the personality of the client fits with such an informal term.

Opening: In your first sentence, get to the point. Why are you writing? What are you asking for? Avoid an interminable lead-in. Today's prospects have neither the time nor the inclination to wade through streams of verbal ore before hitting pay dirt.

Core content: Your audience is looking for evidence that you are the right firm to do the work. This evidence typically consists of the eighteen factors, often called "hot buttons," listed on the following pages. Not all the points mentioned may be germane to your marketing letter, but be prepared because on all of them the client will need answers, if not now, then later. The order shown is a suggestion; let your appraisal of the client determine the sequence of points, and which ones to include.

Questions: You will no doubt have questions as to size, budget, and timing of the project, the nature and schedule of the selection process, and the names of competing firms. Decide to strike a good balance between seeming too nosy too soon and a legitimate need to know.

Your objective: Make it clear what you want out of this exchange—an invitation to follow up with more detailed credentials, an appearance before the selection committee, or more information. Be frank and clear. What you have written will not do you much good if the reader can't grasp the aim of your letter.

Conclusion: Keep it short and upbeat. Leave the impression that you're a good firm to do business with. Be cheerful without being exuberant—spirited, respectful but not ingratiating, enthusiastic but this side of wild-eyed.

Name and signature: Don't type your name if it's printed on the letterhead. You may indicate a file name, but in very small type.

Common Pitfalls

When you review a draft, ask yourself these questions.

• Is the lead paragraph too long before you get to the point? Is the point buried in the paragraph?

• Is the style out of character—yours or the client's? Beware of turns of phrase that are either too glib ("Hey man—we dig this gig.") or too formal ("We beg to respond to your invitation to state our interest in being considered for the design").

• Is the letter too long (or too short) for your message? The initial marketing letter should fit on one page or at most two. If you run out of things to say after half a page, you're probably not telling the clients what they want to know. If you're still at full steam at the end of page two, you risk overburdening the reader with more information than is wanted. If in doubt, get an opinion from an associate.

• Is the material arranged in an illogical flow?

• Is the ending too drawn out?

• Does the ending lack a clear request?

Unless told otherwise, send by mail—and by express mail if you want to confirm delivery. If sending by e-mail, the same rules apply, with a few adjustments as noted in chapter 11.

Hot Buttons: What the Client Wants to Know about Your Firm

Push these "hot buttons." The client needs to know whether your firm:

1. has an understanding of the client's goals and needs. Of all the hot buttons, this is perhaps the most critical. If your research has been on target, you'll know what's right.

2. offers experience in the client's project type. Most clients will require that you have handled their type of project before, whether it's a shopping center or a middle school. This places you on the defensive if the project is your first shopping center or middle school or seismic consultation or public park, but it challenges you to cite similar experience at a previous firm—if you have had it—or to make a strong case for original thinking unjaded by too much prior experience. Think of Eero Saarinen, Jørn Utzon, or Will Bruder, some of whose best work—airport terminals, concert halls, libraries—was done on never-before-tried project types. Highlight your problem-solving ability by citing other work, not necessarily in the client's building type, showing how you tackled certain challenges and resolved them.

3. possesses a record of good relations with prior clients. Offer—but do not at this point enclose—testimonial letters from past clients and/or the readiness of those clients to answer questions about the caliber of your performance. This information can make or break your chances, so make a habit of obtaining such references soon after each job.

4. benefits from a high ratio of repeat business. For prospective clients, the ratio matters and can work in your favor. Some firms point with pride to a repeat business ratio of 80% (out of every 100 jobs on the boards, 80 are for previous clients; or stated another way, of every $1,000,000 in annual fees, $800,000 comes from previous clients). Few firms do that well. Many firms are happy to reach 50%. Clients won't expect young firms to have built up a high ratio, so you need to show a track record in other areas, such as experience in the building type and on-budget and on-schedule completion.

5. retains a high caliber of staff. Point to the education and experience of your workforce, citing project managers you may assign to the job who have experience on similar projects, and what you look for in people before you hire them. You probably won't cite names at this stage, unless asked. That comes later.

6. has received professional recognition. Cite awards, honors, and major publications in which your work has been published. Stick to the most impressive ones; there will be time later to send full listings. If you are a young firm, list awards from previous firms' projects on which you had a role. Be sure to acknowledge the prior firm.

7. has an effective working procedure. Summarize your process how you assemble your team, who is the point of contact with the client, and any special procedures that have worked for you in moving projects forward, such as intensive on-site fact-finding sessions.

8. has good working contacts with consultants, contractors, suppliers, and public agencies. The client isn't buying just your services; your range of contacts that will make up the project team is also in demand.

9. can control project costs. The best way to prove this lies in your record. Avoid glib statements that you believe in accurate estimates and thorough cost management (who doesn't?), and that you have always managed costs. Instead, provide figures—simple in your letter, more detailed as the job-getting process unfolds. In the marketing letter, try a short affirmation that "on the past twenty-eight projects bids came in to within plus or minus 3% of estimates, and those projects where scope didn't change were built to within plus or minus 4% of bids." (The latter is of course as much a feather in the contractor's cap as in the architect's.) Younger firms too can boast good track records, albeit based on a slimmer volume of completed work.

10. can control project schedules. Relay your track record of having met design and production deadlines. Indicate that you operate on state-of-the-art project management software.

11. can manage environmental concerns? Cite experience, when appropriate, in such areas as specification of sustainable materials, products, and processes, and in energy-conscious design. State how many of your built projects have a LEED rating and how many staffers are LEED certified.

12. can manage remotely located projects. A remote site, a remote client, or both, puts extra stress on managing the project. Point to past experience in handling this kind of work, especially on overseas projects. One option, often required by clients in such conditions, is to associate with a local firm. Indicate your readiness to do so.

13. owns and applies state-of-the-art production and office systems. Clients expect their design professionals to run their shops at a level of sophistication at least equal to their own. That requires at a minimum a late version of CAD, animation and visualization software, plus project and financial management systems and extranet project Web sites. Since client prospects on occasion visit their main consultants' offices, attention to the efficiency, congeniality, and style of your workplace can win you points. In a marketing letter, an invitation to visit will suffice.

14. is adequately capitalized. No client wants a consultant who has trouble meeting a payroll. Such cases have been known to occur and do not sit well with clients (the reverse is also true; as noted, check out your client before you go for the job). You are not expected to attach an income statement and balance sheet here, but an indication that your office is solid is welcome. If you are invited later to submit a proposal, a bank reference, if not requested, is certainly in order.

15. has a preferred method of compensation. If not in the marketing letter, certainly at later stages of developing the project the client will want to know your wishes as to the fee arrangement—percentage of construction cost, multiple of labor cost, unit cost, lump sum, or whatever. Chances are the client will have a preference.

16. is available. Does your firm have the capacity to take on this project? A few years ago an architect with a moderate practice of mainly single-family houses was invited to take on the commission for designing a main house, a guest house, and assorted collateral buildings for the wealthy head of a major corporation. The architect had always had a strong conviction for limiting his firm to about twelve people, so rather than staff up for this commission, he decided to risk putting several other client prospects on hold while he took on and completed the new job. Not every designer is sanguine to this degree.

17. has minorities well represented. Most firms make a sincere effort to recruit and hire women and minorities. Some client categories, such as public agencies, make a point of requesting this information.

18. is firmly interested in the job. There's nothing a client—or, for that matter, any buyer of a product or service—likes more than a vigorous appetite for the job. It's a good way to end your letter.

Sample Letters

SCENARIO

You are the marketing partner in an eight-person, eight-year-old firm located in New York City. Your firm has a mixed practice made up mainly of institutional work including small to midsize projects such as schools, community facilities, healthcare facilities, and fire stations. You have learned that the Soames Foundation will underwrite the costs of a community center on a site at West 141st Street near St. Nicholas Park in Harlem, New York City.

The architects will be chosen by a Selection Committee appointed jointly by Community Board #10 and Elizabeth Sanchez, executive director of the Foundation. The Center will house day care, senior citizen recreation, community social functions, staff offices, and a learning center. You have followed up with phone calls to the Soames Foundation, and were told, as the first step, to write a letter to the Selection Committee. The letter will indicate your eagerness to design the project and spell out reasons why you should be considered. List enclosures.

The Selection Committee will review all letters and invite a short list of architects to respond to a more detailed Request for Proposals (RfP) at a later date.

LETTER TO OWNER

Ms. Elizabeth Sanchez
Executive Director, Soames Foundation
347 Nelson Street
New York, NY 10001

Dear Ms. Sanchez:

I write on behalf of Smith, Huang and Abercrombie because we would like to be your architects for the Harlem Community Center.

Your staff informed us that the Center is to include space for day care, senior citizen recreation, community social functions, staff offices, and a learning center. After reviewing your preliminary program, we understand you have the following key concerns:

• The Center should be a magnet for the community, a meeting place for citizens of all ages and backgrounds.
• Construction should employ as much as a possible local labor.
• Construction is to get under way no later than four months from the date you select your architect and must be completed within eighteen months thereafter.

• Your budget is $2 million, to include construction, fees for architects and engineering consultants, and interior furnishings, but not site acquisition costs.

We offer the following qualifications:

• Five years of experience designing buildings and spaces that meet today's demands for an efficient and pleasant environment.

• A 95% track record of meeting clients' schedules (5% accounted for by strikes and unforeseen materials shortages).

• A 100% track record of meeting clients' budgets.

• We have always worked smoothly with local communities and local public agencies and citizens boards which must approve all new construction in this neighborhood.

• We aim for energy-conserving buildings. Over three-quarters of our buildings have received a LEED rating of silver or higher.

• Minorities are well represented on our staff, and 40% of our employees are women, including one partner.

I include illustrated fact sheets of past projects. Note that 75% of projects are for previous clients. Our last two projects involved designing community centers in the Bronx and on Staten Island. Both designs were featured in the *New York Times* and *OCULUS*, the magazine of the New York chapter of the American Institute of Architects. Both centers have become highly popular community gathering places. Our center in the Bronx was awarded a 2006 national honor award by the American Institute of Architects.

Please call or e-mail us so we can tell you more about our firm. Be sure to visit our Web site at www.sha.com for further details about our firm.

Your goals are ambitious but realizable, and we will assign to your program our most experienced staff.

Sincerely,

Ella Braithwaite

Partner

Enclosures: Firm description; eight project fact sheets; reprints of articles showing our work.

SCENARIO

You are Chen Associates, a consulting engineering firm specializing in high-tech structural engineering. The San Diego architectural firm of Lloyd, Oswaldsen and Associates is interviewing structural engineers for a new terminal for Alpha Airlines as it readies its qualification package for submittal to the airline and to the San Diego County Administration. Your practice includes the design of large-span structures using tensile or thin-concrete technologies. Lloyd, Oswaldsen is at this stage undecided as to the structural system for the building, as the program for it is still incomplete. You have worked with the firm auspiciously on previous projects, but so have many of your competitors. Write a letter to Henry Lloyd, partner-in-charge, stating your eagerness to be part of the design team.

LETTER TO PRIME PROFESSIONAL

Henry Lloyd, Partner
Lloyd, Oswaldsen and Associates, Architects
12860 Coronado Blvd.
San Diego, CA 92118

Dear Henry:

I am told that Alpha Airlines is planning to replace its present terminal building at San Diego International Airport with a new terminal. We at Chen Associates are eager to be part of your design team, and this letter is to highlight the benefits Chen will bring to such an association.

As you know, we have worked together on other projects, such as the La Jolla Stadium. The experience was gratifying for both our firms as well as for the client: the work was completed on time and on budget, and yielded excellent publicity in local and national media.

Chen Associates has made a point of laboring at the cutting edge of long-span technologies, and I'm convinced the Alpha Airlines project is a logical opportunity to break new ground in providing large, uninterrupted, uplifting, and secure space for the tired or jaded traveler.

Despite the "first-time" quality of much innovative large-span work, we have never encountered problems of safety, budget, or schedule, during either construction or occupancy. That's due in large part, we feel, to the high quality of our engineering design and project management staff and the currency of our computer design software. Our financial management software has allowed us to pinpoint costs related to structure up to the last moment before projects are sent to bid; on the past twenty projects we have been within an average of 4% above/below bids. Our computerized construction contract/document system is, if you recall, compatible with yours, thereby cutting the risk of errors to a minimum.

If selected, we would assign our most experienced designers to the project, including Fawn Carvalho, who worked with you on the La Jolla Stadium.

Please tell me what additional credentials I can send you to strengthen your submittal. We have a striking PowerPoint presentation, printed four-color descriptive sheets, a twenty-minute video of the La Jolla and Las Vegas projects, and an animated CD-ROM on our firm.

I'm excited at the unique opportunities contained in this work, and hope we may resume our previous fine relationship.

Kind regards,
Louis Chen
Principal

COMMENT

Note that this letter is more concise than the Braithwaite letter, because the writer knows the recipient and has worked with him before.

SCENARIO

Unlike the Chen letter, which is from a structural engineer to an architect for a specific project, the following letter is from a consulting mechanical and electrical engineering firm sending a letter to architects with no special project in mind. Compare the two letters. This is an actual letter and does a laudable job in pinpointing the firm's strengths. (The recipient's name and address have been changed.)

LETTER (GENERAL)

George Porter, AIA
3500 Fifth Avenue
New York, NY 10000
Re: Mechanical & Electrical Engineering Services

Dear Mr. Porter:

We are a consulting engineering firm and would like to enlarge the circle of our clientele. This letter is intended to introduce us to you.

Our office has practiced consulting engineering for more than forty years; we have designed over three thousand mechanical/electrical systems and installations for office buildings, office tenants, shopping centers, department stores, apartment houses, hospitals, and schools.

There are approximately forty people on our staff in the New York headquarters; we have maintained for the past thirty years a European branch, operating out of Paris, and also a branch in Parsippany, New Jersey. Our offices are divided into four departments: Heating and Air Conditioning, Electrical, Plumbing, and Computer. These departments comprise an integrated engineering office capable of handling all phases of mechanical and electrical design, as well as material quantity forecasts, economic feasibility studies, engineering-oriented sections of landlord-tenant leases, and energy conservation criteria development.

Presently most of our drawings are done on AutoCAD Release 2005. We also have computer systems that permit us to analyze the economy of operations, available energy sources, and maximum-investment returns. We have developed a method that permits proceeding with the tenant space design before the tenant layouts are finalized. The computer keeps track of the construction phase, too: documents, quantity of material used, and percentage completion.

Our forte is economical design, in terms of initial investment and operating cost. Furthermore, thanks to the integrated and computer-assisted design operation, we can produce the work most speedily, while maintaining the highest quality.

We would like an opportunity to meet with you at your convenience to present our expertise in more detail.

Very truly yours,

Sidney W. Barbanel, P.E.

SCENARIO

Albinoni Contractors, Inc., has invited four architectural firms to submit credentials for a design-build project. Albinoni will select one of these firms as part of its team to promote the new 200,000 sq. ft. central public library for the city of Indianapolis, budgeted at $60 million. The award hinges on a bond issue to be voted on nine months hence, but the city wishes to sign up the design-construction team earlier so the team can play a part in promoting the project. Albinoni has used design-build on medium- to large-sized building projects over the past eight years, mostly institutional work such as educational and healthcare facilities. Its record for delivering on time and on budget has been good, but sporadic cases have been reported where design members of the team have been unduly pressured to change design concepts and product specifications to save money. Your firm, O'Shaughnessy & Cohen, has previously designed libraries, and you have worked in the public sector but not on any design-build projects. You feel winning this project will open up new opportunities for you in the library facilities market and as a profit-making participant in future design-build ventures. Write a marketing letter to John Albinoni, CEO, whom you have met briefly at various civic lunches but with whom you have not had a professional relationship, requesting to be his architect and head of the design team.

LETTER FROM DESIGN-BUILD TEAM LEADER

John Albinoni
President, Albinoni Contractors, Inc.
4 Elm Street
Indianapolis, IN 46206

Dear Jack:

My firm would like to join yours to form an effective design-build team that will win the contract for the new central public library for the city of Indianapolis.

We understand the city intends to select a design-build team to carry out the work, and plans to do so by April 30 in order to give voters a chance to scrutinize the various teams' proposals before they vote on the bond issue in November.

Therefore, we see it as critical to develop a design package, cost estimates, project delivery schedule, and accompanying marketing materials that will impress the voters with the benefits they will receive through construction of the new library.

Our firm is well equipped to help you reach this objective:

• We have designed in the past eight years four public libraries of over 150,000 sq. ft. each, for Louisville, Sacramento, Gary, Indiana, and Youngstown, Ohio, as well as smaller but technically advanced libraries for school districts in those cities, and for the Kincaid School in Houston. These libraries were built on budget, and all were delivered on time except for the high-school library in Youngstown, which was delayed four months due to bankruptcy of a major supplier.

• The four public libraries attained instant acceptance in those cities, yielding several favorable reports in the local press and TV media, as well a write-up in the annual library issue of *Architectural Chronicle*. We can send you visual materials, including videos, CDs, and several PowerPoint presentations to demonstrate the kind of materials we are able to place before the voters.

• Over the years we have often appeared at public meetings to make successful presentations to community groups. We have videotapes of such sessions should you wish to see them.

• We have worked steadily over the past ten years with a small group of highly skilled, dependable professional consultants in structural, mechanical, electrical, and civil engineering, with landscape architects, as well as with two of the nation's most eminent lighting designers and an acoustical consultant in wide demand. These consultants know our procedures for delivering contract documents, and we know theirs. The result will be a smoothly operating team that will mesh well with your own staff.

• We have a record of cordial relationships with general contractors, and will be glad to send you a list. They will tell you that we always combine fresh design thinking with a realistic eye to its cost implications. Indeed, we respect value engineering and believe that it is possible to combine quality design with rigorous management of costs and schedules.

• Our in-house CAD and computerized project and financial management software will allow us to link with your systems to maintain a high level of communication with members of the design team and with your own staff. I invite you to visit our offices so you can see the advanced state of our design and production systems.

We welcome your suggestions as to the best type of contractual arrangement between you and our firm. Please visit our web site, www.osc.com, for greater detail, including links to animated tours of facilities we designed.

We look forward to being part of your team. This is a special opportunity for both our firms.

Sincerely,

Maurice O'Shaughnessy

Partner

Enclosures: List of clients (past five years); fact sheet of completed libraries.

COMMENT

Note that this letter extracts from the list of hot buttons those that differ in focus from a more traditional contract with a traditional client, especially a concern for value engineering, costs related to scope, management of the design team, and ability to produce on a fast schedule.

SCENARIO

The following was an actual project and letter (the recipient's name and address have been changed). The writer's firm was one of two still in the running for the commission to tackle the planning and construction needs of a county school system in south Florida. It is clearly not the first correspondence between writer and receiver, but it packs a wealth of marketing savvy and a unique arrangement into a tight space. The superintendent of schools had asked the two finalists to submit a convincing document to accompany his recommendation for an architect to the county school board. The writer, the late William Caudill of the firm then called CRS Associates, had known the superintendent for years and was able to adopt a decidedly informal tone. The letter recaps the firm's understanding of the issues in a fast-growing school district that already had an inventory of inadequate schools.

LETTER TO OWNER

John Brown
Superintendent of Schools
Broward County
1 Coconut Avenue
Fort Lauderdale, FL 33302

Jack, I've done my homework:

A. WHAT YOU HAVE

1. The Board of Public Instruction of Broward County, Florida, is operating on the advanced edge of primary and secondary education—individualized instruction, team teaching, and ITV being the major educational methods used.

2. Recently constructed elementary and middle schools most vividly show in no uncertain terms manifestation of the team concept, which appears to be synonymous with the "open plan" idea.

3. Broward County schoolhouses make up a 3D history of education in this country, ranging from the forty+-year-old two-story mission-type schools through the self-contained finger-plan multilateral lighted schools, to the compacted open-plan EFL-inspired plant. Broward busted the box.

4. There are not enough schools to go around, even by busing. Double sessions are inevitable unless drastic management and technological changes are made to deliver schools at a faster rate.

5. The new schools are going up too slowly to take care of rapidly increasing enrollment, and, in some cases, rather wastefully—overhangs that protect

neither people nor windows, unnecessary geometry for small auditoriums, false structural expressions, and mansard "roofs" that are not roofs. Unfortunately, the new schools lack the amenities—those human values which the 1926 Northside Elementary School possesses.

6. The old schools need both air-conditioning and functional conversion. For example, the self-contained classroom—a splendid teaching tool for a specific job—simply will not do for another task (team teaching), like a cotton-picking machine is no good for threshing wheat.

B. WHAT YOU SHOULD HAVE

1. For one thing, you need better schoolhouses to match your fine curriculum. The school—the most important and expensive machine for learning—either helps the teacher teach or gets in the way. The old schools deter. Broward County's commitment to high-quality education is a commitment to high-quality facilities.

2. You need faster ways to plan and construct schools, such as fast-track, critical-path, and system building.

3. You need more economical ways to beat rising construction costs and inflation, making use of techniques mentioned above, plus sophisticated programming that separates "wants" from "needs," pares the "fat," and sets up early computerized cost controls. You need to work fast with effective teams of many specialists.

4. You need to supplement local talent/experience with outside expertise that can help the school board, the superintendent, and his staff initiate these new ways—better, quicker, and more economically—to provide those urgently needed high-quality facilities.

5. Overriding any one of the methods suggested is the need for a high-level centralized team to motivate and manage the school planning/construction program that brings into full play the coordinated efforts of users, designers, manufacturers, and builders. Such a management team must be systems-oriented, must have the sensitivity to human values as related to the physical environment, and at all decision-making times must have empathy for the child and the teachers.

C. HOW YOU CAN HAVE WHAT YOU SHOULD HAVE

1. You need outside talent/experience—a team of experts whose members are highly competent in both system building and management of planning/construction programs.

2. You asked if our team is qualified and available. We are on both counts.

3. Availability? Say "frog," we'll jump.

4. Qualified? We are twenty-four years old, a team of highly competent specialists. Baltimore (public schools), Hartford (public schools), New York (higher education); each can vouch for high professional performance of our team concerning the aspects of management. Texas (mental health), Merrick, Long Island, and SCSD [School Construction Systems Development] substantiate our experience in system building.

5. People? Consider these members of our team [there follows a listing of seven individuals with experience in school building systems development, school design, project management, research, fast-track construction, and building technology].

If you want to take quick action (you need to), pick up the phone anytime and call [lists phone number]. Talk with either me or [my assistant] Jan Smith, and be assured we will schedule two or three key staffers (specialists in management and system building) to fly immediately (on us) to discuss our services—scope and cost—with you, your staff, and your board.

You wanted action. You got it.

Bill (William W. Caudill)

Reproduced courtesy of the CRS Group.

COMMENT

Some of the references to then state-of-the-art school education concepts are dated, but the letter is a fine example of sparkling yet spartan, staccato writing, effective salesmanship, and an upbeat ending. Note the generous and effective use of "you" compared to the more self-serving "we"—this letter contains only six "we's" but a convincing sixteen "you's"!

Marketing Letter for Firms Just Starting Out

As a recently organized firm, you cannot fall back on a long list of completed projects, honors, awards, and clients. Instead, you need to focus on work in which you took an active part as an employee of another firm; highlight outstanding school work; mention travel and foreign languages where appropriate; show a solid grasp of CAD-based design, animation, and production; and vaunt the fresh look and enthusiasm brought to a job by designers with modest experience but a solid mastery of the design process.

SCENARIO

You have learned that the Washington County school district is looking for architects and interior designers to convert a 500-pupil, thirty-year-old open-plan elementary school into enclosed classrooms, and to rejuvenate an obsolete wiring and communication complex into a modern, broadband system that will accommodate emerging electronic instruction techniques. Here is one way to write your letter:

LETTER

Ms. Nefertiti Jones
Superintendent of Schools
Washington County
1 Elm Street
Middletown, AR 70000

Dear Ms. Jones:

I recently visited Polk Street Elementary School, and I agree the facility needs urgently to be modernized to make way for the progressive teaching techniques you have planned for your school district. This includes above all the enclosure of classrooms and a wiring and communications network and capacity that will allow you to access the wealth of resources on the Web.

I believe that my firm, Izumi Associates, can make this happen.

Before starting my own firm in 1996, I worked for six years as a designer and project manager at Perkins & Will in Chicago. While there I was lead designer or project manager on four elementary and two middle schools, all with educational demands similar to yours. Half the schools were new, the other half renovated. Of these schools, two were published in the *Architectural Chronicle* and received honor awards from the American Association of School Administrators, the Chicago Chapter of the American Society of Interior Designers, and the Midwest region of the American Institute of Architects. Those client references are yours for the asking.

My firm offers both interior design and architectural services. You need excellence in both fields to achieve your goals.

As you select architects and interior designers for your three-firm short list, be aware that Izumi Associates, while not a large or old-line firm, offers you several advantages. You secure the solid professional background of its staff, our firm's close physical presence twenty minutes from the site of Polk Street School, and a state-of-the-art computer-aided design, presentation, and production system. This will allow you and your colleagues to preview the various design schemes in three dimensions.

If selected, we are also ready to present, at your request, the design schemes to parents and teachers in the community.

Please visit our Web site, www.izu.com.

Sincerely,

Donald Izumi, Partner

Enclosures: Six project fact sheets.

For the special challenges found in communicating with overseas clients, see chapter 16.

Following Up the Marketing Letter

When and how to follow up on a marketing letter can be a puzzle. Contacting a nonresponsive prospect calls for firmness and tact. Chances are the client's silence is for reasons out of the client's control; or the decision has not been made or has been postponed; or a decision has been made but is not to be disclosed at this time. It makes sense to initiate the follow-up sequence with a mild phone call on the lines of "I'm calling to follow up on our letter (or presentation) of June 12. Is there more information you require?" This commonly reveals the status of the decision. When testing the lay of the land this way, begin no less than two and no more than three weeks from the time you mailed the original letter or made the presentation.

If voice-mail messages begin to pile up unanswered at the client's end, send a letter or e-mail on the lines of "We are still interested and look forward to your decision." If that doesn't work, a more outspoken letter may be in order, such as the one following.

SCENARIO
Five weeks after your firm, Bruyère and Ivanov, made a proposal for the Pontefract Laboratories' new clean laboratory building, and after two follow-up phone calls and no response, you resolve to write a letter.

LETTER A

Dear Dr. Pontefract:

We have not succeeded in reaching you by phone to discover when Pontefract Laboratories may be expected to reach a decision in choosing an architect for the proposed clean laboratory building.

We are anxious to hear from you as we have pending commitments to which we must assign staff and resources we had planned to reserve for your project.

We were glad for the chance to share our qualifications with you, and we continue to hope for your response. We'll be happy to deliver any added information you may need.

Sincerely,

Peter Ivanov

COMMENT
If this doesn't work, save your hounds for a more promising fox.

If the answer is that you haven't made the cut or that the work has been assigned to another firm, a gracious response is vital and can serve to ferret out the reason the client went to another firm. Some firms request and often receive helpful pointers over the phone on why they weren't chosen. Most firms include a mild pat on the back for the successful competitor.

LETTER B

Dear Ms. Kenworthy:

We were disappointed not to have been chosen to design your new sculpture museum, but thank you for your helpful feedback on why we were not chosen. We believe that Gómez and Partners whom you selected will do a fine job for you.

We enjoyed the chance to show you our work, and we look forward to another opportunity to work with you.

Sincerely,

George Oban

Partner

Never burn your bridges.

3 Marketing Brochures and Portfolios

The brochure and the portfolio are your ambassadors. Whether each is printed, on a CD-ROM or videocassette, or appears on your Web site, it represents you when you cannot appear in person, when the client prospect doesn't find it convenient to meet you face to face, or, in the case of the portfolio, when the client is looking at your work and not at you, even though you may be sitting across the desk.

Let's first define terms. The brochure is a text-and-illustration aggregate of your firm's qualifications in design, project management, and technological know-how. It is used as a pre-interview submittal or as a post-interview leave-behind. It is posted on your Web site. The portfolio is an illustrated album of an individual's work, usually intended to advance an applicant's cause for competition, admission to graduate school, or hiring.

The Brochure

The brochure conveys to an audience your firm's vision and professional record. How you build your brochure depends to a large degree on how you respond to certain questions.

Marketing intent. Is the immediate purpose of the brochure an initial overture to a client prospect? Supplementary matter to a proposal? A leave-behind after a verbal presentation to a client? A device to entice the media? A joint venture partner? A tool to attract gifted job applicants? All of the above?

Shelf-life. What shelf-life is reasonable before changes in projects, services, and people make the printed version obsolete?

Tactics. Will a fat and complex brochure place you at a disadvantage compared to a leaner but more sparkling and less formidable package by your competitors? Or vice versa?

Focus. If your current marketing target is a college dormitory, why clutter up a brochure—and the client's time—with pictures of mid-rise office buildings, hi-tech manufacturing facilities, and children's science museums?

Best medium. Do your chief prospects prefer to soak up their information from the printed page or through another medium, such as the Web?

Budget. How large is your budget?

Inventory of completed projects. If you are an emerging firm, how large is your inventory of completed projects?

The days are gone when a single, bound brochure had to satisfy every need. In this fast-paced age, the single, printed brochure is obsolete the day it leaves the press. A brochure—and from now on I use the term to mean any system of prepared promotional materials about your firm—has to be tailored to the demands of your marketing plan.

To construct a brochure, develop a series of modules for assembling into a package targeted at a specific selling situation. The modules should be brief enough so they can be updated simply and cheaply; this beats updating and reissuing an entire brochure. A "brochure" posted on a Web site avoids most of these concerns, and is far simpler to update. (On the minus side, some clients may not yet be organized to look for and/or absorb Web-posted brochure information. High-resolution graphics, such as photographs, may take too long to download if the client has a dial-up connection to the Internet.) Following is a listing of key brochure modules.

Firm description and vision
Project fact sheets
Services fact sheets
Staff resumes
Client liaison process
Client listings
Past project listings
Publications and honors listings
Article reprints

Web-Based Brochure

What separates the Web-based brochure from the printed brochure is not so much the writing as the organization, although it is risky to downplay the importance of clear writing on the Web site, where it is easy for a frustrated visitor to scroll beyond a particularly obfuscated passage—and, if there are too many of those, simply log off and visit a competitor's site.

Here are dos and don'ts when planning or revising a Web site for your firm:

• Do not think you can take your printed brochure and simply post it lock, stock, and barrel on your Web site. Instead, think content and arrangement through from the ground up. (That doesn't mean you cannot use text and pictures from your print brochure—chances are that most of them are stored electronically anyway, and you can edit the text. Decide whether resolution of the pictorial material is high enough to use on the Web).

• As noted, avoid large files, because you do not know how many of your prospects have narrow bandwidths and slow modems. These days most companies are connected by DSL, cable, or T1 lines, where downloading is quite rapid. If you have qualms about a significant segment of your clientele being equipped to view or download large files, break them down into smaller files, or compress them using zip software.

• Provide a response mechanism. Clients and prospects should be able to link to further detail, such as staff resumes, project descriptions, and posted reprints of published articles. Encourage clients to respond directly to you with queries (another use of such a feature is for job applicants to complete a form and submit it to you on-line—see chapter 8).

• Updating. Never let the Web site get out of date; keeping it *au courant* says reams about your firm; so does the opposite. A weekly update is usual.

• The benefit of a Web-based brochure is that you can show information without limit, and in a wide range of formats. These may include animated building walk-throughs and various forms of representing projects, before and after completion.

• The key to good client Web reception lies in navigation, the path provided as the visitor moves in, forward, sideways, or back again. Choices include a guided tour, with or without shortcuts; multiple choices; or a mix that may comprise guided subsections, such as all your healthcare facilities projects or all your LEED-rated HVAC consulting work.

Adapted in part from remarks by Nancy Yen-Wen Cheng, University of Oregon.

Your Web-based brochure, thanks to its graphic nature, depends less on the written word than does a printed brochure system, which allows you to read and turn pages at leisure. Writing for the Web brochure has tighter demands:

Keep it brief. There's no place for long lead-ins. The only place on the web brochure calling for an extended text is your vision statement and firm philosophy, which is discussed below. Don't try simply to post your printed vision statement on the Web. Break the statement into key points; write tight (check out the Eight Principles in chapter 1). If you see the statement getting too long, try posting a short, one-paragraph distillation, with a hyperlink to the full statement.

Organize project descriptions in problem/solution sequence. Limit yourself to five to eight lines; supplement with image captions.

Even in this day and age creating a viable Web site is still a specialist's job, free guidance from eager Web site software vendors notwithstanding. Check out the consultants and entrust the development to them. Be sure they leave you with an operating manual that your IT director and Web manager can work with.

Firm Description and Vision

This is the place to state your firm's vision, describe your outlook on the world of design and construction and the firm's place in it, point to eminent accomplishments in the past, identify specialties, name key players on the team and their attainments, and provide an upbeat picture of the firm without reading like a press agent's handout. A concise vision statement follows:

Write a vision statement for the "description of the firm" module in your print brochure and for posting on your Web site. The statement must capture what your firm stands for and what you offer better than any other firm. Steer clear of vague, high-sounding declarations; focus instead on specific attributes or accomplishments.

VISION STATEMENT

• First, we create a building that identifies with its use. We work to develop an idea with you as to "what the building is." What will the building be used for? Who do you want the building to attract? Based on its use, can we create a building that epitomizes that use?

• Second, we work with the client to develop a palette of building materials that will create an appropriate image. For example, if the image of a client is known to be strength and longevity, then we may use materials that make the building feel solid and permanent. If a client's image is to be seen as innovative and cutting edge, then perhaps we use materials that explore advances in the technology of building materials.

• Third, we tend to stay away from trends. Architecture and buildings should be timeless. We design today and build for tomorrow. If a building is timeless then it will always exist to tell your story.

©Jay Rimatzki 2002

COMMENT

This statement zeroes in on a specific aspect: how do we work with you to arrive at the right design? It conveys a strong aura of commitment to the client's goals. You may want to add a passage on how you handle staff diversity, the environment, sustainability, and other concerns, or you can bring those matters up in later discussion.

Perhaps add material on how you organize projects for good client liaison, or you can place this in a separate module (see page 52).

Keep this piece to two pages or less. Illustrate it with a few good project shots—for atmosphere only—and perhaps a view of your offices with staff at work. Showing headshots of principals is two-edged: it risks making the piece instantly obsolete if the partner leaves (easily fixed on a Web brochure); and if a member of the selection committee has a thing against men with beards, for example, you may have a strike against you.

Project Fact Sheets

One fact sheet per project makes it simple to assemble only those projects needed to impress a selection committee. Select significant projects (completed where possible)—buildings, furniture, interiors, master plans, landscape designs, graphic design and wayfinding systems, exhibits, and product designs. Charge someone in the firm with the task of assembling the key data about each project as soon as it's completed; it will smooth the effort of writing the fact sheet if project data are recorded before the project manager starts on a new project and lets the facts slip into oblivion. In the project folder, include photography and the simplest, clearest drawings available.

If your firm specializes in certain building types or consulting services—sports facilities, for instance, or tensile structures—develop a one-page cover sheet with two or three paragraphs describing your specialty, or develop an independent brochure on sports facilities or tensile structures. For the Web, set up a link to each specialty.

Whether printed or slated for your Web site, the fact sheet should contain the following parts:

Headline.
Description, as brief as the size of the project allows, stating the problem and your design solution.
Endorsement (excerpt from a flattering letter from a client, or a published media comment) (optional).
Statistical box score (area, cost, major materials, structural, mechanical, electrical, and communications systems, LEED rating). Make concise, as this type of information may not make exciting reading for the client (optional).
Credit box (names of clients, architects, engineers, interiors and landscape architects, other consultants, photographers, your firm's project team leaders).
Photographs (interior, exterior) with one-line captions and photograph credits.
Drawings (site plans, floor plans, landscaping plan, axonometrics if not so intricate as to be unintelligible, computer-generated models.)
Firm's contact person or telephone/fax/e-mail data.

See the following examples of headlines and project descriptions.

PROJECT FACT SHEET A

Science, Music & Technology Building
Buckingham, Browne & Nichols School
Cambridge, MA

The new classroom building responds to the village character of BB&N's Lower School Campus, and its sensitive setting in a residential area. The "house" offers four classrooms for science and technology, a large new teaching and performance space for dance and music, and a third floor for the lower school community. Outdoor and enclosed porches provide small spaces for collaboration and special projects.

Distinctly contemporary, the new building deploys traditional New England materials: cedar siding, slate roofing, and stone foundation walls, but it simplifies their application, and sets the building in the landscape. The interior exposes the construction systems, promoting students' understanding of the building's assembly. The design provides long views to the playing field and the campus, welcoming daylight, natural ventilation and the changing seasons into the classrooms.

From a fact sheet forming part of a brochure on completed institutional projects by Ann Beha Architects. Reproduced by permission.

PROJECT FACT SHEET B

Oak Knoll School of the Holy Child
Summit, NJ

Oak Knoll's 1950s "gymatorium"—a multipurpose space for assembly and liturgical functions, drama and music performance, and physical education—was suffering from problems typical of such facilities: it lacked the appropriate configuration and ambiance of a first-rate auditorium, was too small to be a good gymnasium, and created scheduling nightmares. In implementing our ongoing master plan of the campus, we first created a new freestanding gymnasium for physical education, freeing up the old gymnasium for fewer and more coherent uses. The new steeply raked seating yielded a significant bonus for the school: enough space beneath the sloped seating to allow us to create a large formal conference room.

An accompanying illustration (not shown) carries this caption:

Carpeted floors, fabric-wrapped acoustic wall panels, painted sheetrock wall, and ceiling panels all help control and focus the acoustics, making the auditorium as functionally flexible as it is attractive.

From a fact sheet depicting recently completed schools by Butler Rogers Baskett. Reproduced by permission.

PROJECT FACT SHEET C

MIT School of Architecture

The School of Architecture and Planning is located within MIT's prominent "main group" of monumental neoclassical structures built in the early 1900s. Over the years, the main space—three corridors off a central rotunda—has been virtually abandoned and the facilities of the academic departments were scattered in twelve different buildings. The goal of the renovation is to reunite the academic departments, studio, and review spaces and to create a coherent identity for the school on the three floors within this main group.

By reconfiguring the space around the dome, the renovation unifies the critical mass of studio and review areas, creating a symbolic new "heart" for the school. The new plan creates an ambulatory around the dome where exhibitions, a café, and design reviews enliven the space with views to dome coffers.

In addition, the relocation of two of the corridors to a position adjacent to a windowless attic wall creates large, windowed studios and one continuous orienting view through exhibit and studio display areas.

Between the gallery and studio, new roll-up doors offer flexibility for students to expand either the studio space or the review space. The new studio spaces are fully wired for computers and sophisticated telecommunications, with power supply and network connections at every student desk, and provision to upgrade the network as more advanced technology becomes available.

A new exhibit, thesis, and conference space is developed in the departmental office wing around a huge volume containing Frank Stella's 1994 mural *Loohooloo*. The 97-foot long, 3D, acrylic-on-molded-fiberglass painting completely encompasses a new conference room from floor to ceiling, creating an exciting visual environment.

From a fact sheet by Leers, Weinzapfel Associates. Reproduced by permission.

PROJECT FACT SHEET D

Puget Sound Air Pollution Control Authority

The new offices for this Seattle environmental agency are in the two top floors of a turn-of-the-century office building that has been newly renovated. A skylit atrium was created to provide an organizing central element. Open work areas, a library, and conference rooms surround the atrium, and get natural light from it. A new connecting stair is located in this space, reinforcing the sense of community in the work place. The kites provide a Northwest air motif. The materials and design are direct, bold and clear, reflecting the agency's desire for a high level of design within the parameters of a public agency budget.

From a fact sheet by Paul Segal Associates, Architects. Reproduced by permission.

Service Fact Sheets

If your firm's output is not a tangible product such as a building or landscape, but a service (see list below), consider developing a series of fact sheets that describe each service. Do this only if these services generate enough billings, or are projected to do so in your marketing plan, to justify creating sheets.

Examples of services may include: research, feasibility studies, client facilities inventory and database development, environmental studies, energy conservation investigations, programming, construction management, software development, commissioning program management, and transit planning studies.

In your text, cover these points:

Describe the service.
Tell the client why it's significant (helps the environment, reduces operating costs, speeds construction, enhances quality, improves community participation).

Describe briefly major accomplishments in this service.
Name the partner who directs this service; list major personal qualifications.
Give "how-to-contact" information.
Include endorsement or excerpted quote from a happy client.

Whether you enclose staff resumes with your brochure or with a proposal depends on the circumstances. Typically, brochure resumes comprise one sheet or one screen per significant person. For proposals, transcribe each prospective team member's biodata from your database into a narrative that shows how this person's talents will enhance the job.

Opinions vary on how to organize a person's brochure resume—listing or narrative? chronological order? most recent effort first or last? include a photograph or avoid it? On the whole, the most useful arrangement is:

Name and title.
Snappy sentence or two summarizing person's role and chief contributions in the recent past.
More detailed narrative of person's contributions (start with most recent, and work backward).
Education and licensing (weave into a narrative or list).
Personal information (marital status, children, place of residence, age) (optional).
Photograph (optional).

For a staff resume write-up, see the following example. (See also organization for proposals in chapter 4 and job applications in chapter 8.)

Elena Karageorgiu, Partner

Elena heads the firm's school planning and design services. Since joining the firm in 1998, she has contributed as a designer, and later as an associate and partner, to the planning and design of six suburban and inner-city high schools, three schools for grades K–8, and two facilities for special education. As partner in charge of Powell High School, St. Louis, she devised innovative, economic ways of building flexibility into the school, giving educators the option to apply new teaching methods with minimum need for renovation. On Thomas Middle School in Hannibal, Missouri, she incorporated into the design a simple but effective system for computer access in all classrooms and the resource center. All projects in which she had management input met clients' budgets and schedules.

Before joining Smith, Karageorgiu and Smith, Elena worked for six years at HOK in St. Louis, where she was project manager on several institutional buildings, including schools and small health facilities.

Elena has bachelor's and master's degrees in architecture from the School of Architecture at Washington University, St. Louis, and a master's degree in education from Columbia Teachers College, New York City. She is registered in the states of Missouri, Kansas, Colorado, California, and Ohio, and has the NCARB certificate.

In 2004 she received a special citation from the American Association of School Administrators for her contributions to school planning. School projects in which she took a role have been published in the *St. Louis Post-Dispatch*, *Architectural Chronicle*, and the *American School Board Journal*. She is the author of *Schools and Education: Design Matters*, published in 2002 by Plato Press.

Client Liaison Process

Few items cause clients, new and seasoned, more anxiety than wondering how they will get along with their design professional. For example, what process does the design professional intend to establish to get the design started, and the work completed on time, on budget, at the specified quality, and with minimum friction all around?

Therefore, a page that depicts how your firm sets up the job, who will coordinate it and connect with the client, and what sorts of controls you have in place to manage costs, schedules, and quality are very useful in pursuing a job. (As noted, you may also incorporate this information into the initial firm description page of your brochure.)

As you write the page, avoid peppering it with vapid generalizations about your pledges to place the client first in all things, and vague pronouncements about your commitment to see that the project is built as designed, on budget, and on the money. If you do this, your page will resemble the page of every competitor who hasn't bothered to define the firm's strengths and has fallen back on clichés.

Try writing a 400-word statement about your firm's process, then compare it with the following client liaison statement.

As soon as a new client signs our agreement, Callay Associates appoints an associate of the firm who manages the project from beginning to end, under the overall guidance of a Callay partner. The project manager stays in constant touch with the individual assigned to the project by the client. The partner in charge is on call to the client at all times.

The project manager establishes a schedule for delivering the project, including an estimated completion date, and updates daily schedules with each activity identified with a start and estimated completion date. By monitoring this schedule daily and relating it to key milestones and final completion, the project manager is able to adjust activities and bring added staff and other resources to bear to keep the client's project on schedule.

Callay Associates also helps in organizing the client's staff for making sound, timely decisions. Where appropriate, we bring our design team to the client's site for highly focused planning sessions in which the client's staff and future users participate in reaching design decisions.

The client's budget is a critical factor in our thinking. Like the client, we abhor surprises. From the start, Callay Associates makes sure the scope of the client's project matches the client's budget. If not, we propose alternatives that bring the budget in line. Callay selects products, materials, and construction methods that offer the best performance for the cost, both to buy and to operate. We run frequent cost estimates at all phases of design, using our in-house estimating staff; we also retain outside estimators to check on our work. As a result, on our thirty most recent projects, final estimates have averaged within plus or minus 3.5% of final bids.

Callay Associates operates with a state-of-the-art computerized management system. We produce contract documents on the latest-version CAD software, and routinely share project documentation with consultants at the various phases—and with the client's representative as necessary—thereby reducing the risk of error. On complex projects, we recommend a project ftp site or extranet.

The project manager consults with the client to schedule presentations and to obtain approvals at key phases of the work. After the project is completed, Callay Associates helps clients resolve any post-occupancy issues.

Client Listings

Past clients intrigue future clients. List clients for whom you have done work in the past fifteen years, organized by type of project. In the case of very large firms with vast numbers of clients, make up separate sheets for each building type or project category. Choose clients who are likely to give you a good endorsement, but to add a note of realism do not omit clients with whom there were honest differences and who will be fair if contacted. Provide each client's city, state, and/or country, but avoid names and telephone numbers so as to keep some control over who is being contacted. As a courtesy, inform past clients they are to be on your list.

Past Project Listings

As with client listings, project listings give the client a flavor of the firm. Divide projects into categories. Include the name, location, area in square feet and metric, completion date, and a one-sentence description (such as "first coed dormitory on the St. Paul's campus"). Avoid cost figures—inflation may make older projects seem cheaper than they were; also, does the figure include site costs, fees, fixtures, furnishings, equipment—who knows? Best omit.

On your Web site, where space is not at a premium, you may include more facts and crosslink to project fact sheets and added illustrations.

Publications and Honors Listings

Clients may or may not be interested in books and articles written by members of the firm. Include them if the client committee is heavily academic or the project involves government-sponsored research, where technical review panels are impressed by published works.

On the other hand, every client wants to know what honor awards your firm's projects and its staff have gained, and who has published articles about your work. That kind of third-party endorsement is gold.

Introduce the list sheet with a short statement, such as the following:

The following listings reflect the views of others about our work and our people. The listing is divided into three parts: works written by our members; design honors awarded to our firm (personal awards are listed under each member's resume in another part of this brochure); and articles in the press about our projects or staff. Note that since 1990 Callay Associates has received thirty-two national or regional honor awards for design, and our work has been published at least once in each of the ten professional journals covered in *The Architectural Index.*

Article Reprints

Have the graphic designer of your brochure develop a simple holder for article reprints. Unlike twenty years ago, when magazines came in all sizes, today's magazine formats vary little. This makes it simpler to fit all reprints into one holder. Arrange with the journal's reprint department to fix typos or errors of fact. Most journals recommend waiting until the article appears before ordering reprints (ordering a press overrun ahead of time saves on some costs but creates others). Be sure to check if the journal is able to forward an electronic file of the article so you can link it to your Web site.

Containers and Binders

You may develop three sorts of binders for your brochure.

• A folder made of stiff paper and die-cut pockets. The folder should be big enough to accommodate reprints from standard-format magazines. Some firms cut small diagonal slots into the pocket flaps for slipping in a business card. Typically, you put inserts in the right-hand pocket and your transmittal letter in the left. Large or multidiscipline firms may develop a folder for each specialty, and print the name of the firm and the specialty on the cover. Decide how many pages you are likely to insert, so the folder is neither too stuffed nor too empty. Assume that the client won't reassemble the inserts in the order you planned, so mark the order of each insert with a numeral.

• A mechanical binder with a transparent acetate cover sheet and a plastic or metal spiral or ring binding. You can bind in the transmittal letter, and not have to worry about the inserted items getting lost or wrongly reassembled.

• A permanent binding. You keep fact sheets, etc. in inventory, then select appropriate pages for a specific client or project and bind them permanently between preordered hard covers imprinted with your firm's name. The process is expensive. It may impress some clients with its extravagance, but alienate others for the same reason.

Smaller or emerging firms, with fewer projects to show, fewer articles and awards to their credit, and fewer dollars to invest, have other ways to bring their experience to the eyes of client prospects. As a partner in a young firm with a limited marketing budget, you should decide whether your dollars are better spent elsewhere, such as on increased travel and "sales calls." This may mean more frequent travel to distant interviews, stepped-up bird-dogging, and investment in first-class photography, while reducing the role of printed brochures and similar "indirect" marketing products.

Here are suggestions I give smaller firms for reducing brochure size while still communicating credentials:

• Combine in a single, four-page piece a description of your firm and its vision; how you work internally and connect with clients to keep projects on track; photographic images of two or three significant completed projects with short captions; listings of clients and of previous and current projects (if the list is short, give it more detail); and a listing of published articles. Don't hesitate to include work and activities from prior firms, so long as you acknowledge the fact.

• Insert one-page resume sheets of key firm members.

• Add top-quality prints of selected projects, with short attached descriptions and box score (area, cost, year completed, principal consultant credits, photo credits).

• Add article reprints. These can be expensive for the small quantities you need; some firms order extra copies of the magazine and enclose a copy, with the article marked.

• Review sample texts in the larger-firm brochure discussion above, and use them as guides to develop more concise versions for your own use. Simple brochures can be very effective even for larger firms. I once judged a marketing materials award contest; after looking at a great number of expensively produced brochures, my colleagues and I gave first prize to a clearly low-budget entry consisting of a brilliant, two-page, typed statement printed on the firm's fine letterhead, along with top-quality prints of four recently completed projects, with caption material attached to the backs. It isn't always the dollars that matter, but the insight that puts them to work. See the examples of low-cost projects with impact shown simply through good photographs, with brief captions attached, on pages 102 and 103 (top). Often these images with captions are mailed independently to lists of clients and prospects.

The Portfolio

The portfolio differs from the firm's brochure because it is a personal document. Whether you are applying for a grant or scholarship, for admission to graduate school, or for a job in a firm, you develop a portfolio to strut your work. The portfolio is essentially a one-person brochure.

A design portfolio tends to be heavy on images and light on writing. That doesn't mean that you can ignore the written parts. These may include:

Transmittal letter
Statement of purpose
Descriptions and captions for design images
Resume

The mechanics of designing and producing a portfolio are covered in Harold Linton's work *Portfolio Design* (see Resources).

Student Portfolios

As a student, you will need a convincing portfolio to impress a granting agency or foundation and, above all, the interviewer at what may be your first employer. The core of your portfolio is examples of school work, especially drawings. Unless you elect to drag around full-size examples in a large portfolio carrying case, your drawings will need to be reduced to folder size. This risks losing a lot of detail, so you may have to simplify your full-size presentation drawings so they can be read at a reduced size. If the interviewer is amenable, bring a PowerPoint presentation.

Observe the top design magazines. They simplify routinely; often designers edit out any complexities (such as toilet fixtures; window lines; sometimes even door swings) before sending drawings to the journals. You should go through the same editing process. One way is to scan the drawing into Photoshop, then remove surplus lines. Be sure to select only your best projects. No employer or foundation grants committee has the time or patience to look at every line you ever drew. Make sure your drawings are clearly identified—you may need to write short captions. Identify key spaces with "labels" or a legend.

Then attend to your written material. Even if you present the portfolio in person, include a leave-behind customized letter of transmittal that dwells on your enthusiasm in being chosen, and summarizes (no more than that) your qualifications. Include in this letter what you will presumably be telling the interviewer in person—namely, your purpose in looking for work with the firm or in soliciting a grant from the foundation. Avoid pat generalities; be frank and open. Finally, include your resume (check chapter 8 for ways to write a strong one). Also review chapter 2 for good letter-writing technique.

Proposals $\boldsymbol{4}$

Proposals are marketing tools of the first rank. Clients issue requests for proposals (RfPs) to qualify vendors of design and other services on large or complex projects, and to look for specific qualifications as they seek the right firm to do the work. Clients do not, as a rule, select their design professionals only from proposals, but also do follow-up interviews. Since clients may expect a high number of responses to their RfP, the proposals allow them and their staffs to review qualifications at leisure. The far more time-consuming mode of face-to-face interviews follows once a short list of firms is established.

Writing the winning proposal therefore requires a blend of marketing savvy and effective packaging, made up of focused writing and catchy visuals.

A typical RfP for design services includes a statement of the desired result, a description of the circumstances of the project, the delivery schedule, the budget (not always included at this stage), a detailed description of services required, and instructions to proposers as to the form or format for submitting the response. If there is a point system for the evaluation, it is described here. Some RfPs request a prescribed or "closed" form of response. Closed forms include the federal SF (for Standard Form) 330, described later in this chapter. The format for "open" forms is left to the responding design firm. An example of an actual RfP is shown later in this chapter.

Whether or not to respond to an RfP is a business decision. Factors to consider include the size of your backlog, your proficiency in the design type being solicited, the odds on the work being "wired" to another designer, the reputation of the client, the odds on a long-term relationship, and the size of the fee. (Being "wired" occurs when designers who help the client develop the RfP—because of special expertise—are sometimes rewarded by receiving an inside track in the competition.) The parts of a proposal ordinarily included in the response to an RfP (listed on page 58) comprise a framework. From it we will focus on certain proposal components where the quality of writing is critical and may make the difference between a winner and an also-ran.

A typical proposal comprises the following parts. You may consolidate some parts if the proposal is modest in scope, but be sure all the subject is covered.

Cover
Letter of transmittal (sometimes attached to the cover, sometimes
    bound into the proposal, sometimes both)
Executive summary (or abstract)
Table of contents (for long proposals only)
Statement of your understanding of the problem
Scope of offered services
Organization of the team and reporting relationships
Resumes of key team members, including recognition
Proposed schedule for completing the work
Record of experience on like projects
Firm honors, awards, and publications
References
Fee (if asked; usually sealed)
Other supporting materials (project description sheets, slide sleeves,
    reprints, CD-ROMs, diskettes)

All parts of the proposal are critical. Lists of projects and clients and personnel resumes need to be rewritten from your database and adapted to each
project proposal. Other parts are written from scratch. These include the letter of transmittal, the executive summary, the statement of understanding of
the problem, the scope of services, and the personal qualifications of key proposed team members.

As noted, proposals are often evaluated on a point system, with a total of
attainable points ranging from several hundred up to thousands. Points are
awarded for responses to such criteria as clarity of concept, the proposer's credentials and experience, cost effectiveness of the proposal (unless this is a
design-build project, this is usually deferred to a later stage), and readiness to
meet a delivery schedule.

In addition, there are always special hot buttons that your shrewd reading
of the RfP will uncover, even though the RfP may not list them specifically.

Check out the following selection of potential hot buttons (for an exended
list, see pages 29–32):

Concern for environmental features, such as wetlands
An ironclad budget
Proposer's skill in helping promote project to voters, when a public
    project is not yet funded
Concern over operating costs, including energy conservation
A desire for breaking the mold in design, technical innovation, and urban
    planning
Minority participation
An inflexible schedule (start of school or academic year; space leasing
    agreements; scheduling of major concert or art show)
Ability to handle overseas language and practices
Concern for security

As you scan the RfP, you may discover additional hot buttons. Your response to these must be clearly stated in the executive summary, and kept in the forefront as you write the other parts of the proposal.

The following is an actual RfP. It has been adapted to the format of this book. I have eliminated the part of the request asking proposers also to build and operate the facility and help finance its construction. Read the text and note on a pad any hot buttons that emerge.

Southampton, a prosperous township on the south shore of Long Island, New York, resolved to build a new indoor recreational, health, and fitness facility within the town limits. Following are key selected sections of the town's RfP. A suggested executive summary in response to the RfP appears on pages 65–66. Some numbers have been changed to reflect current prices and schedules.

TOWN OF SOUTHAMPTON
Department of Parks, Recreation & Human Services
Community Recreation, Health & Fitness Complex

INTRODUCTION

The purpose of this Request for Proposal (hereinafter referred to as "RfP") is to solicit proposals for the design of a new indoor recreational, health, and fitness facility located in the Town of Southampton (hereinafter referred to as "the Town"). The Town envisions a centrally located, family-oriented facility featuring an indoor pool and other amenities.

BACKGROUND

The Town of Southampton is uniquely blessed with an attractive physical setting that has fostered a rich and intriguing history of events dating back to the colonial period. Still largely unspoiled by urbanizing influences, Southampton draws its vitality from a unique interdependence of farming, fishing, tourism, and the second-home industry. The community is particularly noted for the varied mix of its people, which includes artists, intellectuals, sports enthusiasts, nationally recognized entertainers, and captains of industry, as well as people who support the above sectors of the community's economy. It is this unique balance between all sector interests that we are striving to retain and enhance.

The Town has a population of approximately 45,000 year-round and 85,000 peak seasonal, or a grand total of 130,000 seasonal plus year-round population. Further, it is believed that as lifestyles change, many seasonal homes will be occupied year-round or for most seasons (e.g., all but winter).

Municipally sponsored recreational, health, and fitness programs are administered by the Town's Department of Parks, Recreation & Human Services.

Town programs cover a wide range of topics, including funding of human services projects, art instruction, nutrition programs, senior clubs, exercise classes, senior adult day care, and educational events. The majority of these programs take place in Town buildings.

The Town also sponsors swimming lessons. Although the Town's waterways are its greatest natural resource, Southampton currently lacks adequate aquatic municipal year-round recreational facilities for its residents and visitors. The Town provides swimming lessons to only about five-hundred of its youth on an annual basis, the Town being limited in this regard to giving these lessons in its natural waterways during the summer season. Of the more than a dozen elementary schools, at least four high schools, and one college located within the Town, not one has a swimming pool.

The Town now seeks to create a complex of size and diversity that encourages interaction, involvement, and vitality among all its people. The continued success of Southampton as a resort depends on a successful planning project that will continue to protect these intrinsic qualities of the Town that create a magnet for regional tourism.

PRIORITIES

The Town invites proposals to provide adequate year-round recreational facilities for its residents. The centerpiece for the proposed complex would be an indoor swimming pool to accommodate swimming lessons, fitness classes, leisurely swimming, and competition. It is important to the Town that the pool be readily accessible at all times to members of the public.

The Town is seeking to establish a complex in size and diversity that encourages interaction and involvement of all the Town's residents. The Town believes that a recreational complex that includes, but is not limited to, an indoor pool, weight training room, gymnasium, and aerobic classroom will accomplish this objective.

[There follows a listing of key spaces, with areas.] Spaces include an entrance lobby suitable for exhibitions and other educational and public activities; a pool to be used for competitive, instructional, and recreational swimming; a weight training room; an aerobics room; a gymnasium; men's and women's locker rooms; and a storage area of approximately 500 sq. ft. to hold equipment, supplies, and miscellaneous items.

Also required is an on-site child-care room. Added later may be an outdoor pool and other facilities adjacent to the recreation complex. The facility will also house the Town's Department of Parks, Recreation & Human Services administrative personnel.

The design of a coordinated community-based services delivery system rests with the community, including the active participation of the community advisory network. This advisory network is composed of agency and individual representatives from across the socioeconomic spectrum of the community.

Proposals will be evaluated on a point system (total 350 points) described below.

GOALS AND OBJECTIVES

The Town has the following objectives for the Community Recreation, Health & Fitness Complex with an overall goal of providing integrated services directed towards youth, seniors, and families:

- To work with families, agencies, schools, citizens, and governmental leaders to ensure effective local community planning, development, and use of resources.
- To facilitate the design of specific integrated services for youth, seniors, and families.
- To facilitate the delivery of integrated services responsive to community needs, in a more cost-effective manner.
- To encourage community health and fitness through the use of recreational facilities in a therapeutic environment.
- To make the facility and its programs available to visitors in order to create a magnet for regional tourism.
- To achieve accessibility to the greatest number of residents and visitors.

BASIS OF AWARD

Proposal Content

- Cover letter. The letter must contain a statement of intent, indicating the proposer's understanding of the project.
- Proposer information.
- Abstract [executive summary]. Please provide an abstract of no more than 300 words about your project. It should address, at a minimum, the items listed below. You may also include other information relevant to the project:
    - who will be served by the project and what is their need;
    - the approach you will take to meet that need;
    - the results you anticipate from the project;
    - the project location.
- Scope of work.
- Estimating ultimate results. Based on the needs of the community, what your project will serve and the service(s) your project will offer, an estimate, in measurable terms, of the performance targets you aim to achieve.
- Project management. Provide a statement of qualifications and resume of each member of the project management team.
- Budget.

EVALUATION CRITERIA

Proposals will be evaluated on a point system, with a total of 350 points available. Criteria include qualifications, experience, past performance of proposer and staff, budget, and overall quality of the proposed approach to the program.

A rapid scan of the above RfP immediately suggests certain hot buttons. These include:

A desire to attract families to the township by offering an attractive recreation facility.

A desire to develop town-owned land.

The goal for the complex to serve as a community focus for the town's diverse constituencies, such as well-to-do business people, artists, and sports partisans, thereby boosting their loyalty to the town that is part of their lives.

Preparation for increased year-round living in this historically summer resort township.

Serving the athletic needs of local schools.

Desire to hike municipal revenues through heightened tourism.

Planning Your Proposal

You have gone into a huddle with your partners, decided that according to criteria noted in this chapter the job is worth going after, identified your project team, composed your statement of the understanding of the client's problem, forged your take on the scope of services you will offer, determined the delivery schedule, adapted the resumes of the team leader and team members to the job, and gathered related project lists and reprints.

When responding to an RfP, avoid the kind of writing that has come to be known as "proposalese." Writing a proposal is no different from writing a letter. Yet some proposals read like a cross between a specification for a space station and an insurance policy. Avoid such clunkers as "the undersigned shall initiate, implement, and finalize the contract documents within a time frame of thirteen calendar months" when you can just as well write "we will complete all contract documents in thirteen months." Good English, as noted in chapter 1, can be made to appeal to many client levels—the level of an Intel technical staffer ("influencer") reviewing a proposal to build a microchip manufacturing facility, or the level of the vice president for facilities or CEO ("decision makers"), whose votes help select the winner.

A proposal is not commonly a contract document. If accepted, the lawyers will enter to convert its provisions into a legally tight contract. This does not, however, excuse loose language in the proposal or designer-babble.

Finally, in your concern for style, don't neglect the whole. There is always the risk, with many staff people in your firm tapped to write and assemble the proposal package, for consistency to be lost in the shuffle. Most firms with an active RfP response program appoint a manager to shepherd the process. It's too easy, in the pressure to complete the whole, to lose sight of the written quality of the parts. Every sentence, diagram, and supporting item must bolster the theme of the proposal. Just as a fine building, park, bridge, or interior has its artistic unity, so a skillfully prepared proposal hangs together as a single, cohesive example of good writing (and good marketing).

In your preliminary huddle, canvass your firm for unique qualifications. For example, if your proposal deals with renovating a large, outdated exterior theater in a big city, make the most of a partner with a lifelong interest in the theater who worked as a production stage manager, has a degree in theater and lighting design, and may even own a stagehand union card.

Appoint a proposal-writing shepherd at the start; this person makes assignments for writing text, assembling illustrations, and making sure that RfP requirements are strictly adhered to. The shepherd should develop a simple critical path pinpointing which activities are pressing. Arrange for fact checking, editing, printing, and binding (some clients, especially public clients, may demand up to fifty copies). If it is to be submitted on-line, arrange for suitably attractive formatting.

Even if you are a very small firm, the process for organizing the proposal is much the same. It is like cooking a meal—some items have longer lead times and need to be caught, bought, processed, and cooked earlier than others. A simple bar chart, with days marked across the top and activities listed down the side, is useful to keep work on target.

If the proposal is to be printed and mailed, do not try to save pennies on the delivery. I know of a firm that shipped an important proposal due in Washington, D.C. at 5 P.M. on a particular Wednesday, and thought it would save money by sending it first-class mail. The proposal failed to arrive, and all the effort was wasted. I have known firms to send a staff member by plane to deliver a proposal personally. When you consider that a proposal may be worth $400,000 in fees, it is absurd to try to save the difference between a $400 plane fare and $4.75 in first-class postage. Yet it happens more often than you would think.

Above all, focus on how to make your proposal stand out from your competitors'. First, offer a clear sense of understanding the client's wants and needs (note the difference—what the client wants may not be entirely what the client needs. It's your job as a design professional to point this out). Second, come through with a clear direction as to how you would go about solving the client's problem. Check and recheck the applicable hot buttons. Third, keep your writing simple; avoid throwing a lot of complex terminology at a client. Why waste effort on brilliant content if the message is lost on the client?

Letter of Transmittal

The transmittal letter is as a rule a short note (no more than one page) to the designated client official. Its purpose is to provide a personal touch to the proposal package, to highlight in a simple paragraph what you expect to bring to the table, and in general to set an upbeat tone for your proposal.

SCENARIO

Write a transmittal letter for your proposal prepared in response to an RfP calling for preserving and recycling a historic courthouse as a step in reviving a decaying neighborhood. Compare it with the following example.

LETTER

Ms. Maria Overton
Contracting Officer
State Facilities Administration
2000 K Street NE
Chicago, IL 60690

Dear Ms. Overton:

Attached is our firm's proposal for services in response to your RfP #98-415 for architectural and engineering services for restoring and renovating the historic Van Buren Building on F Street.

We agree that this project will do much to revive a once eminent city neighborhood while adding valuable office space.

Our proposal presents our firm's ability to make good your goal. George Links, our award-winning preservation architect, will be assigned to the project, backed by a team of experienced specialists, with a single project manager responsible to your designated contact person. You will see from their resumes that they are a creative and experienced group.

You will also find a detailed description of the scope of services we propose. We understand you must move into the renovated building by September 2007, and the proposal specifies how we plan to meet your schedule. We also include an illustrated portfolio of similar projects designed by our firm, including the Hay County Courthouse, winner of an Illinois state design honor award, and a CD-ROM with a profile of our eighteen-year-old firm.

We believe this submittal gives you the information you requested, and that it conveys our enthusiasm for the project. We look forward to introducing our entire team as you proceed with your selection process.

Sincerely,
George Grant
Partner
Grant, Grant and Smithfield

Proposal-writing architects sometimes use the cover letter as a letter of introduction to summarize their take on the project. Here is an actual excerpt from a short-listed proposal for the new San Diego Main Library by the association of William P. Bruder-Architect, Ltd., McGraw/Baldwin Architects, and Manuel Oncina, Architect.

The new San Diego Main Library will be the last large American library to be completed before the start of the new millennium. It must acknowledge the finest traditions of the past in which librarians were the recognized caretakers of knowledge. As the concept of the library is transformed into a space-age platform of technology, librarians will be the navigators of knowledge. Their computers will instantly make the collection available to the entire globe. We will no longer define libraries according to number of volumes, but by megabytes! . . .

While some may see the site covered by a building edge to edge, we see a great landscaped public piazza, an energized entry forecourt over which a library of the future magically hovers as it kinetically reaches out to its citizens. Creating a place of sensual power and public pride will be as important as creating a place which seeks functional perfection . . .

The Library must reach to greet the light of the sun as a distinctive sculptural form of timeless civic presence. The opportunity to create a garden in the sky adjacent to reading rooms and collections is an idea that has much more power than creating a mere roof.

A city's main library is where children come to meet their first books. A main library is a place where a city defines its respect for knowledge. A main library is where young adults discover where their lives will take them. A main library is a place where people go for free entertainment and cultural growth. A main library is a building where everyone wins and memories of life begin.

To conceive a library whose architecture inspires the soul and thrills the senses must be the goal. To build a place of pride, pragmatism, and poetry must be the charge of us all.

This text contains a poetic quality unusual in proposal writing.

Executive Summary (or Abstract)

The executive summary is one of the most critical elements of a proposal. It is read by two categories of people—influencers and decision makers. The influencers—the client's technical staff—go through the entire proposal with a fine-tooth comb and make a recommendation. The top official—the decision maker—is usually a nontechnical person, and is certain to be pressed for time. So keep technical verbiage to a minimum, eliminate jargon, and limit the executive summary to three pages or three on-line screens at most.

Write your executive summary last, after the rest of the proposal has been written and assembled.

Thus the executive summary for the Southampton Recreation, Health, & Fitness Complex RfP on pages 59–62 could read as follows:

We understand the Southampton citizens' goal to attract families by offering an attractive facility for recreation, fitness, and health. Given Southampton's special standing in the Long Island region and its broadly diverse community-oriented citizenry, this project will be another valuable asset in a town already rich in built and natural resources.

Because the population of Southampton varies widely, from a constant base to summer peak population, we believe it is in your best interest for the project to be designed to expand as necessary. Conversely, whenever the population diminishes, the complex must be flexible enough so that portions may be dismantled until the need reappears.

The idea for an indoor pool to accommodate multiple uses is practical, but we suggest that two smaller support pools be added. Very small children, pregnant mothers, elderly people, and the infirm can choose these pools instead of having to swim in the heavily used main pool.

Your budget as it looks now seems to us low for what you hope to obtain. To build 35,000 sq. ft. at $250 per sq. ft. requires $8,750,000, which is considerably higher than your stated budget of $6.5 million. We recommend that you approach sources of added funding at the state and federal levels and in the private sector (we are ready to suggest an array of such sources); you may also phase the scope of the work by building certain facilities—such as the pool complex—first, and others as funding becomes available.

Your projected occupancy date is May 2007. We feel this date is feasible provided you select the design team before March 2004 and you authorize design to get under way immediately thereafter. To further ensure that your dates are adhered to, we propose that project delivery be done on a fast-track or phased basis. This may make for earlier occupancy of the buildings and reduce the interest and carrying charges on construction financing.

Added sections of the executive summary would introduce the key prospective team members, describe project management and leadership, and briefly list your firm's main qualifications.

Statement of the Problem

The statement of the problem is a sign from you to the client that you have captured the essence of the client's purpose in deciding to build. But rather than merely throwing back at the client the exact wording of the RfP, convey and, if necessary, express the client's underlying needs in your own words.

Using the Southampton example, consider this wording (excerpts):

- Despite the abundant waterways around Southampton, which are also the town's greatest resource, there is no adequate year-round municipal recreational swimming facility. Of the more than a dozen elementary, secondary, and college facilities located within the town, none has a swimming pool.
- The proposed complex would encourage greater and better contacts throughout the community, and provide a focus for such contacts.
- The complex will also become a source for additional revenue as tourists and summer families take advantage of its facilities.
- The town boasts a diverse community of artists, artisans, show busi-

ness and media people, academics, and sports enthusiasts. The complex will encourage useful interplay among these groups.

- The main indoor pool is the central component and focus of the facility. It will be used for competitive, recreational, and instructional swimming. To encourage active interest, bleachers should be provided to seat up to 750 people.
- The weight room, aerobic room, and gymnasium are to serve all segments of the community, from infants to the elderly. A child-care room will allow parents or guardians to drop off children so they may use the pool and other amenities.

Other sections of the statement deal with integration of various age groups in the town, the need to run the sports facility under professional guidance, charging modest fees for use, and seeking additional financing through direct investment or fundraising.

Covers

Proposal covers should be simple, legible, devoid of cute graphics, and should clearly list the name and location of the project and the name of your firm.

Standard Form 330

On January 10, 2004 Standard Form (SF) 330 replaced SF 254 and 255 as the official form used by the federal government to procure A/E services. The full name of the form is the New Consolidated Form for Selection of Architect-Engineer Contractors (for "contractors" read "firms."). SF 330 became mandatory June 8, 2004. Whereas the federal General Services Administration and other federal agencies used SF 254 to develop and maintain a database of eligible firms and SF 255 to select firms for specific projects, SF 330 consolidates the two into a single form. State and local agencies have also used the form for screening firms, and private sector clients on occasion adapt it to their own selection procedures.

The new form reflects shifts in A/E practice as it embraces new information technology to create, correct, and transmit contract documents, and the reduced federal agency staffs that must process the forms. Each federal agency keeps up its own database of firms. Fill out a form also for each branch office, defined as "key" offices outside the head office. Highlight examples of successful teamwork.

To download the form, including nine pages of instructions on how to fill it out, visit www.gsa.gov. You have a choice of downloading it in accessible FormNet screen-fillable PDF, or Word format.

SF 330 contains little opportunity for writing, with the following exceptions:

- Section E: Resumes of Key Personnel for this Contract, which calls for one page per person in the form, asking for relevant projects the individual has worked on. Indicate in the brief space available the scope of each project, size, cost, and the individual's role. Keep the text tight, specific, and avoid jargon.

• Section F: Example Project that Best Illustrates Proposed Team's Qualification for this Contract, which allows plenty of space for describing the project (one per page), its relevance to the project being sought, such as scope, size, and cost. Focus on features the project has in common with the client's including related challenges and how your solution solved or exceeded the client's objectives.

Newsletters and Other Marketing Tools 5

The previous two chapters dealt with writing in pursuit of actual projects. This chapter takes up indirect marketing tools such as newsletters, news or press releases, and text for design award submittals and exhibit panels.

The Newsletter

Firms use newsletters either to reach client prospects or, internally, to inform and motivate their staff. The client newsletter is taken up in this chapter. The in-house newsletter is discussed in chapter 6.

The external, or client, newsletter is a helpful marketing tool so long as its content provides value. Avoid the common habit of focusing so much on the firm's in-house activities of little or no interest to outsiders that it reads less like a newsletter and more like a house organ.

The newsletter as a modern medium is a way of reaching people who are strapped for time. It can be fast and economical to produce, is versatile, and lends itself to simple but telling graphics. It is easily posted on a Web site (or e-mailed for optional downloading), thereby avoiding the cost of printing and mailing—although there will always be a demand for a printed version. State-of-the-art desktop publishing, equipped with chart-making and page-making software and a good scanner, can make the entire writing, design, and production process fast, cheap, accurate, and, depending on the graphic design, attractive. But your clients and prospects are not necessarily going to check your Web site regularly to read your newsletter. So you need to use a "push" method such as e-mail or postcards to alert them to a new issue.

What matters is the content. Select topics you can link closely with your firm's objectives but, at the same time, spark the interest of prospects in your marketplace. Give them something of value. For example, an architect or consulting engineer active in environmentally conscious design can feature completed "green" projects, along with a brief article by an in-house specialist. A graphic designer whose focus is on signing (wayfinding) can show a recent directional system for an acute-care hospital or airport terminal, two building types in which it's seldom easy to find your bearings.

Do not confine newsletter content to featuring projects. Your firm's expertise most likely extends to other areas such as technical innovation, urban design experience and construction in deteriorated neighborhoods, unusual performance in managing projects, or designs for safety and security.

Before selecting client newsletter topics, consider the following criteria.

Performance. Does the story show clear evidence of good performance, measured by such factors as user satisfaction, productivity (if a workplace or factory), and design recognition?

Budget, schedule. Did the project meet the owner's construction budget and delivery schedule? What about the maintenance and operating expenditures?

Good will. Was there evidence of good rapport with the owner during design and construction?

Special issues. Can the project be viewed as a symbol of your progressive attitude on such matters as the new workplace, social and design concerns for the sick and the elderly, outsourcing and the special challenges of international practice, the adoption of a state-of-the-art lighting or acoustical technique? If you are a multi-disciplinary firm, consider targeted separate on-line issues on your major specialties.

Topics for a Client Newsletter

The following list suggests candidate topics for a newsletter. Note that every article doesn't have to be about a project. Don't be modest about your firm's other accomplishments, such as public or professional recognition of one of your projects or people, or a senior promotion. At the same time, don't try to make a newsletter do the job of the news release. The news release covers a single event, and is therefore immediate. The newsletter deals with many happenings, and a three-month-old event can qualify.

PROJECTS
Recently completed facility or design (photographs)
Significant commissioned new work (models, plans)
Progress images of a difficult preservation job
Recent feasibility report for a major school district renovation plan

PRACTICE
Example of effective completion of problem-ridden (through no fault of yours) project on time and on the money
Innovative use of CAD software to produce complex project involving a large team of consultants and a many-headed client
Innovative teamwork on a design-build enterprise

BUSINESS
Merger (this story has been preceded by a news release)
New joint venture

RECOGNITION (for a project)

Design award from a client association such as the American Association of School Administrators, the Building Owners and Managers Association International, the American Hospital Association

Design award from a society of fellow professionals and its national, regional, state, and local organizations

Design award from a journal published by the above, or by independent journals with reputable award programs

Significant story about a firm's project published in a design publication or the general media

RECOGNITION (for staff or the firm)

Personal honor accorded the firm or individual members. Limit these to professional activities, such as election to fellowship in your society, and civic activities such as appointments to local or federal panels that deal with the built environment

Major speech to a client organization

ILLUSTRATIONS

Projects (completed, if possible)

People

Tables, drawings, diagrams

Be sure not to let the newsletter tail wag your firm's dog. Four to eight pages is a good length. An on-line newsletter may be longer, since it is easier for the viewer to skip to longer Web-based stories via link buttons and there's no cost penalty. Limit the newsletter to three or four issues a year, or you'll end up an unwelcome presence in the client's mailbox or inbox. A rule of thumb is to send out a newsletter often enough so the client is aware of you, but not so much as to be a nuisance. Supply boxes (❏) next to individual items, so the client can check off items of interest and return that page to you for more information. Or, if on line, create an easy-to-use "submit this question" return e-mail option; you never know when a client is on the verge of launching a new project.

When publishing a newsletter, consider these steps:

Planning. Assemble items that have accumulated since the last issue, rank them according to the criteria discussed earlier, and write up late developments. Rank by news value.

Writing. Keep the style simple and informal (observe the guideposts of chapter 1). Eschew material that smacks of self-hype and does little to boost the client's curiosity about your firm. If you have to work with a submitted text, say from a colleague, edit it rigorously to conform to guidelines for good writing (see chapter 17 for tips on how to edit a text effectively). Headlines should be "active" and specific, and should tell a story—e.g., "Patients, staff, and visitors praise interiors of $100-million teaching hospital."

Illustrations. Photographs need captions—avoid forcing the reader to dig for photo descriptions in the text or deduce them from a minimal caption.

Design. While writing matters highly, your newsletter is no better than the quality of its design. Your in-house or retained graphic designer will know how to express your firm's personality with a fresh, eye-catching, and readable design. Basic standards exist about what colors and saturation percentage allow you to read type comfortably, and how small the type can be before you need a magnifying glass. Never allow graphic quirks to get in the way of a readable newsletter.

The News Release

The news release is an inexpensive way to get the word out to clients and prospects—especially if you use e-mail and/or post it on your Web site—but it takes effort. (It makes sense to retain a professional public relations firm when you want to reach the general or mass media, where you are less likely to have good contacts than among the professional media.)

To do a news release, the topic must be worthwhile. Clients and editors receiving your release are already overloaded with messages, so choose your topic with care. It may be a merger, alliance or joint venture, appointment of a new top principal in the firm, completion of a high-profile project that met contract requirements despite adversity, the award of a highly competitive, high-profile commission, or a new product or service—in other words, a single momentous event.

Timing depends on the event. For nonmedia recipients, such as your client database, timing is less critical than it is for a release sent to the media, which work to deadlines. Consult one of the media directories listed in the Resources for deadlines. Monthly magazines commonly write their news columns at least four to six weeks before their publication dates. It makes more sense to issue the release when the content is ready to be spilled. Some releases still include an embargo date ("Do not publish before May 8"), but few media observe this and the attempt is usually futile.

Finally, don't do a news release if your client has resources and contacts far superior to yours. (Some owner-designer agreement clauses actually give the client the sole right to issue a release. At all events an okay from the client is advisable.)

Be sure to maintain a mailing database broken up into one or more of the categories shown here:

Past clients
Current clients
Client prospects
(The above three groups may be further subdivided by building type. If your firm has a major concentration, such as residential, the list may be further divided by single family, multifamily, assisted living, etc.)

Media
(Media may be further subdivided by various classes of print media, on-line broadcast media, and cable media. For details, see chapter 10.)
Web sites and blogs
Employees
Friends of the firm (A vague but profitable category.)
Your clipping bureau

The news release consists of six parts:

Headline
Contact information
Release date (but see facing page)
Dateline
Text
Supplements

Headline. This should be informative, active, specific, and dramatic. It should not be coy, cute, or corny. Be wary of humor: not everybody gets it; it is a dangerous medium and usually ends up offending someone. Here are examples of poor and good headlines.

Poor:
LARGE OVERSEAS COMMISSION

Good:
CHICAGO'S LAMB ASSOCIATES WINS 20-FIRM CONTEST FOR $200 MILLION MIXED-USE CENTER IN MALAYSIA

Poor:
MAJOR PARK GREENING IS ANNOUNCED

Good:
NEW YORK CITY TAPS ELM & PARTNERS TO RENOVATE OLMSTED'S PROSPECT PARK BY 2007

Contact information. List at the top one or two persons prepared to answer questions. Provide their telephone and fax numbers and e-mail addresses. Since business is done globally these days, make sure these numbers are good twenty-four hours a day.

Release date. Optional. Avoid including data in the release that would cause harm if someone jumps the date.

Dateline. This appears at the head of the first paragraph—e.g., "San Francisco, 31 July 2006." It helps to put the event in the context of place and time.

Text. Place the beef up front. Editors begin to cut long press releases starting from the back. Other recipients, such as clients, often lack the patience to read a release to the end. The five Ws are still excellent guides. In the first paragraph or two try to tell the reader the who, what, where, when, and why of the event. As you proceed, keep adding details until you get to the two-page limit, then stop.

Once you have described the event, the release is a good vehicle for piggybacking some background on your firm, especially relevant projects and other accomplishments. Work in a quote or two by key players—avoid the kind of stiff statement that was obviously written by someone else. On the printed version, double-space the text and leave one-inch margins for use by the client reader or editor. If e-mailed, use the opportunity to link to your Web site and to illustrations.

Supplements. The news release is to whet the appetite with basic relevant facts, not to cover every angle. Supplements can include a couple of headshots, a 3D simulation of the proposed project, a site plan of a development, or a page of statistics. Failing that, state in a final line that such material is available and give a contact number. Avoid loading up the release with supplements—the reader, instead of acting on the release, may just set it aside for further study.

SCENARIO

Your thirty-person firm, Brown & Madison, is about to reach its twenty-fifth anniversary, and you and your partner have picked this occasion to announce the handing over of the firm's reins to a younger group of colleagues. Over the years, your firm has designed and had built a large volume of architectural projects, especially residential work of all types and at all market levels. This has earned you numerous design and firm awards, and you now have a substantial backlog. You, your partner, and several of the designers have received honors, professional and public. You wish to spread the word on the changeover to those audiences the firm must continue to depend on for its prosperity.

Write a two-page (maximum) news release, including headline, contact information, dateline, text, list of supplements, and distribution list.

Note: The hard news is the change in ownership of a well-established firm. Collateral news lies in the firm's goals for the future. You can enhance the bare announcements with relevant facts about the new partners/owners, the firm's reputation, and a quote or two from an outgoing and an incoming partner.

Compare your news release with the version below.

NEWS RELEASE

BROWN & MADISON TO RETIRE, JOHNSON AND KIM TO HEAD FIRM;
HOUSING ARCHITECTS PLAN TO GO GLOBAL,
PUSH DESIGN-BUILD

Contact: Emily Woods, Tel: 994/345-9876, Fax: 994/345-9955, e-mail:
ewoods@bandm.com
Release at will

Denver, 30 April 2006. Dale Johnson and Andrea Kim will be the new principals of the architectural firm known since 1978 as Brown & Madison, partner Harrison Brown announced today. The firm will keep its present name until 31 December 2006; after that it will be known as Johnson, Kim and Associates.

"Skip Madison and I started the firm and built it into a respected residential design firm. I now feel it's time for us to move on to interests we've postponed for years, and let a new generation of architects run the firm," said Brown.

Johnson and Kim said they would expand the firm's scope to pursue overseas work. They felt confident thanks to their own overseas contacts and the presence there of several major clients. They also plan to establish a design-build development arm to capture a share of the growing design-build building construction market.

Dale Johnson, thirty-eight years old, is a graduate of Tulane University and Yale University, and has been with the firm for twelve years. He was the designer for Douglas Houses, a seventy-four-unit assisted-housing development in Colorado Springs. Douglas Houses won an AIA Honor Award in 2004 and several local awards for its concern for energy conservation, livability, mixed-income pricing, and the attractive development of the site.

Andrea Kim, 36, has degrees from Colby College and Yale University. She joined the firm ten years ago. Since then she has forged the firm into an expert design and production machine using a highly efficient network of CAD design, presentation, and project management software. The firm now boasts one of the highest billings-per-technical-employee ratios in the country, according to a survey by BXQZ Research Associates.

"We welcome the challenge," Kim told a gathering of employees last week. "We intend, in association with private sponsors and municipalities throughout this region, to make added inroads into the region's dismal housing picture. We have plans to establish a separate design-build outfit. We also aim to exploit a number of bright chances to work overseas."

Since its founding, Brown & Madison has completed some 75,000 units of housing, from custom-designed to below-market-rate to multiunit. These total over $30 billion in construction value. The firm has won forty-six national and local design awards, and in 2000 was the subject of a major profile in the *Wall Street Journal*. It has also designed public schools, primary-care health facilities, and several courthouses.

Attached: Photographs of Brown, Madison, Johnson, and Kim
Photographs of three completed projects

For more information, including a listing of all past projects,
contact Emily Woods or visit Brown & Madison's Web site at:
http://www.bandm.com/transition

news

BRUCE ROSS ASSOCIATES INC.

FROM:	PARSONS BRINCKERHOFF One Penn Plaza New York, NY 10119
CONTACT:	Bruce Ross Bruce Ross Associates Inc. 212/768-1155

JOHINKE NAMED PRESIDENT OF PB CONSULT

New York, NY—Bruce Johinke has been named president of PB Consult, a Parsons Brinckerhoff (PB) subsidiary that provides management consulting services to developers of infrastructure projects worldwide. He replaces Mortimer L. Downey, who has assumed the role of chairman of PB Consult and will continue to participate in key consulting assignments with the company.

Mr. Johinke has over 30 years of experience working with multidisciplinary teams of developers, investors, banks, government authorities and contractors to develop effective solutions for implementing financially and technically viable infrastructure projects throughout the world. He has managed the planning, design and construction of large-scale projects involving highways, transit facilities, airports, ports, and industrial facilities.

"Bruce Johinke has led large, complex projects in virtually every one of PB's markets," commented Thomas J. O'Neill, PB's chairman and CEO. "After a career spanning international borders and the public and private sectors, he is a natural choice to lead a growing infrastructure advisory practice that is becoming increasingly global in nature."

Mr. Johinke originally joined PB in 1987. He has held senior management positions for the company in Asia, Australia and Panama. Most recently, he served as head of PB Consult's international projects group. He also served as chairman of PB Power Asia Pacific and senior vice president of Parsons Brinckerhoff International.

PB Consult serves clients across the globe in all areas of infrastructure management, investment and development—transportation, water and power, and telecommunications. The firm specializes in the areas of infrastructure finance and economics, management and strategic consulting, systems analysis, business process reform, information technology consulting, public sector policy and program management advisory services. PB Consult is a subsidiary of Parsons Brinckerhoff, an international planning, engineering, program management and construction management organization with over 9,000 professionals and support staff in 150 offices on six continents.

11/30/04 ###

News release by Bruce Ross Associates, Inc. Reproduced by permission.

Distribute as follows:

1. Past and current client lists (attach brief, informal notes signed by the partners).

2. Selected design firms, especially those who need to be reminded of your specialty for a possible association.

3. Media lists (professional design, educational, health care, home building, general news media in Denver and twenty selected cities).

4. "Friends of the firm."

5. Local broadcast outlets (radio, TV).

6. On-line.

For a dexterous news release, see the example opposite.

Following is another example of an actual news release. Note the crisp, fact-filled style.

Industry Alliance for Interoperability;
Enabling Interoperability in the A.E.C.FM Industry

Editorial Contact: Julie Brown, 415-824-1795
News Release
At A/E/C Systems '96

IAI SHOWS NOTABLE GROWTH, ADDS BOARD SEATS AND INTERNATIONAL CHAPTERS; DRAMATIC EXPANSION FUELS GLOBAL ACCEPTANCE OF THE IFC STANDARD

Anaheim, Calif., June 18, 1996—Citing global membership expansion and support for its developing Industry Foundation Classes (IFC), the Industry Alliance for Interoperability (IAI) today announced six international chapters, the addition of three new seats on the North American chapter board of directors, and a membership milestone of more than 250 companies worldwide.

The three new directors on the IAI board are: Bentley Systems–Rebecca Ward; IBM–Scott Sherwood; and Turner Construction Company–David Furth. This brings the number of seats on the board to thirteen, including officers. Other companies holding board director or officer seats are: Autodesk, Inc.; Carrier Corporation; HOK; Honeywell Inc.; Jaros Baum & Bolles; Lawrence Berkeley National Laboratory; Lucent Technologies; Primavera Systems, Inc.; Softdesk, Inc. and Timberline Software Corp.

GLOBAL EXPANSION

The TAI was incorporated as an independent, not-for-profit organization in September 1995, with nine member companies in North America. Since then, chapters have been formed in Germany (German-speaking), the United Kingdom, Japan, France (French-speaking), and Singapore. Other chapters are now being formed in the Nordic region, the Benelux, Australia, Italy and other countries.

Each chapter is managed locally, sponsored by a local company and holds two seats on the International Coordinating Council. The North American chapter is sponsored by Hellmuth, Obata & Kassabaum (HOK), Inc. The German chapter sponsor company is Obermeyer Planen + Beraten; the UK chapter is sponsored by John Laing plc.; Kajima Corp. sponsors the Japan chapter; SAA Partnership Pte. Ltd. sponsors the Singapore chapter; and Ingerop Systems sponsors the French.

MEMBERSHIP MILESTONE

The global acceptance and support of the IAI "has been tremendous," said Patrick MacLeamy, Chairman of the IAI North America chapter board of directors. "Since the IAI was incorporated last September, our international presence has grown from just nine members to more than 250 member companies. This demonstrates that the idea of projects defined using Industry Foundation Classes is truly an international concept that meets a universal need."

In addition to the board members mentioned above, a few of the most recent IAI members in North America are: AIA, AT&T, Johnson Controls, MKS-20/20, Naoki Systems, Trane, Turner Construction, and the US General Services Administration. A complete list of all members of the IAI is included in the press kit.

Twenty IAI members are exhibiting at the A/E/C SYSTEMS '96 show. They are:

Member	Booth #	Member	Booth #
AECS Solutions	# 457/2103	Nemetschek	#409
AIA (Masterspec)	# 701	Primavera	#419
APEC	# 2144	Quickpen	#800
Autodesk	# 741	R.S.Means	#300
Bentley	# 1189/1803/2303	Rebis	#657/2203
IBM	# 182	Softdesk	#781
Intergraph	# 609	Timberline	#541
KETIV	# 560	Trane	#381
MC2	# 2151	U.S.Cost	#500
Naoki	# 741	Visio	#349

The IAI was formed to define, promote, and publish specifications for the IFC as a basis for sharing AEC project information globally, across disciplines and technical applications, throughout a project life cycle. It is an independent, not-for-profit organization, open to all companies in the building industry.

# # #

For more information about membership, the IAI, and the IFC, contact: Executive Director Ken Herold, 1-800-798-3375; fax to 1-314-432-3130; send e-mail to iaiexec@interoperability.com; or, visit the Web site at http://www.interoperability.com

News releases are inexpensive to write, produce, and disseminate. Newsletters can be as elaborate or simple as you wish. Therefore, developing these two marketing tools is not a matter of firm size so much as intent. A young firm with a local clientele can keep its prospects informed of new developments in ways other than the sometimes daunting-looking news release—for example, through postcards and similar methods illustrated in chapter 3, and in the color section. Avoid news releases if the subject matter can't support it. Always ask: If I were a client, prospect, or magazine editor, why should I read this?

Client newsletters, on the other hand, are an efficient way of updating past and present clients and prospects every quarter or so. Tell them only what is useful—whether it deals with wetlands or the new workplace or complying with ADA regulations—not just trivial internal activity. Since newsletters can be brief, even limited to a single page, and are moreover easily moved on-line, even small firms should take advantage of this promotional vehicle. For ways to compose a newsletter, refer to earlier parts of this chapter.

A direct route to fame for professional design firms, school faculty, students, and award sponsors is the design award. Awards trigger publicity of all kinds—magazine articles, newspaper profiles, TV interviews—publicity that has been known to snowball into an avalanche of national recognition.

Now that awardmania, or the uncontrolled expansion of award programs, has come to reign as a cultural icon of our society, there are few creative efforts for which there is not some form of award recognition. Typical sponsors are:

National, regional, and local chapters of the architecture, engineering, landscape, planning, industrial, and interior design societies—at professional and student levels

Federal, state, county, and municipal departments and agencies

Civic groups

Professional, business, and general magazines

User associations such as school and healthcare facility administrators, housing officials, and developers

Building product manufacturers, individually and as trade associations

Corporations or individuals seeking to recognize excellence in architecture or another design field (e.g., the Aga Khan Award for Architecture; the Pritzker Prize; the Carlsberg Prize; the Premio Imperiale; the Stirling Prize)

These groups sponsor award programs of varying quality and distinction. If you resolve to enter your projects in an awards program, do it right.

Plan one year ahead to identify award programs you want to enter. This will help you budget the effort and meet early deadlines. Assess the prestige factor of the award, the prize money, and the caliber of publicity the donor is likely to generate (for example, the U.S. General Services Administration Design

Awards is highly publicized and may even get you invited the White House to meet the president).

Are you prepared? Choose projects with a good chance of success, because readying a winning submittal takes staff time and money. Who are the judges (names are usually published), and what type of work is likely to captivate them? Check out with your staff the innovative features of, say, three candidate projects. Note the "selling points" and incorporate them into your submittal.

Keep it simple. Judges or jurors—"assessors," as they are known in some English-speaking countries—are pressed for time, having other business besides serving on juries. They may have to review one hundred entries in a day. Hence they like to have their submittal presentations short, graphically attractive, and focused on the issues.

As a young or emerging firm, watch for special award programs, magazine features, and exhibits geared to you.

Each contest's rules are set by the sponsor, so you have no choice but to follow the rules. All demand some sort of statement—strictly limited as to number of words—that lets you put the best face on your project. *The best way to structure the statement is to start with the problem and follow with your design solution.* Avoid generalized statements such as "due to the school district's rising enrollment," in favor of the more specific "the district's enrollment has climbed 22% in five years and is expected to rise another 19% by the year 2008." As noted in chapter 1, avoid designer-babble, especially if the jury includes laypeople who will rightly resent having to read statements they cannot decipher. Consider these criteria:

• What is the essence of the project and how does it reflect the values of the sponsor agency?
• If it is a design or graphic product, what are its superior aesthetic, technical, and functional qualities; its success in its physical and historical context; and its preeminence in environmental, social, or operational terms?
• If it is a publication, how should you describe its intent and the degree to which the intent was realized through public or professional reaction?
• How has the article's graphic design contributed to its impact?
• Organize your statement into easy sections, preceded by numerals or bullets, for example:

1. the problem
2. the design solution
3. how the owner and user benefit
4. user response (if you can get it)

Edit brutally; make sure every word pulls its weight. Then proof with care: typos are not in themselves mortal sins, but they betray a lack of attention to detail that may color jurors' perception of your firm's professionalism. Throughout the submittal, worry about credits—are all included? Are they correctly phrased and spelled? Are they to be sealed or left open? Are square feet and dollars correct?

When nominating a completed project for an award or prize—whether a design project or a design-related piece of published writing—the same rules apply. (See the criteria listing, left.)

Some sponsors, such as the Pulitzer Prizes, ask you for a one- or two-page summary of the submittal's contents. This makes sense especially for pieces such as a thick report or a long article series that would take a reviewer too long to read in its entirety.

Follow strictly the submittal formats demanded by the sponsor. This often includes type of binder, but with the growing use of on-line submittals, the process is much simplified and less costly: the toughest requirement tends to be the minimum acceptable resolution—dpi, or dots per inch—of photographic artwork.

The following sample design award submission uses the bulleted organization of sections.

SCENARIO

After reviewing candidate projects for a design award, you and your partners have decided to submit your design for an inner-city mosque for resident and visiting Muslims located at a busy intersection on the East Side of Manhattan. The program is sponsored by the City Club and is aimed at recognizing excellence in architecture, interior design, and landscaping.

• The problem was to create a building that combines religious and educational functions, uses modern materials and systems, and retains dignity within the commotion of a busy New York street. It also had to fulfill the architectural demands of Islamic scripture.

• The design solution was to connect modern building techniques, materials, and finishes with the building's form. The mosque is placed at 29 degrees to the Manhattan street grid so as to face Mecca, the only physical demand in Islamic scripture. The interior is a majestic 90-foot clear span, with a grid of four trusses supporting a steel-and-concrete copper-clad dome. A modern adaptation of Arabic calligraphy is used in lieu of animal ornament, which is forbidden. The space is lit by a circle of steel wire-supported lamps, which were derived from traditional circles of oil lamps. To fulfill its cultural purpose, the mosque is flanked by classrooms, a library, and social spaces.

• The center is a popular magnet for Muslims visiting or living in the city, not only on Friday holy days but throughout the week. It supplements the network of storefront mosques that dot New York's outlying boroughs.

Note: This example is based loosely on the Islamic Cultural Center of New York, designed by Skidmore, Owings & Merrill and Swanke Hayden Connell.

Exhibit Panels

Developing text for exhibit panels is rigorous because the viewer is usually even more strapped for time than design award judges. Therefore, as the late Jean Labatut used to tell his Princeton architecture students, "you must achieve the maximum with the minimum."

Panels are of two types: those showing projects that are already award winners and end up as elements in an exhibit; and boards and panels showing schemes and concepts, such as at a school review.

Completed project exhibit panels are commonly displayed through invitation to award events by professional architectural, engineering, landscape, and interior design societies. These societies allocate exhibit space at their national and regional conventions. So do associations of school, college, and health-care facilities administrators, and other client associations that have trade shows. In addition, community gathering places, including local schools and colleges, suburban shopping malls, and museums, are known as venues for exhibits showing design work.

The challenge is to grab the attention of the walking viewer. The viewer may well be on the way from lunch to a seminar, or heading for the car after a burst of shopping, and must be lured by a beguiling panel. You are also competing for attention with perhaps three dozen other panels. Go for uniqueness without vulgarity. Make it broad-brushed, large, and simple. Select one striking image and make it big. (The core of a panel is the illustrations. Drawings should be simplified, not cluttered with lines that don't add to understanding. Poché walls in black or dark; possibly differentiate circulation from programmed space using different colors or tones of black.)

Now concentrate on text. Write a powerful, active-voice headline—tabloid newspapers such as the *New York Post* or the *Daily News* have much to teach as they pack a maximum message into the fewest words. A dull, static title and long-winded, jargon-filled text drives the viewer to your rival's boards.

Write a succinct, perhaps bulleted, text. Use large type (to decide how large, test different fonts and sizes and see how close you have to stand to the panel to read the type). As with award submittals, state the problem, its solution, its benefits, and (if you have it) its acceptance by the users. Use photograph and drawing captions to reinforce the message of the headline and the main statement. But keep captions brief—three to four short lines maximum.

Review the following example of an exhibit board headline and descriptive statement.

SCENARIO

You have been invited to exhibit panels showing your Energy Services Center at the next convention of the Council of Educational Facilities Planners. You are to develop a headline and descriptive text.

COOL CHILLER: UCLA ENERGY SERVICES CENTER GRACES CAMPUS
AND PLEASES WELL-HEELED BEL AIR NEIGHBORS

- Aging, dispersed, inefficient, pollution-causing network of boilers and chiller units supplied campus hospitals, food services, labs, other functions.
- UCLA decides to build single central plant applying cogeneration, using waste heat to produce steam and added electricity.
- Plant is to supply steam, chilled water, electricity to entire campus, and demands very large single-story site.
- No large site available, so plant had to be split into three stories; also must present friendly front due to central campus location and adjacent wealthy neighborhood.
- Design solution features two heat-recovery generator stacks, resembling old ocean liners. Mid-level screens partially reveal high-tech equipment behind.
- Two shades of brick wall in irregular pattern create lively street rhythm.
- Benefits: site is conserved; air quality maintained; money saved.
- Reaction from campus and adjacent high-income communities of Bel Air, Beverly Hills, Westwood: thumbs up.

Sometimes exhibit panels must display planning or research results that cannot rely on striking photography or elegant drawings. The panels show a process or system of organization that can only be conveyed through text and a few charts and diagrams. Examples could include the outcome of an investigation into energy-conserving building systems, or an innovative management process to control schedules on complex engineering projects.

Attract and hold the panel viewer with bold activity boxes linked to a process path, accented by color and clear type. Avoid cramming in too detailed an analysis—viewers are here to be stimulated, not to take a course of study. If intrigued, they will want more; help them by including a name, phone number, and Web site.

Looking ahead, exhibit panels and boards may well become an endangered species. Some architecture schools separated by continents already link together on-line to solve an identical design problem, with results viewed and judged through digitally-transmitted images projected on screens. The time will come when convention exhibits, often last on showgoers' tight agendas, are replaced by on-line exhibits. Viewers will be able to access them in their hotel rooms, at terminals on the convention floor, or at the office before or after the show.

Competitions

The written portions of design competitions are much like the requirements for design awards submittals, except in one case you're submitting a completed or unbuilt project, in the other a design or design concept from which a jury will select a winner (sometimes a runner-up, too).

As always, in providing the written description that supports your design, use simple words and sentences, avoid trying to impress the judges with obscure or convoluted design terminology, and organize your text in the desired problem/solution sequence. Just as your drawings and models should seek clarity, above all—judges tend to pass over designs they don't immediately understand—so your written material must seek not to test the judges' patience with anything beyond what they need to know to make a decision.

Project Writing 6

Unlike marketing writing, which seeks to persuade, project writing is informational. It is designed to convey information or to resolve a situation connected with a project or the business of your firm. It is the most common form of writing by design professionals.

Project writing consists of the following types:

Correspondence
Planning, feasibility, research, and other reports for clients
Investigative reports sponsored by your firm
Internal newsletters or house organs

Clear project correspondence is the grease that runs the machinery of professional projects, smoothly functioning teams, and happy clients.

Some examples and themes of correspondence are:

Correspondence

Letters
Project manager to client (notify of a change in choice of facing material; schedule a meeting; schedule a site visit by client's CEO; review impact of strike by electricians' union; introduce punch list; notify concerning change order requiring budget adjustment; advise on options for ordering and installing high-school computer system)

Partner to residential client (discuss living room furniture options)

Consultant to prime professional (review impact of floods on landscaping plan; identify discrepancies between the location of structural and mechanical systems; list problems encountered by acoustical, lighting consultants)

Partner to head of citizen review committee (schedule public informational meeting of citizens)

Project manager to consultant (discuss lateness of drawings; explain pending changes in seismic code; demand environmental impact statement)

Office business partner to vendor (letter to legal counsel, accountant, insurance representative, rental agent; order computer software updates, hard-ware, office supplies)

Specification writer to supplier (request to send rep with stone samples; request for added performance data on new product)

Project manager to general contractor (alert over community complaints about site noise; ask about delay in preordering steel frame; confirm schedule adjustments; relay concern over excessive volume of RfIs)

Project manager to team (meeting minutes)

In-house memoranda

Managing partner to staff (significant new commission; new bonus plan; opening of new branch office; promotion)

Project manager to partner (request for added staff; forward, with comment, letter received from client)

Social correspondence

Partner to client (invite to share box at Camden Yards stadium; send "thank you" note for successful fishing excursion or dinner event)

Letters　For letter writing to be effective, it must be geared to the recipient's need to know; adjusted to the recipient's ability to understand it; of a length consistent with the nature of the message; clear; and able to get to the point quickly, then stop.

The informational letter resembles the marketing letter (chapter 2), especially in formatting the name, address, and salutation, and getting to the point. It differs in intent, which is to convey information.

To shape the informational letter, use this format:

Recipient's name and address (see chapter 2).

Salutation (see chapter 2).

Opening. State what you are writing about and why it's important.

Core content. Describe the issue—whether you are dealing with latent community opposition to a neighborhood construction project; a consultant's lateness in supplying drawings; a need to review brick samples due to a change in design; or attaching your comments to minutes of the last job meeting with the client's facilities manager. To make this material jump smartly off the page, consider bulleting your key points.

Decision and marching orders. End by pinpointing what the recipient has to do as a result of the situation you have just described, and by when; what you and your firm must do; what is up to third parties, and who is to notify them.

Brief summary.

Closing. End with a cordial greeting or a cool adiós (as warranted); propose the next contact date; and sign off.

cc/bcc. Whom to favor with copies of your message can be a subtle game of politics. It's a way of enlisting a person's support, for instance, without actually requesting it. On occasion, the identity of those on the copied lists may be more significant than the main recipient. Shrewd, politically savvy writers play this game with great skill. Some take it a step further: in addition to typing "cc" at the end of the letter and listing the names of those copied, they send so-called blind copies, or "bcc." A bcc goes to individuals you want to see the letter *without the knowledge* of the original receiver.

Often a letter is better sent as e-mail. This has a subtle impact on the writing style. For details and tips on etiquette, and when e-mail is more effective than the U.S. mail, see chapter 11.

SCENARIO

You are one of two partners in Gómez and Abernathy, a ten-person architecture and town design firm. You have been hired to renovate a two-block deteriorating area at the eastern edge of downtown Cleveland. Your plan calls for tearing down some dilapidated five-story walk-ups that are still 50% occupied and replacing some of the units with infill housing, building a small clinic, and using some of the new and existing vacant lot space for an outdoor neighborhood gathering area to include benches, plantings, a small playground, and a fountain. The project is now in design development. Due to sloppy communication, the community has not been kept abreast of the plan. While most of the area's citizens hope the project will improve the quality of life, many are worried about the final outcome of the scheme, and a strong anti-faction is emerging.

You decide to approach William Patterson, chairman of a local citizens' group, about convening a town meeting at which you will present the plan and answer questions. You write a letter to Mr. Patterson explaining your idea for such a meeting, and suggesting a site, format, agenda, and proposed participation. You plan to follow up with a phone call.

LETTER

Mr. William Patterson
Chairman
East Downtown Cleveland Citizens Committee
800D Euclid Avenue
Cleveland, OH 44100

Dear Mr. Patterson:

The Cleveland 2000 project for which our firm is the architect and town designer is now in design development. When completed eighteen months from now, it will make for a happier, confident community, preserving what is fine, removing what is crumbling, and adding much that is good, including new hous-ing.

We sense that most of the citizens favor the plan. Our project manager and staff have, however, noted some unease over the final outcome, and a strong anti-faction is emerging.

I am writing to enlist your help. I know that some of the doubts arose because the community doesn't know enough about the project and its impact. May I therefore suggest, with your support, that we convene a town meeting to describe the plan? Citizens will be encouraged to ask questions and share their concerns.

To recap the main features of the plan, the community gains a net of forty-eight housing units, a small clinic, and an informal gathering place including benches, plantings, a small playground, and a fountain. It will lose eight dilapi-dated five-story walk-ups and two trash-filled empty lots. The mayor has approved safe, clean, affordable temporary housing for the families displaced by the construction.

Would you contact the community's leaders and discuss a place and time for the meeting? Please avoid weekday daytime so people can attend without miss-ing work. We will prepare a visual display and demonstration to clearly explain the scheme. We'll also alert those of our consultants who should be present.

I will follow up with you this coming Tuesday.

This is a worthy project that will benefit all concerned. With your help and the right communications, we are confident the community will give the plan the support it deserves.

With best regards,
Henry Gómez, Partner
Gómez and Abernathy
Architects and Town Designers

cc: J. J. Smith, chairwoman, Cleveland Housing Agency
       Amelia DeFiore, president, Ohio Community Foundation
       Herb Green, landscape architect
bcc: Thornton Lee, mayor of Cleveland

A case can be made for dealing with this matter by means of a phone call. If you do it you still need to back up a potentially explosive situation by let-ter.

SCENARIO

On a new elementary school, your firm, Gómez and Abernathy, is embarassed to see estimates rising uncomfortably above the client's budget. You had warned the client earlier that the scope was too ambitious for the budget, but the client insisted on moving forward. You must now share the brutal truth with the client.

Ms. Ivana Kopecka
Facilities Officer
Sandusky School District
1 Acacia Street
Sandusky, OH 44870
Subject: Garfield Elementary School

Dear Ms. Kopecka:

I must tell you that estimates for Garfield Elementary School continue to come in well above your budget for the school. We have worked hard to find ways to bring the costs down. We have explored alternative materials for the exterior wall facing, for the lighting system, for the classroom furnishings, for the cafeteria and gymnasium finishes, along with other options. This effort reduced construction costs to a degree, but we have now pared those costs to a point where any added substitutions will bring the school's quality below the standard you want.

The only option that now remains is to reduce the scope of the project. Please recall we alerted you to this possibility in our initial discussions. We recommend that you revise the scope of the work as follows:

- Eliminate two classrooms and one administrative office.
- Reduce the areas of the remaining office by 10%.
- Erect only the shell of the fitness center, for completion later as funds become available.
- Eliminate all but basic food preparation; instead, bring in meals from outside.
- Postpone landscaping except for paving and seeded areas.

While not an ideal solution, we feel that these measures will bring your school in on budget. More, your district will gain a school that provides a stimulating setting for learning and a new landmark in its neighborhood.

To review this in detail, I suggest that Jerry Smith and I meet with you at your office as soon as convenient. Please call me about a date and time.

With kind regards,
Victor Abernathy, Partner
Gómez and Abernathy

cc: J. Smith, project manager

This letter is courteous, detached, and raises the issue of an earlier warning on the scope-versus-cost issue, without rubbing it in. It shows effort on the architect's part to reduce costs, but holds out for quality.

In-House Memoranda

The in-house memorandum, or memo, differs from standard correspondence mainly in the compactness of its content and form. It is the vehicle commonly used for managing projects in-house and for conducting the firm's internal business such as business planning, accounts, human resources and IT management, marketing preparation, and links with branch offices.

The memo comprises the heading box and the message. Include names of the receiver, sender, and those to be copied; the date; the topic; and a file name or number. Many firms arrange these fields in a template with preset tabs. You merely fill in the information. When developing the message, largely follow the format for letters: explain what the issue is, why it's important, who is being tapped to deal with it, and when. Organize this material in short paragraphs, identified by numerals or bullets.

This type of memorandum is now commonly distributed on-line. For an example of a concise internal memo, read the following.

SCENARIO

Your firm, Knudsen, Carlson, and Knudsen has just learned of a new commission won after strenuous effort. As the managing partner, you decide to let the staff know, hand out the bouquets, and make assignments.

MEMO

DATE: 9 June 2006
TO: All staff
FROM: Bob Knudsen
SUBJECT: New project
FILE: KCK-RLK200

FOLKS:

Good news! I just learned that the Magruder Art Foundation has chosen Knudsen, Carlson, and Knudsen to design the building, interiors, signing graphics, and landscaping for MAF's 80,000 sq. ft. art museum near Little Rock, Arkansas. Congratulations to Marilyn DiPaglia and her business development team for this success.

• Here's the designated project team. John Coelho will be project manager, Priscilla Davies will be architectural design leader, Capability Jones is landscape designer, and Kevin Leung will take the IT lead, with myself as partner-in-charge. We'll meet in conference room 2 this Monday at 9 A.M. to kick off the process.

• Our consultants will be: Tension Associates (structural); Bernouilli Engineers (mechanical, electrical, plumbing); Matt Sabin & Associates (acoustical); and Lumen Associates (lighting).

• As is our practice, the team will establish itself as a working group in Alcove B of the main drafting room. Willie Kelly [office manager] will have workstations rearranged in the next two weeks.

• Marilyn DiPaglia will ASAP issue a one-page news release to notify local and national media, as well as the CI section of the client list.

Bob

Meeting minutes may be short or long, depending on whether you include only actions taken or discussion too. Minutes of society chapter or committee meetings are best kept concise and limited to actions taken. Job minutes need to include discussion, to keep absentees and need-to-know persons posted. The record of discussion should be kept also for legal reasons.

Give each major topic a number, the first subordinate topic a number with a decimal, each second subordinate topic a number with two decimals, etc. See the following example.

SCENARIO

As project manager you have just completed the Monday meeting of the design team working on renovation of the old Vedette vaudeville theater on Maple Street. You need to let all know what was discussed and what was decided. Arrange the material either in the order in which it was discussed (see below), or according to priority.

MINUTES

Vedette Theater Renovation
Minutes, 28 February 2006

Present: Jane Talavera, Jane Chang, Charles Mann, William Hord
Absent: Herbert Smith, Sonny Chavez

1.0 Team member reports
    1.1 Jane Talavera
    1.2 Jane Chang
    1.3 Charles Mann
    1.4 William Hord
2.0 Cost estimates
    2.1 Overruns
        2.1.1 Foundations
        2.1.2 Framing
    2.2 Report on labor prices
3.0 Schedule
    3.1 Report and discussion on fast-track bid packages
        3.1.1 Steel
        3.1.2 Curtain wall
        3.1.3 HVAC
4.0 Future meetings

Your writing style should be tight, with unnecessary words omitted; for example:

> 1.2 J. Chang reported that specified glazing system may need substitution due to cost and unreliable delivery. She will explore options and report in two weeks.

Social Correspondence from All Over

On occasion you will be called upon to write on matters that, while linked to business, are so clearly social as to call for a departure from the detached, impersonal tone of most correspondence. Consider the following situation, and the called-for response.

SCENARIO

Your travels as a partner in the eight-person, Atlanta-based office of Heron & Heron take you to Sacramento. This also happens to be the home town of Gene Gerahty, a junior designer who recently joined your firm. Gene gave you an introduction to Mr. Reginald James, a prominent Sacramento businessman and philanthropist. The Jameses ask you to dinner at their large house situated not far from the California Governor's mansion. At dinner, it transpires that Mrs. James chairs the Sacramento Symphony Foundation, a fund-raising society that is looking critically at the size and condition of the city orchestra's cramped current quarters. You sense an opportunity.

The event clearly calls for a thank-you note. The line between a marketing and a social occasion is fine, as in this case. The best approach is to dwell on the social occasion, to mention favorably but not gush about the work of the symphony foundation, mention that both Mr. and Mrs. James had revealed a polite interest in architecture and in your firm, and that you would send them for their amusement a profile article the *Atlanta Constitution* had run the previous month about four young Atlanta firms—yours among them. Keep it brief. Then sign off. If you have personal office stationery, now is the time to use it. Omit your title in the sign-off; it smacks of business.

LETTER

Mr. and Mrs. Reginald James
8 Elm Drive
Sacramento, CA 95801

Dear Mr. and Mrs. James [or Dear Mary and Reginald—it's your call]:

Thank you for having me over to your house last week. It had been a strenuous day, and I was grateful for this chance to unwind in such a pleasant setting and friendly company. It was kind of Gene to suggest the idea.

The challenges facing the Sacramento Symphony Foundation are clear. You bring vigor to the task.

You kindly encouraged me to talk about our firm. To add to what I said, I enclose a story from our hometown paper on emerging Atlanta firms, including ours.

I look forward to showing you our offices should you ever head this way, and your joining us for dinner.

Sincerely,

Charles Heron, Jr.

cc: Gene Gerahty

Research, Feasibility, and Planning Reports

A design firm's work product often ends up not as a built project, but as a report. A wit once remarked that thick reports are *de rigueur*, to justify the fee. As the final product of your work, the report is one of the most challenging projects for the writer. Reports are often an excuse for pompous, jargon-packed language, which has given them a bad name over the years and consignment to gather dust on remote shelves.

The report is especially significant, as it is generally the final product of the designer's services. It is a monument to the designer's skill in doing research or investigating a topic, assembling the material in an arrangement that makes sense to the client, and writing it in a style that fosters easy reading.

Beyond its role as the end product of your services, the report has wide-ranging marketing value: a copy of the report is a powerful attachment or supplement to a proposal or to your brochure or portfolio. As a leave-behind on your client's desk or forwarded to the client's associates and friends, it's an eloquent emissary for your firm.

Reports can cover a wide array of topics:

Feasibility study
Campus master plan
Health facilities merger analysis
Energy use analysis
Environmental impact study
Building safety and security report
Wetlands mitigation report
Building operations and maintenance manual
Corporate workplace reorganization report
Programming study for a primary healthcare unit
School district facilities retrofit plan
Neighborhood housing development plan
Central business district parking study
Integrated product systems development
Building systems commissioning report

The purpose of the report and the way it is to be used set the pattern for its organization and style. A research report on building security and safety prepared for the National Institute for Science and Technology and reviewed by other design professionals and fire, police, and building department staffs can get by with a heavier load of technical terms (but not designer-babble) than a central business parking study widely circulated not only to technical people but also to nontechnical readers such as developers, politicians, and the general public.

A report organized for convenience typically consists of these sections:

Cover
Title page
Client's authorization letter
Table of contents
Executive summary or abstract
Main text
The team
Appendices

Cover and title page. The cover and title page should convey information at a glance. A skilled graphic designer, given the key words, will find fresh and snappy ways to project the message (see the dust jacket of this book). The title page needs to include the name of the project and location, the names of the client and designer, and the report's date.

Client's authorization letter. A facsimile of the letter from the client or agency authorizing the job is sometimes reproduced near the front, especially on publicly funded work.

Contents. A table of contents makes sense if the report is bulky and the reader needs a navigational aid. Smart graphic designers can exploit the contents page, as they do in magazines, to highlight the report's chief parts and help make the report an experience, not a chore. For generations of readers reared on MTV and *WIRED* magazine, such touches are critical to entice readership.

Executive summary. The executive summary or abstract is critical. It has the same role as in the proposal: to allow senior client officials and others to grasp the essence without having to read the whole report—the task of the middle-level technical staff. The executive summary isn't always the same as an abstract. The abstract typically exists so librarians and researchers have an easy time filing the report or finding it in the catalog; an abstract is shorter than an executive summary. Some design firms equate the two terms, and the abstract reads like the executive summary.

The intent of the executive summary is to describe the assigned problem, the methods used to investigate it, and the solutions. No summary should run beyond 750 words (about two typed pages) without good reason. Clients have been known to restrict it to a single page. Your style should be concise without being terse, technical-term free without being patronizing, friendly but not chummy. Identify the main parts of your summary with bullets or numerals.

Main text. Divide the main text into logical sections. Consider three sections or chapters—the problem or objectives of the assignment; the recommendations and their rationale; the process used to uncover the answers. Another way to divide the text is by phases; according to the work done by the different parties to the job; or by key influences on the project.

For example, an environmental report tracking the impact of new construction on a large, sensitive site could divide the text into a chapter on the geography, geology, climate, and vegetation of the site; a chapter identifying the possible presence of cultural artifacts on or near the site, and the historical, aesthetic, and ethical issues involved; a chapter of recommendations on the environmentally proper use of the site; and a chapter containing a synopsis of the field and laboratory methods used.

The style of the main text needn't be as tight as the executive summary, because it has to take up a greater volume of detail. Nonetheless, you need to make sure you cut every word that doesn't carry its weight.

The team. A report reflects the work of its project team, so the players should be listed and their roles defined. Writing this section is much like the resumes segment of a proposal—name, rank, and job title, followed by a few paragraphs detailing this person's role in and contribution to the result. List not only your staff and that of associated firms, but also those on the client's side who contributed.

Appendices. Appendices are where you deposit material that is bulky, awkward to describe, or amplifies the text. Appendices may include economic, demographic, or other statistics; maps and site plans; photographs and renderings; a list of references; and a schedule diagram showing the time implications of your recommendations.

(The following sample executive summary is a broadly fictionalized version of one prepared for the Chelsea Piers Sports and Entertainment Complex, New York City, completed in 1995. Butler Rogers Baskett were the architects and planners; Cosentini Associates were the mechanical/electrical engineers; Thornton-Tomasetti the structural engineers; Edmund Hollnader LA Design PC the landscape architects; and Douglas/Gallagher the graphic designer. Chelsea Piers Management was the developer.)

SCENARIO

Your firm of architects and planners and a developer have been asked by the State of New York to explore the feasibility of converting some decaying piers owned by the state on the lower Hudson River waterfront into a sports and entertainment center that will not only attract New Yorkers and visitors and generate commercial revenue, but also relate to the community. There are four adjacent piers and a connecting headhouse; you are to assess the physical condition of the piers, investigate scenarios for replacing them if necessary, and compare the merits of options that have surfaced for adaptive reuse of the restored piers.

These options can include, but need not be limited to developing: 1) participatory, nonspectator facilities for basketball, ice hockey, swimming, bowling, and sailing; a small children's sports-oriented amusement area; and a range of food-service facilities; 2) spectator facilities for basketball and bowling for junior and high school sports, with these facilities also available for participatory activity without spectators; 3) a marine-oriented facility for sailboats and small powerboats, with appropriate food service and facilities for children; 4) a reduced sports focus, with greater focus on entertainment, to include small theaters for stage shows and film projection, and a larger theater for multimedia entertainment.

Your firm has now explored the technical feasibility of such a project, initial capital investment and possible sources of funding, operating revenues and expenses, the time frame, and likely attitudes from neighborhood and community groups. Your report comprises your recommendations, along with preliminary concept drawings and 3D sketches.

The typical framework for an executive summary of a feasibility report based on such an assignment might appear as shown below. In many cases the shorthand format shown is satisfactory. On occasion, depending on instructions from the client, you should write as a narrative.

EXECUTIVE SUMMARY

PROBLEM

Piers built in 1910 to accommodate new luxury liners. Headhouse designed by architects Warren & Wetmore. Piers deteriorated with demise of passenger liner trade. Piers later used to house the city's automobile towing pound. New uses are to meet demand for recreation facilities, commercial revenue, generous public space, and private financing.

RECOMMENDATIONS

The Complex should have a sports focus, with secondary but significant entertainment functions. Focus should be on participatory over spectator sports, although spectator space should be provided for ice hockey and swimming.

Develop piers 59 through 62 and the connecting headhouse as a single phase, with completion dates staggered over six months. Pier 59 is to house a golf driving range. Pier 60 is to house a sports center consisting of facilities for swimming, running, rock climbing, beach volleyball, aerobics, weightlifting. Pier 61 is to house an ice-skating rink. Pier 62 is to house roller rinks integrated with a public park.

The headhouse is to contain commercial space owned and/or operated by the developer, including such activities as network television productions, a feature film studio, a photography studio, and offices, as well as parking and truck access.

Restaurants and snack bars are to be dispersed throughout the Complex, including a major theme restaurant.

The infrastructure, including the piers, is in poor condition and will require $27 million to rebuild, including structural, mechanical, electrical, and plumbing services, emergency access, lighting, and security.

Public space, indoors and out, will be planned to allow for skyline views.

Because the six-lane 11th Avenue cuts the Complex from the community, an overpass bridge is critical to connect the Complex to the adjacent neighborhoods.

The existing headhouse facade erected after demolition of the original Beaux-Arts structure will remain, but a graphic embellishment program to enliven the facade is essential.

A public esplanade will allow foot access to every part of the Complex.

A lease should be given to a cruise operator to operate cruises around Manhattan Island, and docking should be possible for small boats.

Budget for design, construction, furnishings, equipment is estimated at $100 million, not including infrastructure retrofit. The city has agreed in principle to a combined tax abatement and deferral plan, to expire by the year 2045.

We the architects have developed a series of computer animations depicting assorted views of the proposed Complex.

PROCESS

Inventoried public participatory sports facilities in New York City, especially for ice hockey, golf driving range, basketball.

Consulted state and city authorities as to financing incentives available to supplement private investment.

Explored types of commercial nonsports uses, such as parties, conferences.

Investigated structural condition of piers.

Note how this summary offers its conclusions in short, bite-sized, single-topic chunks that inform but don't bore.

Short Reports

Not every report calls for the depth and detail implied in the foregoing example. In many cases, such as a feasibility study for a fire station on an uncomplicated site, or development of a program for an inner-city primary-care facility, simplify the typical trappings of a full-fledged report.

For example, you could dispense with the table of contents; reduce the executive summary to a simple statement of the problem and your recommendations; and avoid chopping up the main text into chapters, in favor of a single text subdivided into bulleted entries. In case of a fire station or a community center, this breakdown could be:

Objectives
Options
Limitations
Opportunities
Recommendations
Investigative process

In formulating a program for an inner-city primary-care facility, you could split the principal text into the now classic five divisions developed in the 1960s by Houston architect William Peña in *Problem Seeking,* namely:

Establish goals
Collect and analyze facts
Uncover and test concepts
Determine needs
State the problem or program to be solved through design

Emerging firms with limited resources should remember (as noted in chapter 3's discussion of brochures for firms with limited years of practice and tight budgets) that clients are looking for content as much as lavish presentation. That doesn't mean the report cannot sparkle graphically—catchy graphics need not cost a fortune. Focus on a good, straightforward text. Even an office with modest resources should be able to afford having the text edited by an outside editor for clarity.

Investigative Reports

Many firms devote part of their annual marketing budget to publishing research findings gained from experience in practice or as the result of a special interest by a partner or employee. It combines marketing value with a perceived responsibility to share knowledge with the design profession.

Potential topics for investigative reports are:

Energy-conserving designs
Assisted-living housing concepts
New directions in planning public schools
Trends in designing for sports, education, healthcare, retail—or any
    building type in which your firm has experience
Urban design observations from travel
Space-age materials applied to furniture design and construction
Advances using water in landscape design
Emerging concepts in intelligent building design
Techniques for designing sustainably on low budgets
Creating designs and displaying in digital formats

Such reports have many benefits. They are a valuable marketing tool, selectively left with important clients or attached as supplements to proposals. They are an outlet for useful, practical information that otherwise no one would ever see. They are an appealing device for attracting and keeping high-quality staff. They are morale builders for enterprising staff wanting a challenge away from normal routine. In some cases the content carries such authority and widespread application that it is sold, generating revenue to offset costs.

These reports need not be elaborate, although a touch of graphic pizzazz or whimsy accompanied by an engaging writing style helps their acceptance. Still memorable today is a series of travel observations by the late William Caudill from Russia in the early 1970s and Egypt in the mid-1970s. And during the Great Energy Crisis of 1974 Caudill wrote a beguiling report showing practical ways to design energy conserving buildings before the days of $50 crude (see page 105, top left). So as not to overload in-house staff, writing and producing such reports may be outsourced to a professional design writer.

Another form of firm-sponsored publication is the periodical. It is issued several times a year and distributed to staff and clients. It differs from the client newsletter (chapter 5) because its content is so substantial that it resembles a professional journal, and because it lacks internal staff and business news.

An outstanding example of this type of professional, content-loaded publication is the *Arup Journal,* begun in 1986 and distributed three or four times a year to prospects (to win work) and to staff (as a learning and morale-building tool). See cover and sample pages from the *Arup Journal* on page 105.

This fine journal uses significant engineering projects for detailed presentations. Included are photographs, crisp color drawings and renderings, and lucidly drawn details. Above all, there's a direct, jargon-free text that doesn't compound the mystery of structural engineering by using cryptic language. One month, the journal gave over an entire issue to a Sydney speech by former chairman Jack Zunz. The speech was the preamble for an in-depth report on the structure of the Jørn Utzon opera house, for which Arup were the engineers. The journal is much sought after for its content and precise layout.

It is simple to make these reports available also as CD-ROMs and on the Web.

Internal Newsletters or House Organs

While the internal newsletter or house organ is not part of the firm's overall marketing communications arsenal and may not win you new clients, it is a handy medium for partners to confer with staff, boost morale, and reinforce team spirit.

Internal newsletter topics and categories may be:

NEWS ABOUT STAFF
Promotions, interoffice moves
Professional licenses achieved
Honors and appointments
Marriages, offspring
Employment anniversaries
Out-of-the-ordinary work-oriented travel

COMPANY ANNOUNCEMENTS
In house continuing education and other training offerings
Working hours and overtime
Use of automobiles (personal and company)
Health insurance

Sexual harassment guidelines
Maternity leave policies
401(k) changes

DESIGN PROJECTS
New work
Completed projects

KUDOS
Published articles about the firm or its people
Design awards

EXTRACURRICULAR ACTIVITIES
Accomplishments of firm in running, baseball, bowling, or other leagues

Firms need to update employees on what's happening. Very few firms any longer use a bulletin board for this purpose. Most write and distribute an internal newsletter, sometimes known as a house organ, on-line.

The internal newsletter also can serve to link multi-branch firms, and to keep all informed on such matters as anniversaries, upcoming company picnics, congratulations to staff having children, or company athletic achievements.

Write the internal newsletter in a style that is simple, chatty, humorous without being cute, arranged into logical categories, and equipped with telephone extensions and e-mail addresses for follow-up information. The writing, design, and production, just like the client newsletter, are not matters to leave in unqualified hands. Follow the guidelines offered for the client/marketing newsletter (chapter 5). You need not follow a regular schedule; some announcements won't wait. On occasion, invite the staff to contribute opinion pieces; aim for high-quality writing throughout.

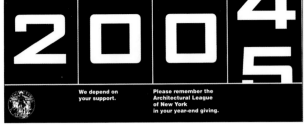

Creative use of type fonts imparts a humorous twist to the front of this end-of-year fundraising reminder from the Architectural League of New York.

Left: A sheet of postage stamps embodied the Butler Rogers Baskett Architects 2003 season's greetings. With design firms increasingly challenged to think up an original greeting to send to clients, prospects, and friends of the firm, BRB decided the postage stamp was a nice metaphor for cheer-by-communication.

Below: Rendered illustrations, such as the Form.Z image of Canary Wharf, London, generated by John Cirka, are dramatic tools for dressing up a firm's brochure and Web site.

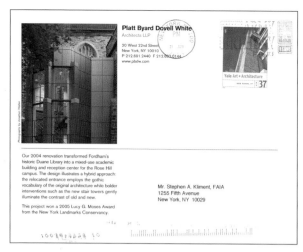

Above left and right: Single project postcards are a simple, direct means for reaching clients and others any time of the year. Architects Platt Byard Dovell White disseminated this oversized postcard (5¾ by 7 inches) showing Fordham University's Duane Library and, on the reverse, their 2004 renovation. Note postage stamp from the USPS's Masterworks of Modern American Architecture series.

Photograph: © Peter Mauss/Esto

On May 7, 2005, **H³** Hardy Collaboration Architecture celebrated the grand opening of **Two River Theatre Company**'s new home, in Red Bank, New Jersey. This is Hugh Hardy's second New Jersey theater, joining the Roger S. Berlind Theatre, at Princeton University, completed in 2003.

The heart of Two River Theatre is an intimate, flexible, 349-seat auditorium. Seating surrounds a modified thrust stage, focusing audience attention on the performers. A 2,500-square-foot rehearsal room doubles as a performance space, further accommodating classes and pre- and post-performance events. An upper mezzanine provides access to the auditorium balcony and a VIP rooms, while back-of-house elements include dressing rooms, a loading dock, and offices.

On the exterior, zig-zag wooden columns support a two-story glass lobby, which becomes a marquee when illuminated at night. An undulating zinc-panel roof wraps the building's two primary facades. Curvilinear forms and rigid blocks of brick mingle a theatrical aesthetic with allusions to the town's history as a commercial port.

Begun at Hardy Holzman Pfeiffer Associates, Two River Theatre was completed by H³. Stewart Jones, AIA, served as principal in charge at HHPA, while Hugh Hardy, FAIA, remained partner in charge, and Geoffrey Lynch, AIA, continued as project architect.

H³ is an architecture, urban planning, and interiors firm dedicated to the design of buildings and spaces in the public realm.

Above: This sheaf of colorful images from the work of architects Holt Hinshaw reaches recipients in a neat cardboard box. Each card is identified by a single word that best expresses the concept of the work featured. The card marked "logic" summarizes the firm's design vision. Projects marked "chilling" and "freight" were designed by Holt Hinshaw Pfau Jones, a predecessor firm.

Left: This folded mailer opens up into a full tabloid-sized newspaper. It is one in a series of mailings to clients and prospects by H³ Hardy Collaboration Architecture LLC. One fold describes the project; the centerfolds show the project at vast scale. This "newspaper" depicts the Brooklyn Academy of Music (pictured here); another describes the Two River Theatre Company.

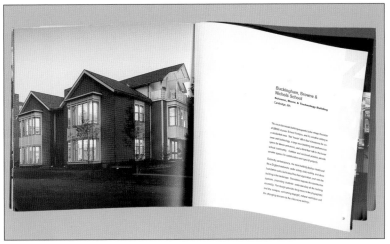

Ann Beha Architects splits its work into two brochures—completed projects and "In Studio" work. The 8½- by 9-inch brochures (about 52 pages each) combine information-packed photos with short, lucidly written descriptive text, such as for the school project above. (See page 48 for descriptive text.).

This 8½- by 11-inch, six-page triptych foldout promotional piece from structural engineer Leslie E. Robertson Associates, R.L.L.P. (LERA) contains an array of the firm's projects. Printed words such as constructible, economical, imaginative, and responsible describe LERA's practice. Shown at right is the Shanghai World Financial Center (Kohn Pedersen Fox Associates, architect). The round hole has been replaced by a parallelogram, whose sides follow the contours of the tower. At left is the Miho Musem, Shigaraki, Japan (I. M. Pei, architect).

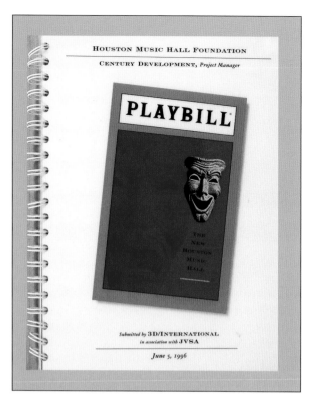

Shown is the cover of the 76-page proposal to the Houston Music Hall Foundation from 3D/International, in association with JVSA. Taking its cue from the traditional Broadway Playbill, the architects pursue the theatrical theme throughout the proposal. Divider pages bear the images of Ancient Greek theater masks and titles, such as Prologue (for Executive Summary), Cast (for Individual Profiles), Script (for Approach/Schedule), and Production Costs (for Compensation Structure).

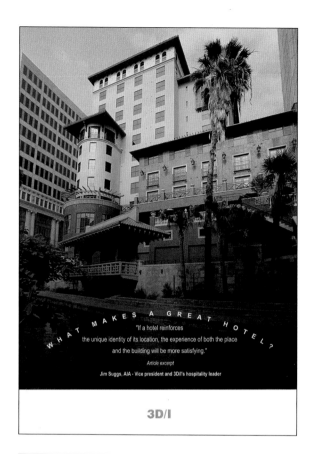

Right, top: This 6½- by 8-inch postcard comes from 3D/International's hospitality division. On the reverse is a concise text and an invitation to visit the firm's Web site for details.

Right, bottom: Several times a year consulting engineering firm Flack+Kurtz disseminates a standard sized postcard with the image of an F+K project and the firm's logo. On the reverse are descriptions of the project and its environmental systems. Shown is the Rand Corporation, Santa Monica, CA.

A Bucket of Oil was researched
and written by the CRS Group to
point out solutions to the oil crisis
of the 1970s. It applies as well to
the 2000s.

The Arup Journal is a newsletter published
two to three times each year. Sixty pages on
average, each issue describes a half dozen
significant Arup projects in clear prose, along
with rendered details and photos, reaching
broad readership among design professionals
and clients.

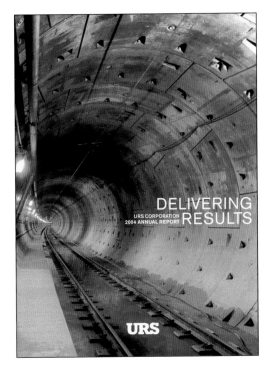

Annual reports are notoriously dull. URS
Corporation's 34-page 2004 report opens
on a colorful photograph of a tunnel. Inside
it offers clear type, an easy-to-read layout,
heavy, semi-gloss paper stock, and more
photographs to project an image of growth
and prosperity.

Covers of @issue: magazine, published by the Corporate Design Foundation, and OCULUS, published by the New York Chapter of the American Institute of Architects, combine powerful images with "cover lines" that give readers an instant idea of the theme, plus clues to the principal articles.

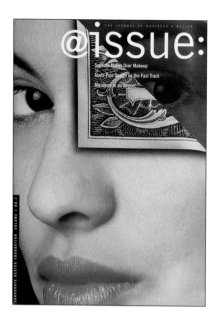

► Cover Story

News May 30, 2005

NEWS ANALYSIS

Power Sector Rebuild Faces Reality Check

Disappointing progress has officials lowering sights to focus on what they can finish fast

Two years and $3.74 billion into reconstruction, Iraq's power system remains an anemic and fragile network of components. Some are newly commissioned, some rehabilitated, some unfinished, but the whole still far short of expectations. Reliability is compromised by shortages of replacement parts and trained operators.

Production is hobbled by disconnects between fuel supplies and generating units. A lack of controls to manage transmission and distribution networks hamstrings delivery and it all is vulnerable to insurgents targeting the work and the people doing it.

Even indirect attacks can reverse hard-won progress, or worse, remove key project members in a flash. U.S. reconstruction officials have seen resources siphoned off by security costs and their control waning with the ascendency of Iraq's Ministry of Electricity. They now are focusing on critical projects deemed most likely to succeed and quickly, canceling others with longer payback time.

But hope still springs in Iraq, and officials say the new strategy soon will pay off as nearly-finished work comes on line.

The Iraqi electric power sector seems always to be on the verge of breaking out. But it then slips back and struggles again to rise even to the 4,400-MW production

▲ **Grinding work.** Power restoration faces complex problems.

estimated before the March 2003 invasion (see chart, p. 11).

On May 10, Ambassador William Taylor, head of the Iraq Reconstruction Management Office in the U.S. State Dept. mission in Baghdad, had relatively good news. "For the last week or so, we've been in the 4,500-MW range fairly steadily," he told ENR in a telephone interview from Baghdad. If that level had been maintained, it would have pushed the average of daily power put on the grid

in May up 30% from the delivery in April. "We are definitely putting more power on the grid," he said.

Five days later, however, another senior embassy official reported, "We've had a rough weekend." Several units around the country went down unexpectedly, joining others down for scheduled maintenance. "One of the lines went down providing transfer of power from the north to the middle of the country," he said. "Always units tripping for one reason or another...usually something minor."

So What's the Problem?
The State Dept.'s quarterly reports to Congress on reconstruction progress explain many of the problems. The most recent was filed April 30. Other explanations are offered through interviews with Taylor and with another senior embassy official in the electricity program, who, by State Dept. policy, cannot be named. Still other insight comes from contractors on the job. Some would only talk on background, but all agree that the problem is that there are lots of problems.

Security tops the list. "The biggest lesson is the importance of a secure environment," says Taylor. "To reconstruct in any effective way with any rational planning, we have to be able to move around

10 / ENR • May 30, 2005 enr.com

This page from Engineering News-Record is packed with aids to ease the reader's task in absorbing the information. Note kicker ("Cover Story") used to classify the story; a strong headline with an active verb; a one-line deck to amplify the headline; a drop-down "T" to accentuate the story start point; and short paragraphs.

Krueck & Sexton designed the sleek new **SHURE TECHNOLOGY CENTER** to complement an existing building and define a corporate campus

By Cheryl Kent

Shure Technology got a bargain when it bought a sprawling, brand-new, architecturally bold headquarters from HALO, the bankrupt company that commissioned it. Shure had just spent two frustrating years on fruitless negotiations for a site for its new headquarters elsewhere in suburban Chicago. Purchasing the existing building in Niles, seemed to put the company exactly where it wanted to be in a space that projected a strong image to the public and featured state-of-the-art systems (such as silent, polished steel-and-glass elevators with exposed mechanical systems) and the amenities to satisfy prized employees. It was a big step up for a company that had been housed in separate factorylike buildings for decades.

Above: Page from Architectural Record shows the headline combined with the deck, a drop-down initial "S," and a picture caption integrated into the column. Right: This page deftly uses a pull quote, a.k.a a scan—a sentence of key text enlarged to help readers as they scan the magazine. Scans also add graphic interest.

Researchers are developing new types of solar cells, including those made from organic chemicals and others using "quantum dots," which harvest more sunlight than today's cells.

Foster and Partners developed a CD-ROM about the firm (above). It was attached to a descriptive page (shown here) and included free in subscriber issues of Architectural Review magazine. The disk includes video "walkabout" clips of key projects, a clear, simple statement of philosophy, partner information, the Foster firm's Web site URL, and an e-mail address for inquiries.

This 50-page, 5½- by 8-inch booklet extols the virtues of simplicity and ingenious use and reuse of available materials and objects in contemporary Cuba. The cut-out stencil cover wraps around the bound pages, which are printed on recycled paper. A sample spread shows a motorcycle made out of bicycle parts and the bodies of old buses (left), and a walking stick made from a bicycle part (right). The booklet is number 32 in the Pentagram Papers series. Design and production express the low-cost theme of the subject matter.

This three-panel foldout mailing piece from architects Pasanella+Klein Stolzman+Berg Architects, P.C. features several views of the Williamsburg, New York Community Center. A warm red cover (not shown) includes comments on the project by New York Times reporter David Dunlap.

Writing in Design School 7

A critical mark of the well-rounded design professional is skilled communication through writing and speech. The groundwork takes place in the design schools, where the prevailing focus on design must be expanded through a deeper concern for the written and spoken word.

Only after a year or two in a school of architecture or other design discipline do students realize with a shock that academic life isn't made entirely of design; there is, in fact, a copious volume of writing to be done, as indicated in this partial list:

Themes and papers for the history, theory, or professional practice course
Text for presentation boards
Reports for courses in technology, engineering, and materials
Essays and exams for required humanities courses
Job applications at graduation
Grant and scholarship applications

For an inspiring look at the role writing plays in an architect's career, see the short essay *Just Write,* by the architect, artist, and educator Paul Rosenblatt, of Pittsburgh.

JUST WRITE

My mother is a writer, as was her mother, my grandmother. I never thought of myself as a writer. Growing up, I was the class artist. I never thought much of my class assignments as "writing," per se. They were homework, pure and simple.

My late father was an architect. His father, my grandfather, was a tailor. Growing up, I tried on many professions: artist, graphic designer, theatrical stage designer, architect. I went to college and graduate school, studied art and architecture. Went to work as an architect. Got licensed. Began to practice and teach architecture. I never thought of myself as a writer. Not once.

Of course, all this time, most of what I had been doing was writing. From writing class assignments in elementary school to high school term papers to book reports to essays to specifications notes to refereed journals to magazine articles and book reviews to talks and lectures to memos to meeting notes and contracts and letters of agreement. To my great surprise, most of what I do as a successful professional architect today is write.

So I'm learning to think of myself as a writer. I am still a practicing architect and installation artist. I still design buildings for people: houses, galleries, workplaces, schools, libraries, restaurants. And I still create site-specific sculptural installations. But I also write. A lot. I write reports to my clients advising them about their facility planning. I write letters to contractors. I write meeting memoranda. I write book reviews for the local newspaper. I write essays and give talks about art and urban development issues and the architectural scene. I spend a lot of time hunting and pecking at the keyboard on my laptop.

So, I'm a writer. I just turned forty years old and I'm just beginning to realize that this may be what I'm best at doing. I'm learning the name of what I do. Or maybe, for an architect, I'm a pretty decent writer. Whatever. I like to write. I like words. I'm glad I have never stopped writing. You can call yourself a writer, too. Just write.

By Paul Rosenblatt. Reproduced with permission.

There are many ways to hone writing skills. Course writing assignments in history and theory, professional practice, research, urban design, construction technology, and environmental studies can all serve as training grounds that you, as a student, can exploit. You'll deepen your awareness of the written word and sharpen those skills to your advantage, and obtain better grades and more attractive job offers.

Before you settle down to carry out a course writing assignment, read through the following useful guidelines for clear writing. While they will not (necessarily) make you into an Ernest Hemingway or a Toni Morrison, they will give you a leg up in writing clear, understandable, and, above all, effective prose. To paraphrase Marshall McLuhan, if your message fails to clearly convey your purpose, you have no message.

Guidelines to Effective Writing

Your first concern in developing a clear style is to stop thinking of the act of writing prose as an awe-inspiring venture. A lot of your writing will be for your studio critics or course lecturers. These individuals are people first and faculty second; therefore, don't throw a lot of convoluted text at them. If you want to get your instructor into an amiable frame of mind, giving you the benefit of the doubt between an A and a B grade, make sure your writing doesn't suffer from an excess of formality and difficult construction. Writing style and talking style should not be that far apart.

Poor wording:

The new business school campus is characterized by a monumental scale incompatible with the context of the surrounding built volumes.

Better wording:

The new business school is out of scale with its neighbors.

Another aid to clear writing is to keep your sentences short. Writing long sentences that make sense takes a talent well beyond yours or mine. It's hard to balance several ideas in a single long sentence and still make sense. You'll do far better to limit your sentences so each makes a single point. This may give you a string of shorter sentences, but you'll have no problem with stating your message clearly. A good rule of thumb is to limit sentences to twenty words. This doesn't mean that sentences longer than this don't communicate; it's just that much harder. If you find a sentence getting out of hand, it's all right to use semicolons to divide it.

Poor wording:

For my thesis I elected to investigate the science of acoustics and to explore its role as a determinant of architectural form, knowing that spatial acoustics are influenced by the shape of the room, the volume of the space, and the absorption of the room's surfaces across a range of frequencies, and that the construction of the edge walls, floors, and ceilings have an impact on acoustical comfort.

Better wording:

For my thesis I decided to investigate the impact of acoustics on architectural form. The acoustics of a space are influenced by its shape, the volume of the space, and surface absorption across a range of frequencies. Key factors in acoustic comfort include the materials and construction of edge walls, floors, and ceilings.

Avoiding Designer-Babble

Consider the benefits and limitations of using specialized designer lingo. Designer-babble or jargon is the use of words in strange, exotic forms, or using common words to denote uncommon meaning. As a student, when searching for models of good writing, avoid passages of text that have a supposed cleverness of verbiage that is in fact muddy or obscure; it usually conceals an absence of content. Used by small groups of like-thinking designers, jargon can serve as a kind of handy shorthand. But beware of assuming that everyone outside the group will understand your meaning when you refer to "syncopated plastic adjacencies" and "referential disconnects."

Do not, however, confuse designer-babble or jargon with technical terms. Every profession and trade has its own terminology to conduct business. For example, there is no way a structural engineer can get by without using such terms as *shear, moment, deflection, point loads, stayed cable,* or *space-web.* If you are writing a class report about Gothic architecture, you may well have to use such terms as *triforium, finial, lancet arch, ogee window,* or *half-timber.*

But don't lose sight of your audience. Your instructor will have no problem with such terms. But as soon as you begin to combine technical terms into oblique sentences and paragraphs, you won't impress your instructor so much as cause annoyance. Your instructor may be devoting a weekend afternoon to grading your class's papers; the last thing he or she needs is to wallow in a sea of verbal obscurity.

How can you tell when you cross the line from clarity to designer-babble? Put yourself in the shoes of the reader. Rigorously screen every phrase in your text. Whenever you have the slightest doubt as to the meaning, simplify the word, the phrase, and the context.

Note that after you go into professional practice, your reports, proposals, and correspondence will be read by several levels of reviewers. First are the client's technical people, and they will probably grasp your design terminology. But most clients lack technical staffs; even when they do exist, most key decisions, such as the selection of design consultants, are typically made at a higher level. That level includes administrators, politicians, senior management executives, selection boards; these are made up of laypeople. You don't want to alienate these individuals with obscure terms and references. If some technical terms cannot be avoided, insert a small glossary. Better be safe than sorry.

The following "before" and "after" instances are based on examples of designer-babble in chapter 1.

Before:
They are articulating their experiential experience.

After:
They drew on their prior experiences for the design of their new home.

Before:
Projects are either investigative or accommodative.

After:
Designs either stretch the envelope or echo current practice.

Before:
Activated axiomatic topologies of nonnomadic tribal elements . . . have been interpreted within the archaeological context of the site.

After:
The architect selected design features typical of nonnomadic tribal cultures and fit them into the archaeological nature of the site.

Another tip for getting your message across clearly is to choose words that have specific meanings. English, like most other languages, has words that range from the specific to the vague and indefinite. The vaguer the term, the greater the chance of misunderstanding. It is true that a hammer is a pounding device; a chicken is a mobile egg-producing grain-consuming unit; a door is an interspacial transition element. But you'll make more sense as you write class assignments to use words on the lines of hammer, chicken, and door.

Note the following example from the design of facilities for education:

Poor wording:
Modem-accessible outlets were dispersed on a two-foot module throughout the instructional spaces.

Better wording:
Dataline jacks occur on a two-foot module in every classroom.

Keep It Simple

Closely linked to the need for specific rather than general terms is the use of simple terms and phrases. To "rank" a list is surely better, and less pretentious, than to "prioritize" it. For other examples of dos and don'ts, see page 21 in chapter 1.

In this entrepreneurial society, such hip journals as *WIRED* and *Fast Company* have caught the excitement. The buzz shows up not only in invigorating, untamed graphics, but also in the writing. Two ways to achieve writing with impact and excitement are to use the active sentence form and to include deliberate references to people in your text (discussed below). Be sure to apply both these guidelines and you'll note in a flash a higher level of appeal in your writing. See the effect of the following sentence, which uses the passive form. It is taken from a student's report on landscaping design for arid zones.

It was decided that plant types requiring a high year-round level of rainfall would not be selected. Instead, planting would be kept to a minimum; various methods of finishing the landscape through special ground colors and textures were chosen by the designers.

Why not write:

The designers decided to avoid rain-thirsty plant species. Instead, they put in very few plants, and embellished the landscape by means of special ground color and textures.

People

Be sure to work people into your writing. Nothing turns readers on more than an infusion of individuals. The public media have operated on this principle for years; the trend has now infiltrated professional and business publications. The well-attuned journals make a point of weaving people into their text. You should do this too, even in unglamorous situations, such as the following examples. Your professors and mentors are more likely to identify with your message if written as though people were involved, rather than as a dry-as-dust event carried out by anonymous participants. So avoid the "before" examples here and turn to the solutions for a better way. (In these examples, the "after" versions are somewhat longer, but much more direct and appealing.)

Before:

Community elements took exception to the methods used by the city in securing their input into the planning and design process. *(from a half-page handout to the judges at the review of a problem for a new community center)*

After:

Several mothers of young children, headed by Mrs. Bess Wright, complained to John Olsen, a member of the city department of housing and community affairs, that his department was making decisions without checking with families in the community.

Before:

The community will benefit by converting the old warehouse into a library, day-care center, and neighborhood meeting place. (from a student presentation)

After:

The converted warehouse will benefit everyone in the community. Parents can drop children off in the day-care centers. Students and their parents, as well as visitors, can use the library, and young and old can meet and socialize in the warmly appointed ground-floor spaces planned for this purpose.

Making Your Point

Above all, your writing will flow more clearly when you are clear in your own mind as to the points or argument you want to make. Whether you are presenting a project at a faculty review or writing an essay or other written assignment in a history or structures class, begin by asking yourself, "What is my message?" You will simply fail to communicate if your reasoning is muddy and your basic logic flawed. Before you even hit the keyboard, list on a pad the points you want to make, arrange them in a sensible progression, eliminate—if you can—all but the critical ones, then start to write. A useful tip is to try to express your message in a single sentence, then keep that sentence in front of you as you write. If you are able to write such a sentence without trouble, chances are that your writing will flow clearly and easily. If not, go back and rethink your argument or approach.

For two excellent student papers, see pages 118 and 120.

Gender Bias

Forty years ago a woman student looking around her in the design studio would see almost nothing but men. In 2004, 42.1% of those enrolled in bachelor's degree programs were women, up from around 30% in the late 1990s. For years, however, writing patterns in the design professions failed entirely to reflect this change in the makeup of the student body.

Guidelines for avoiding gender-explicit writing fall into four types:

- Find a word that is gender-independent (e.g., manufactured, not man-made; staff hours, not man-hours; drafting staff or even drafter, not draftsman). Avoid inventing awkward-sounding terms: use "chairman" or "chairwoman" (if you don't know the gender, use "chairperson" or, if you must, "chair") or "council member."
- Ignore the situation, and state that whenever you use "he" or "she" you mean both. This is a copout.
- Each time you face the possessive form *he*, write *he/she, his/her, him/her*, etc. This is virtuous but clumsy.
- Use the plural whenever it makes sense. Note that the plural (they, their) is gender indefinite, whereas the singular is gender-specific (he, his; she, her). Take advantage of this.

Refer to chapter 1 for more detailed examples of gender-neutral writing.

In the sixties the use of what was then known as sexist language was very much a *cause célèbre*. Today the battle is not won. But attitudes have changed. Positions are less sensitized, more laid back, more tolerant.

That doesn't mean that gender bias in writing or speech is not critical. It has re-emerged more as a general awareness than as a cry to battle. Just as Calvinist doctrine preaches that you cannot achieve grace through good works alone, but that hard work, moral virtue, and business success are evidence of grace, so awareness of gender-free prose tells your instructors, contacts, and prospective employers—many of them women—that your writing aims for a new, higher standard. In the end, as a student you should let yourself be guided by whether your text, or anyone's text, makes a serious effort to avoid references to male or female stereotypes.

You can also safely take an example from the daily and professional press. As you read articles, note how the media—sharp reflectors of language—use gender-independent language. Your instructors, too, are aware of the problem and can help you sort out awkward situations as they emerge.

Above all, be aware. Write a lot: avoiding gender-specific writing comes steadily with practice.

When to Break the Rules

Rules in writing are designed above all to convert an obscure text into one that its audience can understand and use. That doesn't mean you cannot bend or break a guideline if by so doing you enhance your meaning or impact. Shakespeare, who loved short words for their punch, wasn't afraid if the occasion was right to insert a long word. The long word stood out by contrast, and added emphasis to the text, as these examples show:

> Blow, blow, thou winter wind,
> Thou are not so unkind
> As man's ingratitude.
> —*As You Like It,* II/7

and

> The sense of death is most in apprehension.
> —*The Tempest,* III/1

I do not recommend breaking the rules as a regular habit. But if you can get away with it to accomplish a stronger, justifiable text, go for it. Ernest Hemingway once allegedly lambasted an editor for daring to correct a split infinitive in his manuscript. "When I split an infinitive," he supposedly said, "I [bleep] want it to stay split."

Writing an Essay

Among the most common assignments of students in schools of engineering, architecture, interior design, and landscape design is the written essay, often known as an article, theme, paper, or report. Sometimes the assignment is linked to a studio problem in which the instructor calls for a written summary or digest to accompany the drawings, model, or animation.

Look first for the instructor's intent. Are you to write a succinct report on a lab test on concrete mixes? An assessment of a historic style? A review of a significant contemporary or historic interior? A discussion of professional ethics?

Set down your ideas derived from your examination of the material, background research, and your own thoughts. Roughly record this data: use a handy notebook or computer screen. Don't worry about how it looks or the order of the entries. The main purpose is to brainstorm and trigger a stream-of-consciousness thinking process.

Next day, review the assemblage of notes and scribbles, and begin to impose a logical order. A close scrutiny of your notes will almost always suggest an arrangement of the material. Usually it will look like this:

Introduction—define the topic and why it's important (5%)
Subdivision of topic into principal subtopics—these should show how each
    subtopic or subtheme builds on the previous one (10%)
Discussion of each subtopic (six, each 10%, say)
Conclusions (20%)
Restatement of topic and its importance (5%)

There are variations to this approach. Today's media like to kick off every article with a chatty little paragraph of human interest ("Jane Rodriguez was crossing Michigan Avenue after lunch when she stumbled into the pothole that had survived the spring road repair campaign . . .") before the article lumbers on to a discussion of road paving materials. This has merit if you are trying hard to capture the reader's attention; when an instructor must correct thirty papers, it can work well. But use this kind of opening only to set the scene; move on promptly to the core topic.

Once you begin writing the body of the article, recall the guidelines taken up earlier in this chapter, and keep the piece simple. Avoid clever turns of phrase, hackneyed expressions or clichés (e.g., "they lived in a *sprawling mansion*"; "the two spaces were as alike as *two peas in a pod*"), and pointless flaunting of obscure terminology. Include your opinions if asked; when you do, make sure they are supported by facts.

A few seasoned writers claim to be able to compose as they write. The act of writing, they say, stimulates their brain cells to create the proper ideas and ways to frame them. If this works for you, and your instructors like your work, great. If not, you'll do better to clarify your ideas *before* you write them down.

Consult a manual of style (see Resources) to make sure your format, punctuation, and arrangement of references (and footnotes, if you choose to use them) are consistent. Do not imperil your grade by neglecting these important parts of writing.

Above all, have a clear point of view: lacking such a point of view, no amount of verbal acrobatics will help you compose an effective essay.

Note these two examples of papers by students who completed their assignments with distinction.

SCENARIO
You have been assigned a building (or a related group of buildings) around which to write an article suitable for submitting to a professional architectural magazine. Plan to visit it during hours when it is accessible. Spend whatever time you need to walk through and observe it as a whole as well as observing its parts. Bring a notebook and, if you wish, a sketch pad and a camera. Record what you see, then develop a 1000-word article describing the building as well as giving it your assessment.

The article is to consist of these five parts:

1. Title or headline
2. Deck (a twenty-word expansion on the headline)
3. Description [Cover as many of the following points as feasible, not necessarily in this order]:

    Context (relationship to its site and to adjacent buildings)
    Style
    General configuration and massing
    Principal materials (exterior and interior)
    Structural system
    Electric and day lighting
    Interiors and furnishings
    Special spatial features (e.g., atrium, grand stair)
    Access (parking, ADA—Americans with Disabilities Act—concerns)
    Landscaping

4. Your conclusions and evaluation
5. Credits (architect, consultants, owner, sources)

Devote about two-thirds of your text to description, one-third to conclusions and evaluation. You may include up to two pages of illustrations.

ARTICLE A

MANTYNIEMI
Raili and Reima Pietila Design
Official Residence for the Presidents of Finland
by Patrick Brown
[Patrick Brown wrote this piece as a student in the author's course at the School of Architecture, Washington University, St. Louis.]

The President's new residence in Finland was a ten-year project for the husband-and-wife team of Raili and Reima Pietila. They won the national competition for the building in 1983. The house was completed shortly before Mr. Pietila's death in 1993. The building is the first to be designed specifically as the president's residence. The president has lived in various existing manor houses since Finland became independent in 1918. The house obviously has tremendous symbolic importance for the people of Finland. Nature was the source of inspiration; the house is very well integrated into the landscape. Finnish artists from a variety of disciplines collaborated on the project. The result is a complex, unique, and highly articulated building. Mantyniemi is an important expression of Finland's national character.

The name Mantyniemi means "pine tree cape." The building sits on a sprawling, wooded site that juts out into the Baltic Sea. Though the setting is rural, the house is actually in Helsinki, a 20-minute drive from the city center. The vegetation on the site is typical of a Finnish forest—mostly pine and birch trees, with ferns, astilbes, and moss covering the ground. The trees on the site were meticulously preserved during construction. The landscape designer supplemented these trees with other native vegetation to create a garden that does not rely on bloom for beauty.

Mantyniemi consists of three buildings—a gatehouse, a servants' building, and the main house. The main house is approximately 25,000 sq.ft., and contains the reception rooms, the private quarters, and the office wing. The building stretches out along the contours of the site. The entrance facade faces north and is clad in granite. The south facade faces the sea and is almost entirely of glass. The office and staterooms are to the east, at a higher elevation, whereas the private living area is to the west, at a lower elevation. The reception rooms—including the dining room, two drawing rooms, and an office—spread out in a fan-shaped pattern. A corridor to the north links these rooms to the flanking office and private wings.

The architects integrated the house into the Finnish landscape. They considered both the specific conditions of the site, and the geological and climatic conditions of the country. Finland has been emerging from the sea over the past 15,000 years. Helsinki is rising at the rate of sixteen inches per century. The house responds metaphorically to this fact. Mantyniemi seems to be rising from the glacial deposits of the site. At the same time, from the south, the building has a crystalline form, like an ice formation that is draped across the rocky site.

The architectural expression of the interior is complex and sculptural. Folded white planes form the ceiling and walls. These surfaces capture and reflect the white sunlight of Finland. Because of its northern location, the sun angles in Finland vary greatly from winter to summer, creating a variety of effects. Concealed spaces between the ceiling and roof are filled with warm air in winter, to provide insulation in the frigid climate. The lower ceiling rises two feet just inside of the southern windows, giving the impression that the glass extends beyond the roof. The south-facing windows are very tall and narrow, because the architects thought that a short window was not appropriate for viewing the tall, slender pine trees that surround the house. These windows were originally designed with small, branch-like mullions. This idea was abandoned, however, because very heavy window frames were required for security reasons.

One of the most striking things about the house is its complexity. I had the opportunity to visit with Raili Pietila at her home in Helsinki [in the summer of 1997], after I visited the house. She showed me the huge volumes of technical specifications that were required to build Mantyniemi. There are, for instance, over 150 doors in the house, and only a few are the same. The form of the air ducts and the slats that cover the openings are not recognizable as HVAC elements. Elements such as lighting and fences—even the long stainless steel poker that hangs next to one of the main fireplaces—were specially designed.

Artistic collaboration played a key role in creating Mantyniemi. Finnish artists designed the landscape, furnishings, tapestries, artwork, and even the table settings in the house. A staircase links the public and private portions of the house. Along the wall of this stair is a huge ceramic relief work by the artist Rut Bryk. The quality of the welds in the staircase does not equal the craftsmanship of the adjacent artwork. Still, the design quality of the house and its furnishings seem to complement each other. There is a uniform softness of tone to all the fixtures within the house. What one notices most of all is the variety and intricacy of the reflections of sunlight in the house.

Mantyniemi stands as a testimony to the creativeness of the Finnish people. As a national symbol, this building sends an invaluable message as Finland steps up its industrial production. Perhaps the quest for gold will not inflict upon Finland the mediocrity so characteristic of development here in the United States. Instead, Finland has in its geography, climate, and people the means to achieve a unique national expression.

Curiously, not all Finns like Mantyniemi as strongly as I do. I talked to a number of people in Finland, and they are not as proud of their president's residence as I think they should be. Apparently, the current president has made some unkind statements about the house. He likens the experience of living in this house to "living in an Alvar Aalto vase." My friends tell me that he thinks the house is cold, impersonal, and museum-like. The current president is also apparently too overweight to move through some of the house's narrow passageways. This commentary seems to have harmed the Finnish people's opinion of their "first" house.

I'm not sure what this portends for the future of Finland. Emerging nations tend to want to avoid being different, and prefer to imitate their wealthier neighbors. Mantyniemi is a masterpiece. Will the people of Finland fulfill the promise of Mantyniemi? Will Finland maintain its cultural identity as it gains in economic strength? It remains to be seen.

CREDITS:

Maj-Lis Rosenbroijer, landscape architect

Antti Paateru, interior architect

Irma Kakkasjarvi, textiles

Reijo Paavilainen, Kinni Paharinin, Rut Bryk, Mais Kaarna, contributing artists

SOURCES:

"The President's Residence, Mantyniemi, Helsinki," by Olga Gambardella, *Domus*, May 1994.

"Raili and Reima Pietila, Mantyniemi, The Residence of the President," by Raili Pietila, *A+U*, June 1995.

"Finland's New Presidential Residence," *Progressive Architecture*, September 1994.

Reima Pietila: *Architecture, Context and Modernism*, by Malcolm Quantrill, Rizzoli, 1985.

Reima Pietila, "Intermediate Zones in Modern Architecture." Museum of Finnish Architecture, Helsinki, 1985.

Patrick Brown's interview with Raili Pietila, July 1997.

COMMENT

This is a well-argued article, with an accurate, penetrating description clearly based on a site visit. The writer expressed his opinions and, aware of a surge of praise as well as criticism around this building, nevertheless forged a well-balanced article. Note the short, snappy sentences and the virtual absence of jargon.

ARTICLE B

A HOUSE FOR HEALING
A New AIDS Residence Gives Hope to New York's HIV+ Homeless
by Gonzalo Fernandez
[Gonzalo Fernandez wrote this article as a student in the
School of Architecture and Environmental Studies at
City College of The City University of New York.]

Almost twenty years since the first case of AIDS was diagnosed, a cure is still out of reach. Nowadays patients are living longer, however, thanks to new combinations of drugs and treatment. But there are many people who cannot afford treatment because they are homeless. In 1990 a group of people of different minority groups formed Housing Works Inc., a nonprofit organization that provides permanent housing and medical and social assistance to New York's HIV+ homeless population. Since then they have helped more than 30,000 New Yorkers with housing and medical and psychological treatment throughout the city. In June 1997 Housing Works Inc. opened a new building that provides housing and assistance on site for residents of the Lower East Side.

The AIDS Residence and Day Treatment Center is located at 741–749 East 9th Street in Manhattan and was designed by Allan Wanzenberg and Associates. This five-story, reinforced concrete structure was built on two adjacent lots forming an L-shape, with the longer side facing East 9th Street. The shape of the site and local zoning regulations forced a long, narrow, design.

To preserve a residential atmosphere, the entrance is announced by a glass marquee in front of a glass wall. The lobby is also kept at a residential scale with no grand spaces or information boards that might hint at a health institution; a reception desk and waiting area give a private atmosphere that helps residents feel that they are in a secure and private environment.

The common spaces are located on the ground floor. A foyer or corridor divides the game room and the dining room. The game room is in a comfortable setting with game tables, a TV set, and plenty of sunlight. This space is also used as a meeting area for local community groups that visit the center. The dining room seats 80 people three times a day. Next to it is the "sun porch" that leads to the garden. Yet this space receives no natural light because it is located in the north facade and faces a six-story building.

Nevertheless, the residents use the porch as a secluded and quiet space. At the moment the garden is under construction. The design was provided through the generosity of landscape architect Edwina von Gal who donated her time and resources to completion of the project. The design consists of small pockets of bamboo trees along a paved weaving walkway ending in a water fountain. The design was conceived as a self-maintaining garden because of the limited funds allocated for its maintenance. Also on the first floor is a retail space run by the Center. This space will house a small diner for the community and will be run by residents as part of their work training.

The day treatment center is located on the second floor surrounding the double-height lobby. The three departments that form the center (administration, clinic, and social services) face one another. This is done for two reasons: one is to provide a feeling of service and openness for the clients; the second is for efficiency, as only one receptionist and waiting area service the three departments.

On the next three floors are the suites. Each floor has its own laundry room and lounge. Each suite is on average 300 sq. ft. and completely furnished. To nourish a sense of independence no two studios have been decorated in the same way. The furniture was donated by high-scale patrons and corporations such as Crate & Barrel (furniture and china) and Samsung (appliances).

Some of the pieces were designed as modules that can be changed or combined in many ways as the residents' needs change. On the roof is the community room overlooking the World Trade Center where residents can meet as a community in a friendly and familiar atmosphere.

The simplicity of the design, the distribution of the spaces, and the finishing materials ably provide the residents with comfort and a sense of independence. But most importantly the Center provides an atmosphere in which they can feel like functional members of the community.

Reproduced by permission.

COMMENT

This is a well-documented report on a sensitive and timely topic. It aptly combines description and assessment. Sentences are short, the style simple and clear, and the vocabulary straightforward.

Essays and Papers

Here is a method for organizing a writing assignment in a history and theory class.

As the Modernist movement moves into its second century, it is becoming the subject of history, both as an architectural style and as a sociological event. A movement is growing to anoint as landmarks some of its best-known examples. You are to write about this phenomenon. Refer to any precedents where a social, religious, or economic movement spawned a design style which, in its turn, came to acquire historical status and pressures to preserve its prime examples. Write 1000 words, and support the essay with illustrations.

1. Begin by reviewing sources. This will disclose a number of styles that emerged from religious, social, political, literary, or economic roots. One is the Gothic style. Another is the Baroque. A third is the Arts and Crafts movement. A fourth is Deconstructionism. Analyze these styles for causes and effects. Then examine Modernism. Finally, hazard a projection as to Modernism's future in the new millennium.
2. Create an outline with relative lengths for your own use. For example:
   Introduction (5%). State theme, why it's significant.
   Precedents (15%). Origins, evolution, spread, demise, opposition to, and revivals of one or two historic styles.
   Modernism (10%). Origins, growth, emergence as a style, impact of 1932 International Style show at the Museum of Modern Art, New York.
   Criticism (10%). Sterility attributed to Modernism; its temporary eclipse by Postmodernism.
   Revival in the 1990s (20%).
   Comparisons of Modernism to selected historic styles (20%).
   Key players and their roles (10%) (e.g., Gropius, Le Corbusier, Mies van der Rohe, Rudolph, Venturi, Derrida, Meier).
   Conclusion (10%). Modernism, today and in the future.
   References.
   List of illustrations.

Master's theses and doctoral dissertations are, at least in many schools of architecture and design, extended forms of studio work that culminate in a public review. They differ from regular studio problems in the amount of research and investigation required and, especially in the case of the dissertation, in the depth and length of documentation.

Schools differ in their demands. Some place greater weight on research or theory; others focus on the design solution to a (preferably) realistic problem, and often demand of the student several solutions, with one then chosen for final development. Some schools consider the investigation and the design of equal weight, figuring that in the world of professional practice both aspects are essential.

Theses place a premium on original thought and findings. Dissertations raise the bar a notch either by demanding totally new ways of examining an existing theme (for example, water as a design element), exploring a new theme (phenomenology in design), or inviting research into a currently pressing theme that demands the intense scrutiny of a dissertation (such as computer-aided design; intelligent buildings; desert landscaping; the new workplace).

The volume of writing demanded of the doctoral candidate is colossal. Key components of the dissertation include an abstract or summary; a statement of the problem, argument, or issue; development of the argument—typically the central and longest segment; and conclusions. The design complements the written work, displayed on boards or through other media, with writing to identify the drawings and, often in a short sentence or paragraph, to give the theme of each board.

The text of the dissertation is commonly targeted for a faculty committee, at times augmented by guest professionals and lay persons. Because of these outsiders, and because it is good practice, the writing should be straightforward and clear. While use of arcane terms whose meaning is clear to some of the faculty judges may bring a short-term benefit, it makes no sense over the long haul. Even if you are committed to an academic career, where such writing is unhappily quite common, as a candidate you are on firmer ground using a broadly accepted vocabulary and simpler language forms. Dissertations are sometimes published; your chances for publication improve when your work is well organized and clearly written. Avoid the instance of a father who wrote to the *New York Times* that his son, a college student, had earned consistently poor grades for his well-thought out, lucidly written reports. When his son decided to muddy his thinking and convolute his style, he began to receive straight A's.

A student presentation board or set of boards—the outcome of a design studio problem or thesis—has an immediate selling job. It raises or lowers your odds of winning a good grade. It could also get you possible overtures or offers from visiting judges. Whereas the convention exhibit panel has to stand and "speak" alone, the student's board is supported by the student's own verbal presentation and possibly a 3D model or PowerPoint show. Many of the precepts for trade show exhibit panels still apply, however. Refer to chapter 5 on exhibit panels (page 82).

Simplicity is important—of drawing, text, layout. Typically, you must communicate concept, circulation, structure, form and finishes, siting and landscaping, choice and application of energy sources, lighting, and probably acoustics.

You then must choose between too much clutter or too many boards. Normally the studio critic determines the number of boards. The verbal presentation tends to rework what shows on the boards, but as a savvy student you can use the boards as a platform for orally embellishing your solution. How to choose and organize the spoken word is covered in chapter 13.

As you prepare presentation sheets for a pinup or faculty review, remember that drawings alone are not enough. What you write or letter on your boards is just as critical in conveying your design intent.

The written message typically includes the title, an explanation (brief or long, depending on the type of problem) of the concept, and important drawing labels or legends. The amount of writing may be substantial when you seek to explain a technical, financial, or management issue.

Consider both the content and the form of your text.

Content. First, make sure your theme or argument comes across. Whether it's the reorganization of a huge, 4000-student high school into small, 500-student units; a community college that respects its context; a midrise suburban commercial building that complies with green standards; the design of a two-mile bridge span; or a contemporary workplace environment that's totally flexible—say so in an easy-to-read headline. For text of some length, use a verbal shorthand to avoid unnecessary items such as articles (a, the) and useless adjectives and adverbs. Divide the text into small, logical parts, and assign a number or bullet to each part. Study tabloid newspapers; they are expert in compacting mounds of information into the least number of words. You probably cannot rival "STIX NIX HIX PIX" (Small-town moviegoers ignore hayseed films), but something along the lines of "ABANDONED WIRE FACTORY IS SITE FOR COMMUNITY COLLEGE" does the job.

Format. Whether your lettering is by hand or machine-generated, what counts in the end is whether it can be read. Even if your review jury is sitting close to the boards, don't irritate them with lettering so small that they have to rise every other minute to pick out the text. Test letter height in advance to see how far it can be easily read. You'll do better to edit down the number of words and make them larger than to cram too many words on to your boards. Use the lettering on your board as simple but useful cues to your oral presentation.

Common Faults

Certain faults appear and reappear in student writing. The list that follows offers suggestions for avoiding them.

Tighten sentences—make fewer words work harder.

Shorten paragraphs—twenty lines should be ample.

When evaluating a project, avoid unspecific, essentially meaningless words such as "interesting," "impressive," "intriguing," "amazing," "surprising." Be specific, or explain why and how something is "interesting."

If you wax poetic about a building, do not get so carried away that your text reads like a publicity release.

Be sure to include basic credits—i.e., the client, the primary design professional and associated firms, the principal consultants, the contractor, and the photographer (essential if your text is to be published).

Some schools of architecture and design offer courses on verbal communication skills. These are not "English 101" courses, but are geared specifically to the writing demands of the design professions. The course typically takes up principles of good writing; gives uses and abuses of technical terminology and jargon; and shows how to write letters, proposals, reports, brochures, e-mail, and the other written work products of a typical practice. Also usually covered are tips on making a lucid oral presentation. Such courses give students a double payoff: early warning about the career benefits of clear writing and speech, and the opportunity to master the art by practicing it in class.

Think of the principles and suggestions in this chapter as guidelines, not as rules. The intent is to spur in your mind an attitude, not to think of suggested practices as dogma. With practice, these guidelines become second nature.

The Student's Job Hunt

In the booming design and construction climate of the early 2000s, graduates from design schools, especially those at the top of their class, created a job hunter's market. Some large design firms even sent in recruiters. But building construction is notoriously cyclical, and an economy that roared in your first year may be sliding when you graduate five years later. This places a premium on marshaling your assets in a convincing way as you apply for a job.

As a student your volume of practical experience is limited, so make the best of what you have. Consider:

• Your school work, especially studio work in building types that are a specialty of the firm you're courting, or projects that won you a high grade or that graphically sparkle. Also consider an in-depth, well-written report on a technical or design topic, or an assignment for a design writing course.

• Practical summer or part-time experience. Focus on accomplishments rather than on activities, whether in the office or in the field. Even menial work is significant because it gave you an inside look at the operations of an office.

• Computer experience.

• Travel (don't list cruises in Norwegian fjords unless you can demonstrate a design benefit).

- Published writing on design or construction topics.
- Languages, but only if your knowledge is technical and fluent.
- Social or other contacts to make your prospective employer take notice.

Be sure to focus on germane professional items; shun entries such as this one, sent to me by a recent graduate who was obviously short on relevant skills: "High school: junior and senior years, member, later secretary of the Jefferson High School Chowder and Marching Society."

Consider the following successful student resume.

SCENARIO

You are about to graduate with your first professional degree. You decide to prepare a one-page list-style (as opposed to narrative-style) resume that places you in the best light for a solid, entry-level job offer. You have worked summers for professional design firms as well as in a retail store.

A STUDENT'S RESUME

GEORGIA DUPLESSIS
1-A Avenue of the Elysian Fields,
New Orleans, LA 70100
T: (504) 123-4567, F: (504) 123-4568
e-mail: gduplessis@cpr.com
Web site: www.geodup.net

EXPERIENCE
Summer 2005. Portofino Associates, architects, Baton Rouge, LA
Technical assistant
I reviewed the firm's archives under partner's supervision, then reorganized them for easy access. Researched and compiled sources to aid designer of new Botanical Garden, freeing her for added assignments.

Summer 2004. Haussmann and Moses, urban designers and planners, Fenton, TX
CAD operator
I drew base plans for master plans for inner-city districts in Dallas and Fort Worth, using AutoCAD 2004, Form Z 5.0, and Photoshop. I created original map symbols that proved effective and more flexible than off-the-shelf symbol libraries. Also took part in field surveys.

Summer 2003. Neiman-Marcus, Houston, TX
Assistant office manager
Duties included secretarial support of office manager and three buyers, using conventional and on-line media, and customer service. I diplomatically handled numerous complaints to the satisfaction of customers and my boss, even persuading one to drop a lawsuit over an accident that the customer conceded was her fault.

EDUCATION
2000–2003 Colby College, Waterville, ME. B.A., 2003
2003–present Tulane University, New Orleans, LA. B.Arch. (graduation date was expected 2006, but postponed due to disruption of curriculum by Hurricane Katrina)

PROFESSIONAL AFFILIATIONS
Chaired Tulane chapter of the American Institute of Architecture Students (organized conference to plan the Gulf Coast reconstruction).
Member of Tulane Cercle Français. Cercle traveled to West Africa to study natural temperature control techniques.

PUBLICATIONS
"A Student Looks at the Design Professions," *Architectural Chronicle*, May 2004
"The Getty Museum as Urban Design," *CRIT*, May 2005

SPECIAL SKILLS
Fluent on common computer software including CAD, spreadsheet, database, and word processing on Mac and PC platforms
Fluent in technical Spanish and French

HOBBY: Mountain hiking [optional]

REFERENCES: Available on request

Your resume should always state an accomplishment, not merely an activity. A little narrative is added in the summer jobs held, for a more personal touch.

Be aware that employers cannot ask you questions about your race, sexual preference, or religion. There is nothing to prevent you from inserting such information, but it could place the interviewer in an awkward position and thus is best left out.

Arrange your material on the page so each heading is in bold type and the dates stand out. Be sure to incorporate important key words, such as "exceeded," "launched," "created," and similar proactive terms.

For detailed examples and samples of writing correspondence, brochures, proposals, reports, texts for exhibit boards, and other written products, refer to chapters 2–5. Turn to chapter 10 for writing for the media. Finally, refer to chapter 1 for in-depth tips and examples of clear writing.

8 Job Prospects

Nowhere does the quality of your writing count more than when used to advance your own career prospects. If you are a graduating student looking for your first job or a restive employee in a design firm, government, or a corporate or institutional facilities agency who is looking for a change; if you are a junior faculty member seeking a tenure position or promotion; or if you have your eye on a juicy grant that will take you to Harvard or Rome or afford you time to pursue a cherished project—your chances depend greatly on how you present yourself through the few pieces of paper that will serve (along with references and an interview) as your ambassadors.

Career options for design professionals include:

> Private practice
>> design
>> project management
>> technical expertise
>> specification writing
>> estimating
>> office administration
>> construction contract administration
>> business and general management
>> business development (marketing)
>> information technology (IT) management
>> public relations and communications
>
> Government service
> Corporate facility staff
> Education
> Writing/journalism
> Product development
> Research
> Real estate development

Applying for a Job

This chapter tackles the most common categories of applications and submittals (for developing a winning dossier for academic promotion or tenure, see

128

chapter 9). It also offers guidelines on writing a letter of reference that will enhance your protégé's chances.

You usually look for work in one of seven ways:

1. Identify a firm you want to work for, and apply;
2. Look in the classified section of the newspaper or browse the Web sites of known firms;
3. Contact a recruiter who specializes in design professions;
4. Send the word out over your personal or electronic network;
5. Advertise in print;
6. Scan electronic job boards (see pages 130–131);
7. Network aggressively.

There is another variation, known as informational interviewing. Here you visit target firms with the understanding that they have no openings but use the interview as a way for both parties to get to know each other, and thereby create contacts.

Play out as many of these scenarios as you need to. Whether you are a graduating student or have been in practice for years, follow this procedure:

1. Assemble your assets. *Do not merely list activities; focus instead on successes and accomplishments.*
2. Develop a resume, cover letter, and attachments. Some combine the cover letter with the resume, but it is better to separate the two.
3. Send the package. Use first-class mail, private express mail, or messenger. Send by fax if requested by the firm, but some fax machines print on flimsy paper and weaken your impact. Send by e-mail or CD-ROM if acceptable to the firm. More and more firms post a job application template on their Web sites. You complete the various fields—some mandatory, some optional—and submit.

The Resume

You may organize your resume as either a narrative or a listing of your qualifications. A crisply written narrative is better able to convey character; a listing can transmit a greater volume of facts. Use the first or third person, whichever seems most comfortable to you.

The main attribute of a winning resume is that it mentions accomplishments and results, not merely activities. Use specific verbs such as "increased," "completed," "exceeded," "launched," "built." Terms such as "conducted," "coordinated," "managed," "administered" will do only so long as they are seen to culminate in a worthy result. Avoid phrases such as "participated in," "researched," or "was team member" as they give no clue as to the success or failure of your efforts.

List your past activities—most recent ones first. If you have a long record of positions, list them by type of work or position. Reviewers read from the

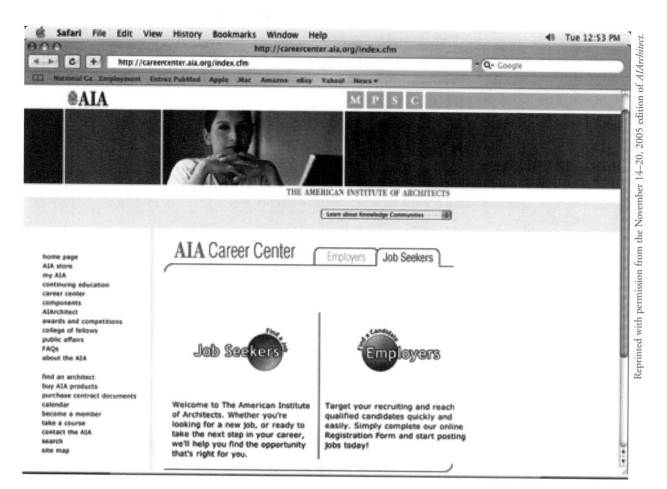

Examples of Web site job boards from AIArchitect (above) and the American Council of Engineering Companies (opposite).

top down; chances are what you did last week is more relevant than what you did eight years ago.

Include in your resume the following items, assuming there is something positive to say about each item (as a student or recent graduate, the amount of information will be more limited; how to deal with this challenge to your advantage is covered later in this chapter):

Positions held and results achieved. Be quantitative if you can (percent under budget; millions of dollars in project-managed construction; successful initiatives).

Publications. What you have written—so long as each is germane to design—and media where your work has been published; focus on quality over quantity.

Education. Stick with colleges, unless you went to a secondary school whose status or location could help your case.

Computer savvy. List software you know, especially CAD or management software, with its version or release; and programs you have written or adapted.

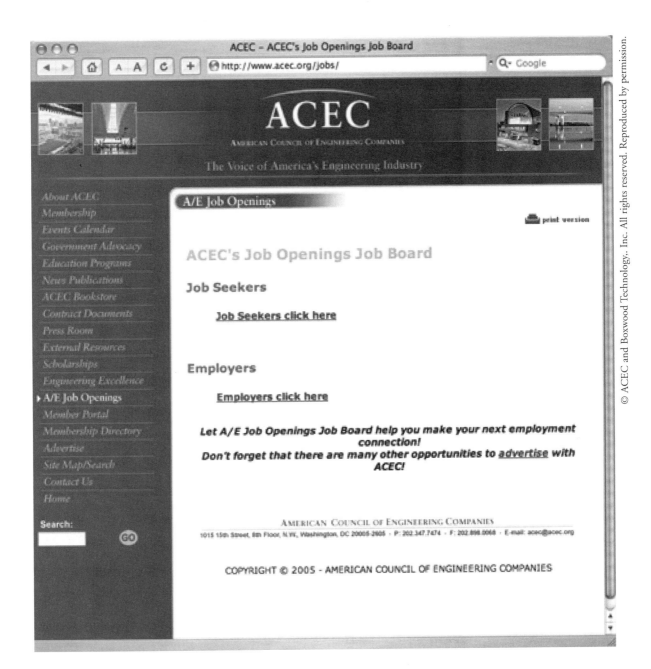

Registrations. Name states, and whether you have a certificate from the National Council of Architectural Registration Boards (NCARB), the Council of Landscape Architectural Registration Boards (CLARB), or the National Council of Examiners for Engineering and Surveying (NCEES). Include overseas registrations.

Travel, where relevant. "Photographed examples of mud architecture as used in modern low-rise office construction in India for an article in *Texas Architect*" beats "traveled to India, Pakistan, Russia, Thailand, Bali, and Malaysia."

Languages spoken or understood, especially design and construction terminology.

Military service, where relevant.

Cover Letter

Your cover letter should be short—two-thirds of a page—but needs to dwell on the following:

- What you are interested in, and why (say this up front).
- Show enthusiasm for working for the firm. Research the firm so you know its strong points and marketplace. (Unfortunately, when responding to a classified ad or in dealing with a recruiter, often you may not know this.)
- Special qualifications. Select them from the resume and briefly restate them here.
- Indicate readiness to travel. Many firms with global practices look for globetrotter staff.
- Show confidence. Use words like "will," not "would"; "must," not "should."
- Ask for an interview.

Let the content determine the length of the cover letter. If you are a student, don't pad it with irrelevant efforts. If you are a mid-career practitioner, gear the length to your audience, including only those items that will help your cause. If you can, determine the name and title of the person to whom your letter should be addressed.

For an example of a cover letter, see page 134.

Enclosures and Attachments

Strengthen your message with enclosures and attachments. Include page-size reproductions of projects relevant to the job or the executive summary page of a key feasibility report. Make sure each is clearly identified and captioned, with a brief statement as to why it is relevant. If the job sought is an academic one, enclose a listing of published work.

Double-check the graphic quality of the enclosures. Eliminate any but the most engaging and clearest items. You do not want poor artwork to torpedo an outstanding written message.

Indicate that more material is available on request.

The Computerized Resume

Some employers, especially high-technology companies with a high volume of job applications, now process resumes electronically. They use optical scanners to identify desired skills by searching for industry key words, phrases, or acronyms—such as "chief designer," "project manager," "JAVA," "AutoCAD Release 14," "top 5%," "fluent Mandarin."

Computerized scanners are said to prefer nouns over verbs. Key nouns such as those listed above may get noticed more than action verbs such as "exceeded." Insert the important verbs anyway; not every firm scan-reads resumes—that is more the province of large corporations and recruiting agencies than of the design professions.

You may also find preformatted resume-writing software packages that reflect some employers' wishes for easily identifiable key words (these packages vary from the one-size-fits-all to more targeted ones). The template for the job hunter is often contained on the employer's Web site. You complete the requested fields and click the "submit" button. If this option doesn't exist, download the software from the Web site, complete it, and fax or mail it back. Even though the submittal may be on paper, feel free to burn and enclose a CD containing images of your work.

Here are added tips for on-line resumes, as suggested by Max Messmer, chairman of Accountemps, a job search services company:

- Target your resume. Don't broadcast your resume indiscriminately.
- Format your resume in a commonly used language such as Word, or in plain text so most computers can read it.
- Send it in the correct format. Some firms have firewalls or antivirus software that discourages e-mail attachments. If you're not sure, paste the text of your resume into the body of the e-mail.
- Use the subject line wisely. For example, include the title of the position.
- Prompt the recipient to keep reading. Include an introductory message. on the lines of a cover letter described elsewhere in this chapter.
- Provide hard copies. Print on quality paper and bring to interviews.

No matter what the medium, your bottom-line motto must always be "think accomplishment, not activity."

For a discussion of the student's job hunt, see chapter 7.

Changing Jobs

Once you are into your career, you are likely to change jobs several times in your career.

SCENARIO
You have worked at Gazebo Associates, landscape architects, for six years, and you feel it's time for a change. Your heart is set on working for Green & Associates. They have advertised in key local newspapers and their Web site for a designer and production person, and you decide to go for it. Here is one possibility for your cover letter and resume. Their advertisement:

LANDSCAPE ARCHITECTS
For a versatile Filmore County firm. Degree, plus 4-6 yrs exp in design, constr docs, production & field superv. Communications skills essential. 2 yrs of office AutoCAD 2000 or later exp required. Mail resume and enclosures to Green & Associates, 4 Eucalyptus Street, Rosefield, MS 38000, or complete the form by visiting www.green.com/contact.jobs

Ms. Olivia Green, Partner
Green & Associates
4 Eucalyptus Street
Rosefield, MS 38000

Dear Ms. Green:

I'm confident that I'm the right staff person for the position described on your Web site and in last Sunday's *Boston Herald* and *Mississippi Times.*

You will see from my resume that

- My experience includes four years in the office of Michael van Nyhuis, where I worked on developing contract documents and later did field supervision on projects that included the Riverfront Walk in Minneapolis and four mid-sized parks in Columbus, IN. All came in on budget and were completed on schedule.
- I was recently promoted to associate project manager, only six years after graduating from the landscape architecture program at the Harvard Graduate School of Design.
- At Harvard I was deputy editor of *Harvard Design Magazine.*
- I received the Rich Travel Prize and used the money to document through sketches and notes the great English eighteenth-century natural parks at Blenheim and Althorp, relating their message to today's environmental practices.
- I have fluent mastery of AutoCAD 2004 and LandCADD, and related software.

I have studied and worked out of state since I left for graduate school, but my Mississippi roots go back four generations. I'm anxious to return to this state and bring my experience and enthusiasm to work in your firm.

I look forward to an interview with you.

Sincerely,
Mary Ellen Brown

Encl:
Resume (one page)
Project sheets (Minneapolis; Columbus, IN)

MARY ELLEN BROWN
6C Brattle Street • Cambridge, MA 02138
T: 617/459-2001 • F: 617/459-2002
e-mail: brownme@mzu.c
web: www.maelbr.net

EXPERIENCE
2001–2005
Mary Ellen Brown began as a designer in the office of Michael van Nyhuis. After eight months as a junior designer and production person, she was promoted to

associate project manager and a year later to project manager. In that position she coordinated the design, production, and later field supervision of two significant landscape projects designed by Mr. van Nyhuis: the Minneapolis Riverfront Walk and four midsized parks in Columbus, IN. Both projects had tight budgets and in one case faced persistent poor weather during construction, but were completed on budget and on schedule. Both projects were published in *Landscape Architecture* and *Garden Design*.

1999–2001

Brown's first full-time position was as a designer in the San Francisco headquarters of the architecture, interior design, and landscape architecture firm Vancic & Ericson. There she completed, in record time, under partner Janko Vancic's direction, schematics for the three-acre St. Absalom park, playground, and fountain on Russian Hill. With the partners' support, she completed a detailed management report on the workings of a large, multidisciplinary firm, which she developed into an acclaimed paper presented at the 2000 northwest regional convention of ASLA in Seattle.

COMPUTER SKILLS

Expert use of AutoCAD release 2004, and LandCADD, augmented by custom creation of landscape symbols and textures. Also Adobe Illustrator, 3D Studio Max, and Atlas and Foxpro linked to GIS.

EXTRA-OFFICE EXPERIENCE

On a Rich Travel fellowship, Brown spent six months at Blenheim Palace and Althorp House researching Georgian parks developed under the influence of Capability Brown. Identified and sketched every tree, flower, and shrub species in the two locations; her report has come to be used as a text in the landscape architecture curricula at the University of Pennsylvania and the University of California at Berkeley.

The other six months of the fellowship Brown spent in post–World War II new towns, including Cumbernauld and Milton Keynes, tracking intended versus actual uses of open land.

EDUCATION

In 1999 obtained a B.A. from Mississippi State University.

Graduated summa cum laude in 2001 with a Bachelor of Landscape Architecture degree from the Graduate School of Design, Harvard University.

REGISTRATION

Brown holds the Council of Landscape Architectural Registration Boards (CLARB) certificate.

References are available on request.

SCENARIO

Some employers demand submittal by fax. You are a structural engineer and found the following advertisement in the newspaper:

ENGINEER

Growth-oriented consulting engineering firm has outstanding opportunity for a self-motivated structural designer accomplished in innovative structural design, with significant management skills. Constructive team member. Good communications skills. 12+ years experience required. Submit resume by fax to: Levy Associates, attn. William Thomson, FAX: 404/201-0000.

FAX COVER PAGE AND RESUME

COVER PAGE

TO: William Thomson, Levy Associates
FAX: 404/201-0000

Mr. Thomson:

I saw your advertisement in Sunday's *Atlanta Constitution*. I have long admired the work of your firm, and would like to be part of the team. I have held positions of increasing responsibility at three of the nation's most eminent structural engineering firms.

After you have reviewed the attached resume, I look forward to the opportunity of an interview.

George A. Williams, PE

(Note that Williams decided to send a "listing" resume instead of a narrative, the brevity suggested by the required fax format. The firms listed in the resume are real, but the applicant's positions and functions are fictitious.)

RESUME

George A. Williams PE
400 State Street
Oak Park, IL 60300
Telephone: 708/210-0001 (home)
Facsimile: 708/210-0002 (home)
e-mail: gawpe@mzu.com
Web: www.gaw.com

WORK EXPERIENCE
Leslie E. Robertson Associates, New York, NY, 1999–present
Senior engineer. Leader of design teams on 20 high-rise and other large buildings. Project engineer on 15 renovation, facade investigation, and repair projects. Launched investigation into methods to protect high-rise office buildings from damage from natural or human causes.

Arup, New York, NY, 1994–1999
Senior engineer. Project manager for 30 large-scale preservation and conservation projects. Developed advanced technique for nonintrusive analysis of the building fabric.

Thornton-Tomasetti Group, New York, NY, 1988–1994
Designer on 12 buildings ranging from 4 to 32 stories. Realized improved coordination between owners and contractors using project Web sites.

EDUCATION
Georgia Institute of Technology. B.S. in Civil Engineering, 1986
Columbia University Graduate School of Architecture, Planning and Preservation. M.S. in Preservation, 1988

REGISTRATIONS
P.E.: New York, Georgia, Massachusetts, Colorado, Texas

MEMBERSHIP
National Society of Professional Engineers

TEACHING
Adjunct professor, City College of City University of New York

PUBLICATIONS
Composite Structure Materials. Titanium Press, 2005
Conserving Historic Structures. Vernon Press, 1998

LANGUAGES
Technical Spanish (fluent)

References on request

The Portfolio

The portfolio is a packet of personal qualifications. Consider it when your materials are more graphic than written. It contains chiefly reproductions of completed design work, suitably annotated, and is typically accompanied by a transmittal letter and a resume. For details, see chapter 3 on portfolios and Harold Linton's work *Portfolio Design*, described in the Resources section.

Grant Submittals

Winning applications for grants and awards follow tactics similar to those used in successful job applications. You are pitching your skills to a person or a committee who very likely doesn't know you and who will match those skills against certain criteria. Your chances of winning depend on how shrewdly you select your good points and how lucidly you write them up.

Grants sponsors typically offer money or prestige or both. They provide funds that permit a winner to do independent work. Grants may be applied to research and travel leading to exhibition or publication. Recipients are usually individuals, but in some cases institutions are eligible. The best-known grantors in the design fields include the John Simon Guggenheim Memorial Foundation, the Graham Foundation, the National Endowment for the Arts, and the J. M. Kaplan Fund. The New York Chapter of the American Institute of Architects offers grants from the Allwork, Stewardson, Keefe, Norden, and LeBrun Funds. Grants can range from $2500 to upwards of $30,000. The Boston Society of Architects administers the Rotch Traveling Scholarship. Some grants tend to favor recent graduates; some, practitioners in mid-career; and some, scholars. The Loeb Fellowship program, for example, is one year of mid-career for study at the Harvard Graduate School of Design. Contact local chapters and headquarter offices of your professional society for sources of grants.

Students are eligible for a variety of important research and travel scholarships. Principal sponsors are design schools. A special program that recognizes written work is the Douglas Haskell Award for student architectural journalism, named after the late *Architectural Forum* editor and administered by the AIA's New York Chapter.

It is up to you to identify and screen awards programs. Deadlines vary widely, as do entry requirements. The Russell Sage Foundation in New York City (www.russellsage.org) keeps a database of charitable foundations, accessible by discipline, among other criteria. Most sponsors send out notices about upcoming grants for posting on design-school bulletin boards and for publication in design journals and society newsletters. In some cases candidates are nominated by their design-school deans.

A large part of the work of submitting is faithful completion of the many boxes common to most application forms. You'll gain the most points, however, by the way you write a component typically known as "the Statement." This asks you why you selected your topic and how you intend to apply the award money.

Your statement needs to deal with these queries, typically in this order:

What is to be the end product of your study?
Why is the end product important?
Who is its audience?
How will it reach the audience?
How will it benefit this audience?
How does it conform to the values of the donor agency?
What are your publication plans?
What are your special qualifications for tackling the project?

Your style should be simple and concise—the 100 to 200 words you are given do not allow for rhetoric; keep technical terms to a minimum and eschew jargon—applications often go through a two- or three-tier review process, and you don't know how many reviewers will be from outside the design professions. The following are abstracts of selected winning grants at the Graham Foundation for Advanced Studies in the Fine Arts.

ABSTRACT A

Julie Campoli, Elizabeth Humstone, and Alex Maclean
VERMONT LAND PATTERNS
Research Leading to Publication

With aerial photography and computer enhanced images, the completed work will illustrate how rural landscapes have changed over time. It will demonstrate to a general audience how the shift from traditional to suburban settlement patterns has created areas of sprawl in rural areas, emphasizing the effect of small scale, incremental development. As they see the land both from the air and through history, readers will begin to recognize these patterns and develop the ability to predict how their own land use decisions will affect the landscape around them.

The book will demonstrate how small towns have traditionally handled growth and how they can be used as models for future development. With aerial views and historic photos and maps of dense downtowns and village streets it will reveal the strong urban tradition of rural areas, demonstrating how a traditional settlement pattern of compact settlements surrounded by open land can sustain development for generations.

The book will feature traditional and contemporary examples of urban centers, neighborhoods, highways, villages, and farm land, highlighting the contrast between patterns and demonstrating alternative approaches. It will illustrate several transformations in detail: a rural road to a commercial strip, a crossroads hamlet to a manufacturing village, productive farm land to large lot housing subdivisions, and the suburbanization of downtowns.

Courtesy Julie Campoli and The Graham Foundation, 1995.

ABSTRACT B

Indiana University Press
DRAWN FROM AFRICAN DWELLINGS
Publication Support

Drawn from African Dwellings will be the first comprehensive study of West African architecture, with a focus on Senegal. The study assumes building practices, living, and ecology are inseparable. It sets into relief some of the structural patterns common to formal aspects of the house (setting, design, decoration, orientation, etc.), and oral traditions and religion. *Drawn from African Dwellings* is ground-breaking in its effort to redefine "tradition" as a mobile, living entity that may not be relegated to the past. Such an understanding will make a critical difference in how we view the growth and change of different cultures that populate the world. The study takes a fresh look at the idea of housing that challenges our preconceived notion of a house as a fixed dwelling or the notion of home related to a Eurocentric view of comfort, security, and individual property.

The book relies on a diverse body of oral accounts and written documentation collected during several years of library research in Dakar, Paris, London, and the United States since 1977, and from extensive field work in Dakar and inland Senegal. Although the information presented is condensed and highly selective, the book comprises 320 pages, 151 duotone drawings, and 225 photographs.

Courtesy Indiana University Press and The Graham Foundation, 1995.

ABSTRACT C

Christiane Hertel
RECONSTRUCTING DRESDEN
Research Leading to Publication

This study is an investigation of the aesthetic and political implications of the reconstruction of Dresden's Baroque center, which was almost entirely destroyed in February 1945. Emphasis is on the rebuilding of Matthaus D. Poppelmann's Dresden Zwinger (1711–28) immediately after World War II, and the current reconstruction of George Bahr's Frauenkirche (1726–43). Reduced to a heap of rubble, its ruin had been declared a war monument dedicated to the victims of Dresden. After the fall of the Berlin Wall in 1989, a citizen's initiative brought about the decision to rebuild the church. This decision has been very controversial.

The primary purpose of this study is a critical comparison of these two reconstructions, their guiding principles, their public perception, and both continuity and discontinuity in the values attached to these two landmarks of Dresden over time.

Courtesy Christiane Hertel and The Graham Foundation, 1995.

Letters of Reference

At some point in a career nearly every design practitioner is asked to write a letter of reference for a professional colleague, student, or friend. An employee (not one of yours) is switching jobs; a designer applies for a one-year mid-career study grant; a firm principal is being nominated for fellowship in a professional society; a practitioner is nominated for the Carlsberg Prize.

When you write a reference letter, consider these issues:

• Use superlatives ("brilliant," "outstanding," "incomparable"). Superlatives are good in a reference letter to ensure that the candidate is not being damned with faint praise.

- Send copies of your letter to the candidate unless instructed not to. That way a successful candidate will be grateful; a losing candidate can't fault you for not trying.

- Obtain the necessary background data on the candidate to help you compose your assessment. Nothing is more embarrassing to the candidate than to have your letter include errors of fact.

If you don't want to write the letter, decline immediately—say you are already endorsing another candidate, or you are busy, or you are going out of town on a long trip.

SCENARIO

Liu Sung-Yee, a former associate, has been proposed for fellowship in the American Institute of Architects, and his sponsor has asked you to write a letter in support of his nomination.

REFERENCE LETTER

Mr. Reginald Hay, Chairman, Fellowship Jury
American Institute of Architects
1735 New York Avenue, NW
Washington, DC 20006

Dear Mr. Hay:

Liu Sung-Yee would be a superb addition to the College of Fellows.

I support his nomination for personal and professional reasons. I have known Sung-Yee for over twenty-one years, from the time he first went into practice as a junior designer in the office of Gómez and Abernathy to his present role as principal of a sixty-person office. In that period he has managed to accomplish what is possible to few. He excels as a designer—buildings and interiors projects from his office have won national honor awards four years in a row. And he has the special gift to inspire students as professor of architecture at the University of Washington.

His designs mark a genius for creating innovative forms inspired by modern structural and mechanical technology and computer-aided manufacturing techniques. Yet he insists on calm and tranquility, qualities that these days are often brushed aside in the race to be original.

There can be no real genius without character. Sung-Yee meets the test in things both small and large. He is totally a man of his word. A promise to return a phone call or to deliver a book review to a magazine is never broken; the word "excuse" is not in his vocabulary. Last year he rigorously took up the cause of a fellow practitioner wrongly accused of unethical behavior by unscrupulous competitors, and obtained his reinstatement. Knowing that the quality of our built environment is only as good as the demands of an enlightened client, he dedicates several hours a month to teaching appreciation of architecture to future clients in the public schools of his native Seattle.

I cannot think of a more worthy candidate for Fellowship, and commend him to the Jury's consideration with the utmost enthusiasm.
Sincerely,
Francis X. O'Connor, Partner
Jansson & O'Connor

This letter is enthusiastic and specific.

Writing in Academe 9

This chapter offers guidelines to help faculty members enhance the impact of their writing to students, tenure committees, journal editors, and book publishers.

Faculty writing typically consists of:

Sponsored research reports
Recommendations on school programs and policies
Applications for promotion or tenure
Comments on or endorsements of applications for promotion or tenure
Scholarly papers (topics include design theory and practice, aesthetics, teaching methods, pedagogy, criticism, technology, history, academic administration, drawing and visual presentation, computers)
Books
Studio problems
Course syllabi

Much of this writing is no different from the reports, proposals, and correspondence discussed in earlier chapters. Where they differ is in the unique subject matter—issues of student performance, curricula and syllabi, teaching philosophy and concepts, and design criticism—which has tended to center in the schools rather than in design practices. Faculty face the challenge of expressing intangible, often theoretical concepts in language that is scholarly without being elusive, and down-to-earth while reflecting the special wisdom expected of the educator.

Academic writing has, often unfairly, been saddled with a reputation for obfuscation. The assumption that critical or scholarly writing has to be obscure to be important—Eleanor Roosevelt is once said to have remarked that you always admire what you don't understand—is not unique to design. Princeton historian James McPherson cited the dilemma professional historians have (allegedly) in reaching broad general audiences, writing in the *Princeton Alumni Weekly:*

Soon after [my best seller] *Battle Cry* [*Battle Cry of Freedom: The Civil War Era*] was published, a member of the program committee of a professional association formally invited me to participate in a session about the book at the association's annual meeting. I was flattered and . . . said yes. Six months later I received an apologetic letter from the same committee calling the whole thing off. No coherent explanation was given, but in my re-reading of the correspondence, it seemed clear that a majority of the program committee felt that a book which had reached a large audience of non-professionals was not sufficiently weighty to merit a session at a professional meeting.

A colleague at a California university recently remarked to me that I would be forced to choose between becoming a "popular historian" or a "historian's historian." He strongly hinted that I was in mortal danger of becoming the former.

Excerpt from "What's the Matter with History" by James M. McPherson. *Princeton Alumni Weekly*, 22 January 1997, reprinted by permission.

Several schools now encourage clear writing for faculty through courses and special interdepartmental liaison programs. For example, the Multimedia-Authoring, Teaching and Research Facility (MATRF) at Clemson University has catered to faculty who wish to write and develop multimedia materials for their courses. Architecture, the arts, and the humanities at Clemson are combined in a single college, at one time headed by architecture dean (and later Clemson president) James Barker.

Some schools of architecture offer elective writing courses to students. These courses do not teach students to write English but to write intelligibly and intelligently on design topics. One such course is taught by this author at The City College of New York. The course involves a simple design problem with the various types of writing that accompany an actual design project. That includes marketing correspondence, proposal writing, reports, client correspondence, requests to be published, and press releases. Architecture schools at the University of Minnesota and Yale University are among a handful of other schools that teach architectural writing to students.

Papers and Research Reports

Articles, papers, and research reports need structure. Despite slight variations due to content and audience, a topic may be broken down as in the following outline:

State and define the topic.
Why is it important? What are the issues?
What are its main components?
What is the role of each component?
Who or what are the principal influences?
What is the likely outcome?
What is the desirable outcome?

What are the arguments in favor of the outcome? Against it?

Is there need for further study?

What are resources for added study?

Notice the structure of the outline. Begin with the topic, break it down successively into its logical parts and details, then begin to retrieve the various strands. At the end, bring the parts together into a conclusion that states an opinion justified by the preceding arguments. An admirable source for developing this attack in greater depth is Barbara Pinto's *Pyramid Principle: Logic in Writing and Thinking* (see Resources), which forces logic into the writer's thinking. This logic will translate itself into better writing.

Most publishers of academic papers will supply an author's guide that spells out the desired format and style; how to deal with footnotes, bibliographies, illustrations, and other apparatus such as the index and table of contents; and in what form to submit the whole. Publisher's guides also counsel on the quality of writing, and you are wise to read those sections before you start, as they define for you what the publisher's expectations are. A favorite general guide is the *Chicago Manual of Style: The Essential Guide for Writers, Editors, and Publishers,* now in its 15th edition.

Journals, such as the *Journal of Architectural Education (JAE)* or the *Journal of Architectural Historians* publish papers refereed by the author's professional peers—usually three to six. Each issue prints the ground rules for accepting a paper. The process is complicated and can take months. *JAE's* guidelines for its authors take up three pages. The object is to yield papers that are critical and fair; sadly, concern for good writing is contained in an inocuous paragraph included by *JAE* as one of seven instructions given to each referee:

> "If necessary, comment on the mechanics of the author's writing, grammar, style, usage, etc. Although specific editing of these is not necessary at this time, it is important to know the extent to which these might influence or impede one's understanding of the article's content."

Perhaps the greatest challenge in writing learned papers is the use or invention of jargon. It's represented in Roger Lewis' cartoon in the *Washington Post* (page 146). For examples of other jargon, see chapter 1.

Isolated examples of designer jargon are often held up for laughter, as in this cartoon. Yet a case could be made that they are taken out of context and that, if you read or listen further, the real meaning will emerge. The reality is that sometimes it does, sometimes it doesn't. On occasion, papers full of difficult language are permitted, because the language is quite clear, but only to a narrowly defined group who use with precision terms that only they understand.

For example, in the late 1980s a group of architects and designers flourished by seeking to transpose from the world of literary criticism the tenets of deconstructionism of Jacques Derrida into the world of design. The architectural champions of deconstructivism borrowed freely from Derrida's arcane vocabulary. Some claim that these closed groups are entitled to confer among them-

Cartoon by Roger K. Lewis, FAIA, first published in his "Shaping the City" column in the *Washington Post.* Reprinted by permission.

selves using what former Dean John Meunier at Arizona State University calls "privileged academic discourse" (PAD) that will help them develop a theoretical base for their work. But is this necessary or desirable? It took an architect and writer of the caliber of Michael Benedikt to discuss deconstructivism in clear language. Study the two excerpts from his book *Deconstructing the Kimbell: An Essay on Meaning and Architecture* (in chapter 10, on writing criticism).

It is hard to imagine that papers composed of obscure references and jargon are likely to fulfill their presumed purpose—awareness of a subject. Any author who makes a practice of communicating in language of limited currency risks damaging a career, mystifying prospective clients or employers, and giving students a signal that obscurity in writing is okay. Recall the sad instance of the college student who changed his writing style from lucid to obscure to improve his grades.

This chapter is therefore a plea for using known vocabulary to express known concepts. Invent new terms for novel concepts gingerly and then only if no word or combination of existing words will do the job. The following excerpts are from a highly successful paper. The subject is the Phoenix [Arizona] Homesteads project, a Depression-era federal effort in rural rehabilitation, affordable housing, sustainable community, and vernacular design. Homesteads is now an historic neighborhood on the National Register. Mary Hardin, while an associate professor at the University of Arizona, consulted on remodeling one of the houses, and in the process came to know the origins and attainments of the project, warts and all. At the 1995 national conference of the Association of Collegiate Schools of Architecture (ACSA), Hardin shared her findings, then wrote up the results, excerpted below.

THE PHOENIX HOMESTEADS PROJECT
Overlooked but Not Forgotten

(The Project)

Ensconced in the heart of Phoenix, Arizona, four miles from the downtown core, is an eighty-acre community that has flourished for nearly sixty years as a verdant oasis in the concentric rings of stucco and asphalt developing around it. The Phoenix Homesteads Project was an experiment in rural rehabilitation, affordable housing, community sustainability, and vernacular design that was surveyed, platted, constructed, and landscaped by the federal government in the midst of the Great Depression. That it came to a free enterprise conclusion and survives as a desirable residential neighborhood is a fact that challenges many of the myths that lend form to the desert city today. Lessons drawn from the project's inception, realization, and ultimate success could inform modern endeavors regardless of the decades that have intervened.

(The Myth of the West vs. Government Intervention)

Accounts of self-sufficient pioneers, scrappy prospectors, and resourceful entrepreneurs who tamed the elements dominate the lore of how the West was won. Explorers on horseback were followed in close succession by pioneers in their covered wagons, prospectors towing mules, and homesteaders traveling the railways and wagon roads.

(Differs from Stereotypes)

The Phoenix Homesteads project, which remains intact as a historic district, merits study as an experiment in cooperative living and working that differed widely from the stereotypes about the development of the West that prevailed during its inception and linger to the present day. Many homesteaders of the late 19th and early 20th centuries failed in their efforts. Some did well enough to gain the deeds to their land; but others gave up within months, forced out by hardships and economic circumstances. In retrospect, they are seen as innocent victims of greedy capitalists, venal government officials, a hostile environment, and an irreversible national movement toward an industrial economic base and an urban-based population.

By contrast, the homesteaders of the Phoenix Homesteads project were successful and prosperous, supported by the government until their personal efforts allowed them to repay their debts in full. Regardless of its socialist origins, the Subsistence Homesteads program concluded in parallel with the American dream; hard-working citizens were able to "pull themselves up by their bootstraps" and enter the mainstream of suburban life.

This project is also interesting as a model for comparison to contemporary affordable housing communities because it incorporated means of vocational and social support as well as residences that used local materials to best advantage. Operating costs of the homes were kept low by the sensitivity to the micro climate, and some costs of living were defrayed by the cooperative facilities (shared equipment, social and recreational spaces) and the edible landscaping.

Professor Hardin moves at a good pace through the subject, using precise but simple language, alternating short and long sentences to maintain interest in the topic.

Studio Problems

In schools of architecture and design, studio problems challenge the studio instructor to distill a program that might normally run to many pages into a single page with enough information to enable the student to create a viable design. Here is an example of a simply stated studio problem.

AN URBAN OUTLET FOR HOME DEPOT

Home Depot, one of the nation's largest suppliers of home repair and construction materials and tools, five years ago launched a bold store construction and renovation program totaling some two hundred stores a year, and plans to continue with the program on roughly the same scale over the next few years.

A key driver of Home Depot's construction program today is the shortage of suitable real estate to accommodate its needs. With that in mind, as well as to enter a market it had not hitherto developed, Home Depot has launched a major expansion into urban areas, including the five boroughs of New York City.

Such an urban agenda raises predictable challenges—parking, loading, vertical vs. the traditional horizontal arrangement of sales area, and, in some cases, landmark law compliance.

Your problem is to design an 80,000 sq. ft. facility at a midblock site in New York City's Chelsea district comprising mainly brick, stone, and cast iron structures dating to the late nineteenth century. The site has been cleared. It has 200 feet of street frontage, a depth of 100 feet and one basement, and a floor area ratio (FAR) of 4. Loading and deliveries are off-street. The block is landmarked: you are free to consider context in your design or ignore it. If you ignore it, you must be prepared to justify your design to the Landmarks Preservation Commission.

The program must accommodate these spaces (there follows a listing of principal required spaces with net square foot areas, and a suggested net-to-total-area ratio of 80%.)

The instructor made the following writing assignments geared to the design problem:

Marketing phase: Letter of interest to the client, proposal, oral interview with selection committee, feasibility report.

Post-selection: Oral presentation to client, letter to community group.

Post-occupancy: Press release, letter to an architectural journal seeking publication, entry on Web site.

> Problem assigned by Stephen Kliment to students at the School of Architecture, Urban Design and Landscape Architecture, The City College of New York, fall 2004.

COMMENT

In few words the program establishes the economic, urban and visual background of the design problem.

Tenure Applications and Promotions

Academic promotion, at some point leading to tenure, is a test of the ability of the candidate and the candidate's shepherds to organize the candidate's dossier or portfolio and state the case for promotion in clear language. The candidate is asking the school and the university to make a long-term, if not lifetime, commitment.

Much hinges on the dossier. Supporting items, such as prior work, are commonly sent to a board of referees—some of whom are chosen by the candidate, some by the school. If supporting papers are obscure because the candidate has used privileged academic discourse (PAD)—that language used by small subcultures as a kind of shorthand to communicate among themselves—the candidate risks opposition from referees who cannot fathom the material. Members of one generation often tend to speak or write what to a different generation seems like mystery-laden language, thereby muddying the odds of a dossier's contents being understood.

Published works heavy on PAD may work in your favor for a time but against you once the materials have reached people who may be mystified and perhaps annoyed by what seems to them obscure or turgid. Each candidate must call the shots on this issue.

Promotion procedures vary with the school or university. Some schools demand a "long form" dossier for in-house use and a "short form" dossier for external use, such as by the provost. The heaviest occur in from three categories of promotion: to associate professor with or without tenure, and to full professor.

Elements of a typical dossier where writing skill really counts include:

- the candidate's self-evaluation
- supporting matter in the form of prior work, such as designs and published papers or reports
- letters to referees from the candidate's department head requesting an evaluation
- letters of evaluation
- letter of recommendation to the dean from the department head

• the dossier's summary page, including a crucial three- to four-paragraph statement about the candidate written by the department head or the head of the promotion committee (this document alone typically goes to the final approval level, usually the university board of trustees).

The Candidate's Self-Evaluation

The self-evaluation must meld the assessment by candidates of their own worth with the values of the department and the university. (Promotions of individuals in a professional school, with their focus on practical achievement, sometimes clashes with the traditional academic focus on research and publication.)

The self-evaluation should document high performance in line with some or all of the following criteria:

• The overall focus or scheme of your work and accomplishment, and its importance to your discipline. This may be research, design, criticism, teaching.
• An assessment of each element of your work—how does it assist the work of others? To what degree does it build on the work of others?
• What is there about your teaching, research, and design work that is in tune with your department's needs, vision, and values? With national values?
• Is your work suited to further development?
• How do you view your educational role in the department, and how have you acted on it?
• How have you told your concerns to others in your field and those outside your field, such as design clients and the general public?
• What has been your role and influence in the intellectual life of the university?
• How have you remained in touch with the professional life of your design discipline, as a designer, professional society committee member, journal editor, consultant?
• If applicable, reasons for a meager publishing record.
• What are your personal aspirations for the future?

An astute declaration of criteria for tenure was created at MIT by former School of Architecture and Planning dean William Mitchell. The document forms part of the school's "Guidelines for the Preparation of Promotion, Tenure and Appointment Cases." The criteria are summarized here with permission. They are typical of major research universities. Direct quotes are from the document.

The standards were created to offer a level playing field for all tenure-track faculty members, whatever their specialty or domain. They are tough and justified by the school on the grounds that "only extraordinary people should be given tenured appointments—particularly in an era of pressing resource constraints and one in which mandatory retirement no longer applies." The school distinguishes three kinds of concerns:

Intellectual leadership
Teaching
Equity and consistency

Intellectual leadership is defined as "a demonstrated track record of recognized intellectual achievement, and consequent stature as a leader in some domain of importance" to architecture and related disciplines. This track record recognizes four models or combinations of models:

Humanities model. This calls for one substantial published book based on a dissertation and one book not so based. It also requires evidence, through letters, of a high reputation among leaders in the field—home and international. At least six scholarly papers in refereed journals may be used to replace the second book.

Science and engineering model. The candidate is expected to produce at least six research papers in refereed journals, plus evidence through letters that the research is important, that it has influenced others, and that its author is a "national leader" in his or her specialization. Also required is a high rank in a listing of workers in that field.

Design practice model. Here the track record can take the form of "a built, published, and critically discussed work." The assumption is that this sort of record is "equal in significance for the field of architecture to the public intellectual track record of a leading scientist or humanities scholar, but is simply different in the form of production." It acknowledges that "publish or perish" for architects and designers can take a different form from the traditional books and papers. The record calls for "at least two major built projects, premiated competition entries, significant theoretical projects"—all published in so-called mainstream design journals. A major published project is seen as the equivalent of a book or "pathbreaking" technical paper. Evidence is needed through letters that the candidate has reached the "stature of a leading designer and design thinker."

Artwork and design thinker model. This model requires "a track record of artistic production, exhibition of work and critical recognition." That means two (minimum) shows with published catalogs, or several "major public installations," reviews by "important critics," and evidence through letters that the work has been "innovative and significant."

Teaching is important but, at least under the Mitchell principles, doesn't take the place of a publishing or practice record. In a telling sentence, the memorandum declares: "Inability or unwillingness to teach . . . is a ground for denial of tenure. . . . Teaching excellence can strengthen a tenure case. . . . But teaching excellence alone, in the absence of the necessary publication or practice record, does not establish a tenure case."

The document admits that under today's more rigorous standards many already tenured faculty would never have made the grade. This should not "be allowed to create ambiguity." Current standards have to be rigorously and consistently applied.

This set of criteria underscores again how critical writing is in advancing careers. Even the tenure route through publication of built designs requires written descriptions that need to be models of clarity.

Supporting Matter

Supporting matter is heavy on published work, such as books, papers in refereed and non-refereed journals, research reports, transcribed invited lectures, articles for the professional press, supervised theses or dissertations; or built or unbuilt designs, suitably documented through drawings, photography, and succinct text arranged in problem/solution sequence.

Referees are independent appraisers of a candidate's qualifications. The letter to referees, typically written by the department head, asks the referees for a fair evaluation of the candidate. Because of the vital impact of these evaluations on the candidate's prospects, how the request letter is couched is very important.

Letter of Request to Referee

The example includes the main components of a letter of request to a referee.

Dear_____:

We are considering the promotion of Professor _____ from the rank of Assistant Professor to that of Associate Professor (without tenure). As we evaluate the case for this promotion, we will take account of Professor_____'s intellectual contributions to her field, her effectiveness as a teacher, and her record of university and community service. To help us make this evaluation knowledgeably and fairly, we need to have the comments of people who can critically assess Professor_____'s qualifications and record.

We would, then, be most grateful to receive your written comments. We realize that you may not be in a position to comment on all aspects of Professor_____'s work, but whatever insights you may be able to provide will be useful to us. In particular, please send us comments on the following:

Her major research, scholarly, or design practice contributions and their significance;

Her standing in her field (an indication of her peers of comparable age, together with your assessment of her relative position in that group, would be especially helpful);

Her potential for future professional growth and leadership in her field;

Her effectiveness as a teacher (if you have personal knowledge of this).

The more precise and specific your comments, the more helpful they will be. We will treat your response with complete confidentiality, as described in the enclosed statement. For your reference, we are enclosing some information on Professor _____'s work. Please contact us if additional material would be useful to you.

To meet our deadlines, we will need your reply by _____. I very much appreciate your help, and look forward to hearing from you.

Sincerely,

Adapted from a letter provided by Massachusetts Institute of Technology School of Architecture and Planning. Reproduced with permission.

Letters of Evaluation

In the letter of evaluation, the referee is called upon to produce a detailed analysis of the candidate's work. The letter becomes part of the candidate's dossier. The ideal approach is defined in the letter of request above. At least half the referees are commonly selected by the school and not by the candidate, thus permitting a frank assessment. Frankness is further encouraged by stiff confidentiality guidelines restricting access to the letter to those who need to know.

With that in mind, the letter of evaluation still must be cast in clear language for a diverse array of judges. Each judge must be able to grasp quickly the salient issues spelled out by the referee/writer.

The referee's letter must address each point suggested in the request letter sent to referees by the department or tenure committee head. A letter of recommendation to the dean from the department head, required in most schools, is a critical component of the dossier. It builds on the report from the departmental promotion committee, and can range from lukewarm to a very strong endorsement.

Dossier Summary Sheet

The summary sheet travels with the dossier and beyond—some schools request that several dozen copies be attached to the dossier for wider distribution. In one section of the summary sheet, the head of the department or promotion committee writes a few "succinct and persuasive" paragraphs (in the words of one school). The aim is to give the essence of the candidate's qualifications. This crucial text is best drafted in rough, left to simmer for a day, then reviewed, tightened, and compared a final time against the substance of the entire dossier. Blessed with the endorsement of the department, this text calls for the utmost care. The following example shows one way to write such a text.

Jana Kopecka exemplifies the best ideals of this department. Appointed instructor only four years ago, she grew rapidly in her specialty: ecologically driven building design. She has proved herself able both to teach the topic cogently to her classes and to document her work effectively for publication in learned technical journals and in professional magazines.

Her talent in generating enthusiasm among her students for a topic that most consider important but lacking in emotional appeal has triggered a strong movement among students and faculty colleagues to found a building ecology center at the school. The center would integrate ecological concerns with distinctive design.

Also to be weighed in her promotion is her unique contribution to the university's responsibility in the urban community. Kopecka has on her own initiative worked with the public schools to bring design awareness into the elementary schools. She has organized a cadre of faculty, local architects, and landscape architects to work with school teachers in leading students to appreciate design and its potential in places where they live, play, and go to school.

Two years ago Kopecka was promoted to assistant professor. Her promotion now to associate professor with tenure will secure and extend her contributions to her department and the University.

Writing for the Media 10

Every design professional and student has sights set on someday writing a piece for the media or having a project published. A few get there by taking up writing as a career, either on a publication's staff or as a freelancer. Most limit themselves to an occasional article at the invitation of an editor; or they write indirectly, preparing text about a building, landscape, interior, or other design project for submission to the editor, who rewrites it more or less drastically for publication.

This chapter offers pointers to each of these contributors. But first, here's a synopsis of the media today, including a glimpse through the curtain of mystery that enshrouds the media's workings. Chapter 12 offers reflections on writing as a career.

Types of Media

Media fall into several categories, depending on audience and formats: professional journals, client-read journals, special-interest magazines, business publications, academic media, general press, newsletters, e-magazines, television and radio, and Web sites.

Professional Journals

Professional journals publish designs by design professionals, articles about the technical or business management framework in which design occurs, opinions, and news. The audience is your peers and competitors. Writing should be geared to the designer's level of understanding of that profession's technical vocabulary. Professional journal writing should not, but often does, contain linguistic flights of fancy that defy comprehension.

Editors as a rule come from one of four backgrounds: design, English, journalism, or the arts. Some journals are blessed with large editorial staffs who do most of the writing. Others have a small cadre of editors who farm out writing to freelance contributors, limiting themselves to editing and some writing. National professional U.S. design journals number a few dozen at most. They are supplemented by regional and local publications. Designers favor publication in professional journals for marketing and personal career advancement reasons, because it implies a third-party endorsement of their work. Also, graphically these journals tend to be of a high caliber, so projects look good in print and as reprints. A significant subset of professional journals is learned journals. Many are published by design schools and are repositories for critical writing and for publishing experimental or unbuilt designs.

Several print media have expanded their offerings by means of links to the Web. Not limited by the economics of print publishing, these e-magazines are able to provide more examples, more criticism, and, indeed, opportunities for reader feedback.

Some on-line journals, such as ArchNewsNow.com, are not extensions of printed versions. They typically offer news items, each linked to an in-depth source. They are commonly free but often require registration. Some are dailies; some weekly. Some, known as blogs, offer a forum for discussion, which is off the cuff, frank and colloquial, and seldom uses the jargon typical of some printed media.

With the decline in the number and size of U.S.-based national publications, we now see regional and local magazines, some independent, others published by professional society local chapters, which fill the gap as vehicles for the work and opinions of design professionals. Many, such as those published by local AIA chapters in Boston (*ArchitectureBoston*), New York (*OCULUS*), and Los Angeles (*LA Architect*), offer quality graphics and editorial content on a level with the national journals.

Overseas, professional media in such countries as Spain, Japan, France, Italy, Germany, and the United Kingdom are of high editorial and graphic quality.

Academic Journals

Academic journals serve as outlets for design thinkers to conduct critical discourse on concerns that surround and sometimes serve as the theoretical basis for design and design movements. Some, such as the *Journal of Architectural Education*, are outlets for the academic community; others such as *Praxis* and *Log*, have a broader base of contributors. Several schools of architecture, such as Harvard and Southern California Institute of Architecture (*SCI-ARC*), publish journals.

Client-Read Journals

Client journals offer design professionals a direct entrée to decision-makers. The audience for these journals are school administrators and school board members, hospital administrators and board members, developers, home builders, public officials, hospitality facility owners and operators, and judiciary and correctional officials. As part of their editorial coverage, they regularly feature stories on the design of facilities. While not all match the visual caliber of the professional design magazines, their written quality is on a par with them, especially those that reach a national audience. Whereas the professional design magazines tend to favor the aesthetics of a project, the client-read magazines focus more on a facility's functional merits.

Special-Interest Magazines

Special-interest design magazines play an important part in shaping the design tastes of American as well as overseas publics. They variously embrace residential design, interiors, garden design, historic preservation, and industrial design. Some, such as *Architectural Digest,* reach audiences as much as ten times larger than do the professional journals. They are handsomely produced, and are written in a style more accessible than that of the professional press.

Without quibbling with purists who consider all media not read by the general public as "business press," my definition is narrower, and identifies as business press only those media that cover business. Examples are *Fortune* magazine, *Institutional Investor, Business Week, Inc.,* and *Forbes.* As building construction contracts approach more than $1 trillion per year, what happens in construction is frequent grist for the business journals' mills. The writing is geared to a business audience and focuses on a building's economic impact on a company, market, or region. Some business newspapers, such as *The Wall Street Journal,* regularly carry reviews of design.

Business Publications

Newspapers and weekly news magazines attract writing on design matters because design has emerged as a popular topic, fueled by the work of star architects and engineers, such as Frank Gehry and Santiago Calatrava, and by the aftermath of massive disasters such as 9/11 and Hurricane Katrina. All newspapers have home and real estate sections, and many urban papers carry critical reviews of buildings, interiors, and landscape architecture. The critics are of national stature (at least two have won Pulitzer Prizes for criticism in recent years). Some newspapers, such as the *New York Times,* in the late 1990s consolidated their design coverage into independent sections, using color for the first time. General news magazines such as *Time* and *Newsweek* have full-time editors in charge of design coverage; the writing style routinely translates jargon into technical prose intelligible to the serious layperson.

General Press

Magazines such as *WIRED* and *Fast Company,* catering to an audience reared on video games and the Web, not only cast their journals in bright colors and space-age graphics, but also include design coverage in stimulating ways. The magazine *@issue:* takes up the argument that good design is good business. Its lively, upbeat graphics practice what it preaches (see page 106).

Newsletters offer a venue for a more clipped style of writing, figuring the reader wants news and wants it fast. Some newsletters publish short features. Publishers of newsletters include the larger chapters of the professional design societies. Some of these publications are of a high caliber. Most are transmitted on-line, suitable for downloading.

Newsletters

The vast majority of TV, cable, and radio channels are designed simply to entertain the public. They tend to contain a low ratio of decision-makers who hire designers. A few programs (such as Charlie Rose on public television),

Television and Radio

especially on cable, regularly interview design celebrities, thereby taking some of the public mystery out of the design professions. Local stations or local outlets of national networks are an added forum for designers keen on reaching the eyes and ears of local corporate and government executives. Interviewed designers are on their own, with the risk of flubbing an interview through inexperience or nervousness (see chapter 13 for tips on handling the spoken word). Many stations do a couple of dry runs and tape the interview in advance.

Writing an Article

Articles about design projects may be constructed in several ways:

- Straight descriptive story, type A. It has no criticism—you assume the project has merit or at least significance, or it would not have been chosen for publication. These design projects are chosen on their own merit and not because they fit a particular type.
- Straight descriptive story, type B. Selected because it is a significant example of a category (a small art museum; the work of a designer under 25; the work of a firm whose principals are married to each other; the work of graduates of a particular school; work designed by left-handed vegetarians). Such articles commonly leave in the air the question of whether the project is published on its merit or because it fits a category.
- Critical review of a project.
- Combinations of the foregoing.

The steps in writing an article vary with each publication, and whether the writer is on staff or freelance. But all follow these basic procedures:

1. Identify your objective. Define exactly why you are writing the article. Is it to introduce the latest work by a celebrity designer? To record a successful blending of historic and Modernist design? To portray a skillful introduction of infill housing into a deteriorated community? Ask if the article is to combine description and criticism and, if so, will you be writing both or is another author tapped for the critical portion? A useful device is to write an interim headline that expresses the essence of the story. The interim headline wording may change before it goes to press, but it's a good beacon.

2. Define the audience. Decide whether the audience is professionals, serious laypeople, or the general public. If the latter, skip fancy terminology.

3. Develop a schedule. The manuscript deadline as a rule is given to you by the managing editor if you are on staff, and by your contact editor if you are a contributor. Work backwards from that date, and establish these internal deadlines:

- Conclude travel and/or research;
- Finish outline (more on this below);
- Complete 50% of the text;
- Complete 100% of the text;

- Insert legends and other non-text material such as captions (as a freelancer you may or may not be required to furnish this material).

4. *Develop a framework or outline of content.* (A much-revered high school teacher of mine left our class with a superb device for building a foolproof framework: "Scan your notes and other source materials; grab a stack of index cards; then record any idea or thought that occurs to you, no matter how dumb, and without worrying about the order; when you are at the end of your source materials, stop; read your notes through several times, and, wonder of wonders! an outline will jump out at you from the page." This teacher assigned to us countless essays based on literature readings, and his advice was good ten times out of ten.) Do it, and you will come up with something along the following lines:

> ***INTRODUCTION.*** Bring in the chief point of the article, in a short, pithy paragraph that pulls the reader into the story. It should be sparkling but not overly cute. People like to read about other people, so if you can bring in an activity by or quote from one of the players on the design project, do so.
>
> ***BODY.*** Pull out your outline, which might have the following subheads or guideposts:
>
>> "Project had five challenges (list challenges 1–5)"
>> "How design team managed challenge #1 (site)"
>> "How design team dealt with challenge #2 (noise)"
>> "How design team handled challenge #3 (scale)"
>> "How design team handled challenge #4 (schedule/cost)"
>> "How design team handled challenge #5 (technology)"
>> "Designer's rationale for design profile and materials"
>> "Smooth/rough spots on project team"
>> "Acceptance by user"

Intersperse the text with short quotes from a designer or client, but avoid an article that is a string of quotations.

> ***CONCLUSION.*** Restate the story's main point, perhaps quoting a major protagonist. Hint at any futures heralded by the project's current status or condition.

5. *Write the article.* Pace yourself. Most writers have periods in their circadian cycles when they think more creatively, have greater stamina, and generally produce more and better copy than at other times, when the most strenuous self-discipline yields nothing. When inputting on the computer, save your text. This good advice is commonly ignored. Most software allows you to set automatic saving at designated intervals. Also, copy text to an external disk or diskette at regular intervals.

6. *Submit the manuscript.* If you are a freelancer, your editor will specify the format. Commonly you will need to e-mail or ship a diskette or disk on specified software and platform, accompanied by a paper copy and originals of any drawings and photographic transparencies. Many publishers still like to receive artwork as transparencies or slides because they allow for better control over printing resolution than digital formats. Your freelance agreement should spell this out, along with requirements for securing permissions and clearances on all material you submit. A typical freelance author agreement is shown below.

FREELANCE AUTHOR AGREEMENT FORMAT

Dear [Author]:

This letter will serve as the agreement between yourself and Smith Publishing, Inc., publisher of Engineering Herald (henceforth called "Smith").

1. You agree to write a 1500-word article provisionally titled "The Impact of Titanium as a Structural Material," tentatively scheduled to be published in the April 2006 issue of the *Herald*. The article should include a description of the metal, its use in construction and nonconstruction applications, its advantages and limitations, recommended connection details, and comparative cost data.

2. Please supply drawn details as appropriate, in camera-ready form. Four-color photographs should be in 4 x 5″ transparency format, cleared for publication. Images in .jpg or .tiff file formats are acceptable subject to prior approval by Smith Publications. Include permissions for all photography and extended text quotes by others.

3. The article is due at our offices by 20 November 2006.

4. Smith will pay you $1500 on acceptance of the article. Should Smith find the article not acceptable, or should Smith decide for whatever reason not to publish the article, you will be paid a "kill fee" of $400.

5. Please submit the article in double-spaced hard-copy format, with an accompanying electronic version in Word for a PC platform.

6. You agree to make any changes requested by our editors for reasons of style, so long as your meaning is not changed.

7. The article is a work-for-hire contract. You agree to assign title and copyright, including all rights in all print and electronic formats, exclusively to Smith.

8. You warrant that the work contains no slanderous, libelous, or unlawful matter, that it is original and accurate and does not infringe on any copyright.

9. Smith will reimburse you for appropriate expenses, including express mail and long distance telephone calls. Travel expenses must be approved in advance by Smith.

10. You agree that you take on this assignment as an independent contractor, and that you are not an employee of Smith nor entitled to benefits furnished to Smith employees.

Enclosed are two copies of this agreement. Please sign both and return one copy to me.

Sincerely,
Louisa Kwan
Senior Editor
Engineering Herald

[Author signature]
[Date]
[Social Security number]

7. Process the article. If you are a freelancer your editor should ask you to review the text in edited or page-layout form, or both. Unless the meaning of your article is changed, do not harass your editor with minor alterations. Respond promptly; odds are the editor at this stage is on deadline, and what may seem to you as a half-day's postponement could mean serious overtime charges to the publisher from the magazine's printer. If you're a staff writer, the edited article will be sent, normally as an entire page, to your screen via your electronic publishing system, with instructions to cut or add copy to fit the space.

Reading Aids

Articles do not live by straight text alone. Respect for the reader spurs the publication to furnish a variety of devices that simplify or speed up the reading experience. They are written by the editor in charge of the story. Here are the most common of these devices (see also the illustrations on page 106):

Headline. The headline is usually set in large type. It focuses the essence of your article. Some editors like a two- to three-word headline that plays on words with a smattering of humor ("Gateway to Haven" for an article about the guest house at the entrance to the residential compound of a computer industry leader). Other editors prefer longer headlines that give more detailed insight into the article ("Larson House Sets New Tone for Fire-Struck Oakland Hillside Community").

In recent years a certain coyness has crept into headline writing in a brave but mistaken effort to entice the reader into reading the story (for example: "Building Jives, But Oh! So Lovely"). It isn't until the fourth paragraph that the point is made: A new building has multiple curves and angles, but none of it works visually or functionally. Don't fall into this trap. Make the headline clear and simple, and let the first paragraph contain the point of the story.

Deck. Decks expand on the headline, seeking to lure the reader into the article. They can run to thirty words and are set in larger type. Some magazines combine the headline and deck (see illustration, page 106).

Kicker. This single word, usually placed near the headline or sideways in the margin, is used to place the article in the context of a regular feature or series ("Practice"; "Criticism"; "Books").

Author byline and identification. Staff writers are identified by name only, as are contracted contributors who regularly provide news stories. Freelance writers receive an author's ID on the first or last page of the article, often also with the other contributors on a separate page. The author's ID should be relevant and specific. ("Vincent Durango, a landscape architect in private practice in Phoenix, advocates designing landscapes using native plant species," not "Vincent Durango lives in Phoenix in a house with seven gables.")

Pull-quote (sometimes known as a scan). Pull-quotes are fifteen to twenty-word excerpts from the text, set in large type and placed in the middle of the text as graphic attention-getters. If this chapter were an article, a practical pull-quote might be "Unless the meaning has changed out of recognition, do not harass your editor with minor alterations."

Subheads. Some magazines punctuate articles with one- or two-line sub-heads placed in midcolumn and set at the standard column width. They need to capture the gist of the next few paragraphs of text. If you are a freelance writer, check out the magazine's preference before you go writing a lot of sub-heads only to see them discarded or replaced by the editor. A new device is to highlight a few key text phrases per page and print these over a gray, light yellow, or other tone.

Photo captions. Captions have a role beyond telling the reader what is in the picture. They are a way of reinforcing readers' skimming of the magazine. Many readers, especially if in a rush or with a backlog of reading matter, never go beyond those captions. Thus, they act as as a secondary route through the magazine. Caption space is precious; write them to make every word pull its weight. Avoid using valuable space telling the reader what is obvious from the photograph. If you are a freelance writer, your agreement will tell you if captions are your responsibility or the editor's.

Other add-ons. These items are linked to illustrations: *labels* identify items in drawings; *legends* (keys to plan spaces identified by numerals) are used when the drawing is too small to accommodate labels; and *credits* identify the owner, designer, and consultants, key team members, and contractors. Some magazines list with the article as many building product and material suppliers as they are able to identify and as space allows; other journals list them in the back.

The Technical Article

The volume of writing about the technology of architecture and other design disciplines is increasing for many reasons: the CAD-based office has become a reality; emerging neuroscience findings are creating a need for adapting buildings better to the physical and emotional needs of the user; novel methods reduce buildings' energy consumption and toxic waste generation; innovations are emerging in landscape and infrastructure design, construction, and management; CAD/CAM allows details to go straight from design to manufacture; the advent of new exterior and interior construction and finish materials such as composites and new synthetics; and sophisticated entertainment and communication systems are finally making Le Corbusier's definition of the house as "a machine for living in" a reality. Writers are in demand to describe and interpret these developments clearly.

• Most writing guidelines for the design article apply to the technical article. In addition, observe these points:

• Owing to the wide range of eligible topics, and the slim odds that a single publication harbors such a diverse range of experts, technical articles tend to be contributed. Since experts often disagree, it's the editor's challenge to ensure an impartial article. Much depends on the choice of author. Few freelancers specialize in every aspect of design technology. Occasional contributors are on the technical staff of design firms, builders, and product manufacturers.

• Editors must screen authors employed by manufacturers with special care. They need to head off favorable coverage of, say, a controversial product or material when an author from a competing technology might take an opposite view. Best is for the editor to pinpoint in advance the conflicting issues, and make sure all sides are raised. The plot thickens when a product manufacturer advertises in the issue. Reputable publishers shield editors from interference, arguing that readers subscribe to get objective information. Realistic advertisers will acknowledge this argument, and won't make a row so long as the article tackles the issue fairly.

• Given the complexity and latent tediousness of many technical topics, writers should complement their text by means of sketches, details, and sparkling 3D images, with distinguishing colors. Word captions precisely, and refer to figures in the text.

• The article should state, in the headline, deck, and first paragraph, the significance of the technical topic to the readers. If your readers are design professionals, the importance could be in opportunities for greater spans, new facing material options, reduced space required for hvac, or more versatile communications. If your readers are school administrators, developers, or hospital board members, compose the piece to fit those readers' concerns—for example, impact of the design on lower operating costs, users' well-being, and increased productivity.

• Keep it simple. No building technology is such that it cannot be expressed in straightforward, simple sentences, using technical language freely when the readers are technically trained, and defining your terms when they are not.

The Practice Article

The practice article may deal with project management, marketing, ownership transition, human resources management, and other topics tied to running a practice. Such articles are typically hard to illustrate, except in some cases through charts and diagrams and by inserting photographs of people for interest. This difficulty places the onus of clarity on the quality of the writing.

As in technical writing, the expertise is likely to lie beyond the editors' offices, because practice comprises such a large and diverse range of topics and issues. Fees, contracts and agreements, legal concerns, marketing, public relations, ownership transfer, project management, estimating, office business administration, employee training, construction contract administration, computerized practice—all of these and more are in a constant state of growth and change.

Organize the material for a practice article into a series of subheads to form a logical connection between points. To make reading easier on the eye, consider arranging material as a list of points, each point preceded with a bullet or some other graphic device. (Don't overdo bullets. Go for a good balance; you don't want an article to read like a punch-list.)

Since practice issues often trigger differences of opinion, a panel debate, duly taped, is an efficient way to gather material. The advantage is that panelists talk a lot more simply than they write. The disadvantage is that panelists always talk too long, so in the end only about 25% of a typical panel discussion is usable; the rest is full of digressions, introductions, and assorted chit chat. Another method is for a writer to take heavy notes, and write up the event as a standard article, inserting a few quotes here and there for effect.

Getting an Article Accepted

Editors seldom accept an unsolicited completed article. They prefer to discuss an idea or topic with you, then give you the go-ahead. Here are the main steps when soliciting an editor's interest in your developing a freelance article.

Overture. Propose your topic to the editor. Submit an idea or proposal to only one magazine at a time. Determine the slant of the editor's interest: aesthetic, technical, management, or some other area.

Preliminaries. Submit the outline, with headings, subheadings, and corresponding word lengths; list proposed illustrations (if the editor knows your work, you may be spared this step, but do it anyway for your own benefit). Discuss length, midpoint and final delivery dates, honorarium, and conditions for acceptance (if your manuscript is acceptable but not published, you can receive a partial fee, known ominously as a "kill" fee).

Development. Conduct the research. Prepare/assemble necessary or desired drawings and photography. Obtain permission for the use of any photography. Write the first draft (and submit it to the editor if requested).

Delivery. Complete and deliver the final draft. Comply with the editor's requested format, probably by e-mail or a typed, double-spaced copy. Deliver the artwork. Drawings will likely be redrawn electronically by the magazine to fit its style. Assemble and deliver credits and permissions. Send a short two- to four-line bio. The magazine will rewrite this to its final form.

Final Touches. Review the edited draft from the editor. Chances are this will arrive by e-mail. Try to concede editorial changes so long as they don't alter your meaning. Respond promptly to requests from the publication—at this stage all are urgent. Arrange with the journal for reprints. Send an invoice for your fee (not all magazines require this).

Criticism

The critic exists in every designer. The temptation to comment on buildings, interiors, engineering feats, landscape design, urban design and planning—especially the other person's project—is never far from the designer's mind. Design criticism is a specialized form of expression that some design professionals do all of the time, and all do some of the time. Good critical writing demands solid academic and practical grounding in one or more design disciplines, a point of view, and the verbal skill to express this to a wide or influential audience. Often the critic's message travels in a limited circle that endorses its point of view, grasps the often esoteric language, and provides the underpinnings of a short- or long-term popularity.

The full-time critical writer bears a serious responsibility, especially if endowed with a large or important audience. Critics often are on staff at newspapers and wide-circulation magazines. Writers such as Lewis Mumford at *The New Yorker,* and before him Montgomery Schuyler at *Architectural Record* when it was still a general-interest architectural journal, were widely read. In more recent years critics such as Ada Louise Huxtable, Robert Campbell, and Paul Goldberger have brought an awareness of design to vast audiences; Huxtable, Goldberger, and Campbell have won Pulitzer Prizes. Good critics provoke a growing public consciousness about design.

Some professional design magazines have editors who take strong stands on current issues; by identifying, supporting, or condemning trends in design, they often influence the way a design profession evolves. Some practicing designers have been critics as well, and a few, such as Robert Venturi, have notably shaped design trends, especially when—as in Venturi's 1966 book, *Complexity and Contradiction in Architecture*—they write in a period ripe for change.

Academe above all has played host to the critic. It provides a fertile intellectual environment, the opportunity for debate in classrooms and common rooms, access to resources, and links to scholarly publishing outlets at university presses and scholarly journals. Critics such as Kenneth Frampton at Columbia University typify the best of these professional critics, though Frampton often demands a second or third reading before the uniqueness of his message sinks in. Like the best critics, he encourages one to see and to think.

Learning to Write Criticism

There is no easy way to teach the writing of criticism. But, as noted, it cannot happen without a broad base of knowledge and a point of view.

Words are symbols of meaning; if the symbol eludes the reader because it is too arcane and removed from common experience, there is no message. Some concepts may take many words to explain; you cannot try to cope with this merely by glibly inventing a host of new words. The challenge is to employ an existing, broadly understood vocabulary to explain complex ideas, not to succumb to the temptation of inventing a new term when the going gets rough.

A fine model is Michael Benedikt's book, *Deconstructing the Kimbell.* In this 1990 work Benedikt, who teaches at the University of Texas at Austin, deftly explains a movement once thought to be short-lived but for years permeated contemporary design attitudes. Benedikt sidesteps the pitfalls of explaining Deconstructivism by using words that mean what they always mean, and assembling them in conventional, nonthreatening sentences. Through his writing,

Benedikt has probably done more to explain Deconstructivism than its champions. Below are two samples of Benedikt's writing, defining and describing a design theory derived from another, nondesign, humanist discipline.

INTRODUCTION

After many years in the air, with the publication in 1988 of Philip Johnson and Mark Wigley's MOMA catalogue *Deconstructivist Architecture*, and the appearance of *Architectural Design Profile 72: Deconstruction in Architecture*, a new "ism" was officially upon the American architectural scene: Deconstructivism.

Grumblings from working architects, historians, and teachers of architecture that it would soon pass, that it "doesn't work," that it's crazy, that it's just a style, that it really doesn't deserve a name of its own . . . all of these are typical of the kinds of things said at the inception of a new movement. Conversely, the notion that Deconstructivism in architecture is actually all over, come and gone, is also mistaken: Deconstructionist concerns, techniques, and terminology are to be found with ever greater frequency in academic journals of architecture, where they are presented with an ever greater air of normalcy. One must, I think, conclude that Deconstruction is very likely to continue to gain influence in the discipline and the profession, if only as a mode of discourse that supports the real and unstated enterprise of all designerly architects (save for feeding their children): the discovery/invention and execution of new formal systems, i.e., styles.

But Derrida's Deconstruction can mean more to architects (and artists) than a transitory aesthetic or a style, and it should not be allowed to devolve into the esoteric, promotional patter and stylish nihilism that it threatens to do. Deconstruction is primarily a philosophy of writing and reading philosophy. But it is also a probing enquiry into the workings of language, ideas, and the whole human cultural enterprise. As a theory, a philosophy, a method, in the hands of Jacques Derrida and others, Deconstruction had a considerable impact on philosophy and critical and literary theory in the late 1970s and early 80s. As a significant component of post-structuralist thought in the late 1980s, it was still making its way through all the arts and all but the "hardest" of the sciences, representing a pattern of thinking whose generality across the disciplines has been unequaled since systems theory in the mid-60s. Deconstruction's destiny, I believe, like system theory's, is to continue to be absorbed into routine intellectual, critical, and even scientific discourse. Already, key elements of its vocabulary have passed into the realm of common wisdom about method, expression, description, and meaning in all these fields, but its name—Deconstruction—and the name of its "inventor"—Jacques Derrida—may well soon be effaced. Who now speaks of W. Ross Ashby, James Miller, or Ludwig von Bertalanffy?

DERRIDA'S DECONSTRUCTION, THROUGH ARCHITECTURE

To read Derrida is to be swept into an uncanny stream of argument, exposition, and altered terminology that knows no rest or single direction. Language is questioned with language; whole passages swallow themselves up and disappear as meaningful. Homonyms vie with synonyms for possession of the argument ... and yet "perfectly good sense" is always there, passing below and over, and just out of reach. One learns to swim in this foreign stream, or not.

One claims to have swum, or not.

It is my contention that very, very few people understand Derrida in any detail, certainly far fewer than claim to. In some way this is the fulfillment of Derrida's ambition, the cause and result of his method. Because it simultaneously uproots and affirms conventional rationality in certain imitable ways, and because it partakes quite freely of neologisms, wordplay, and evasions of resolution, the philosophy of Deconstruction is generative: of arguments, colloquia, papers, books of critical theory and criticism, and, perhaps, of buildings. But understanding Derrida in the first place—the belief that he is indeed saying something clear and deep and definable—is generative too. It has created in the last fifteen years a minor industry in academia of lectures, published interviews, explicatory and ancillary books, conferences, debates, and innumerable bouts of academic one-upmanship.

Through all of this one must move carefully, skeptically, and with companions. Jonathan Culler, in his *On Deconstruction: Theory and Criticism after Structuralism*, educes a number of processes, or principles, from (chiefly) Derrida's writings on Deconstruction that we will find useful. Derrida applies them, of course, to particular texts and (usually by implication) to language as a whole, but he applies them especially to the kinds of texts and the kinds of language that make truth claims and generalizations based on ideas—in other words, to texts of metaphysical ambition. Here we attempt the translation to architecture with a selection of four such essential processes or principles ...

Note Benedikt's skill in conveying abstruse concepts by keeping a tight handle on designer-babble and extra-long sentences.

Book Reviews

Reviewing books is surely one of the most widespread of writing assignments, at school and in practice. Most professional design publications review books. They typically assign this to a staff editor, along with other duties. Often, especially for "significant" books that call for a longer review, the editor assigns reviews to outside writers. Reviewers may be sought out more for their expertise on the book's topic than for their writing skills. As a result, the writing level of book reviews is mixed.

Given meager page allotments and budgets, the book review editor personally writes a series of short (one paragraph maximum) mini-reviews to supplement the few long reviews. These short reviews reveal basic content rather than make an in-depth assessment, and are known in the trade as "flap reviews" because they draw heavily on what is printed on the dust-jacket flap.

On-line booksellers such as Amazon.com and Barnes & Noble also post book reviews and unsolicited, unscreened comments, which often reveal subjective bias.

If asked to review a book professionally for the first time, heed these tips:

• Read the book. Inane as this may sound, it is the only way to make an accurate appraisal. Flap copy and press releases give a good clue as to the intent of the book, and provide synopses of the content. They are, however, written by the publisher and aim to show the book in its best light. You need not pore over a book's every word, but read enough (and skim the whole) to form an impression. Then ask: Does this book meet the needs of its intended audience or not?

• Arrange your material along the following lines:

> Open with a catchy lead-in.
> Give the intent of the book.
> Summarize the content.
> Evaluate key elements of the content.
> Assess the author's qualifications.
> Compare the book to its competition for value and price.
> End with buy/don't buy advice.

You may be tempted to use the review as a vehicle for your own point of view or philosophy on the topic. In some cases, that's all right; but bear in mind that the reader wants first and foremost to know whether to buy the book or not, and only secondarily wants your philosophy. I continue to be dismayed by reviews that broadcast the reviewer's theories but neglect to say a word about the book.

For a book review that largely meets the spirit of these criteria, see the following.

TIMES SQUARE ROULETTE: REMAKING THE CITY ICON,
by Lynne B. Sagalyn.
Cambridge, MA.: MIT Press, 2004 (paper). First published in 2001.
620 pages. $29.95.

O tempora, o mores (oh Times, oh manners)! No longer can urbanist Marshal Berman write about Times Square, as he did in 1997 in "Signs of the Times: The Lure of Times Square" (*Dissent* magazine): "[It is] a human sinkhole, a place where no decent person would willing [sic] go, and where the only helpful thing would be to blow it all away." And blow it away they did. The nice family from Dubuque, Fun City-bound on an affordable package tour (clean midtown hotel room, breakfast and dinner, walking tour of Times Square, airport taxes included) now feels safer than in Disneyland as they march along 42nd Street, not an item of trash in sight, and wholesome souvenirs at every store to take home to grandma.

Alas, gone is the "exotic seediness" that author Lynne Sagalyn, professor of city and regional planning at the University of Pennsylvania, says used to pull in the visitors from all around town, the outer boroughs, and beyond. "Pleasure-seekers and tourists came to ogle, see the bright lights of Times Square, say they'd been there. Titillation. The allure of danger and desire for a new experience involving some degree of risk-taking and thrill-seeking also attracted many to the 'night frontier.'"

Warming to her task of updating her readers on what has become of Times Square, Sagalyn quotes sociologists William Kornblum and Vernon Boggs: "[This is] a place where the laws of conventional society are suspended, people come to seek adventure, to take risks in dealing in the fast life . . . to con and be conned."

The area did not attract the kinds of commercial uses politicians could feel comfortable with. It drew the regulars, in Kornblum and Boggs' words, a "loose-ly connected society of people 'in the life,'" supplemented by the daily advent of transient youngsters, runaways, and an assortment of what Sagalyn describes as "hucksters, chickens and chicken hawks, johns and [small-time pimps]." It was a "reliable economic market for every possible human need."

It was not, however, a market championed by the city's political and business establishment. As far back as 1976, then-Mayor Abraham Beame launched the Office of Midtown Enforcement intended to return Times Square (and its Great White Way—42nd Street between Seventh and Eighth Avenues, which Rolling Stone once called the "sleaziest block in America") to "good commercial uses." Heading the team from 1978 to 1984 was Carl B. Weisbrod, an energetic and conscientious New Yorker who today presides over the Alliance for Downtown New York [or is it "Downtown Manhattan?"] and is an LMDC board member.

The rest is history. An ambitious plan advanced by advertising executive Frederic Papert, sponsored by the Ford Foundation and called The City at 42nd Street, Inc. (it would have transformed, writes Sagalyn, the "entire three-block area from 41st Street to 43rd Street between Seventh Avenue and Eighth Avenues into a combined world's fair, theme park, and cultural showcase for New York," at an estimated cost of $600 million) ran out of steam largely, it was said, because, despite powerful commercial backing, it smacked too many of just one more instance of urban renewal; and because, as Sagalyn quotes former City Planning Commission chairman Donald Elliott, because this was a Mayor John Lindsay project and the new mayor Edward Koch decided to "pull the plug."

Instead, Koch in 1980 organized the 42nd Street Development Project, also known as 42DP, which in due course issued a set of design guidelines along with an RfP for developers. By 1984 two sets of developers had been approved conditionally, but 42DP was beset by difficulties, and by 1989 had attracted as many as 40 lawsuits, writes Sagalyn. Three sets of interests competed for commercial limelight in the area—the sex industry, the performing arts industry, and the real estate industry. The performing arts industry was the first to bring results. In 1988 the non-profit 42nd Street Entertainment Corporation was formed to oversee restoration of several historic theaters along the street. One day Disney's Michael Eisner visited the New Amsterdam Theater, formerly one of the grandest of the playhouses, and despite its sorry state came away with a fierce desire to see it restored to its former grandeur. It opened in April 1997, following by 15 months the opening of the remade New Victory theater. The sex industry moved to a less conspicuous neighborhood south of 42nd Street.

Meanwhile, in 1992 the old 42DP collapsed, and for years no office towers were built in what had turned into a serious recession. But as the recession receded in the late 1990s, large corporations, sensing the optimism and opportunities in the area, began to build—office towers and high-rise hotels at the western and eastern ends of 42nd Street, and north along Broadway. Many of the structures used spectacular state-of-the-art electronic display technology to entertain and inform the troops. At 43rd Street, NASDAQ, the OTC stock market, "plugged in an eight-story 'techno-turret' capable of projecting constantly changing, colorful, swirling images on a 90- by 120-foot screen produced by powerful minicircuitry."

Unique in the literature of Times Square, *Times Square Roulette* provides not only the highlights of the makeover, but the details of the deals, intrigues, and conflicts and pressures that accompany any attempt to bring urban change, especially in a notoriously contentious community such as New York. Sagalyn's style does justice to the effort—lucid, well balanced, and able to capture the labyrinthine byways of what is known as process. No detail escapes her. On page 43 there is even a detailed map showing the location of every theater and every house of ill repute from 37th Street to 47th Street, from Sixth to Ninth Avenues.

That was 1901. The bordellos then outnumbered the theaters by a ratio of about fifteen to one. Today, as the disneyfication of Times Square presses on, it's good to know that our family from Dubuque will have had fun in Fun City, and return home with a clean sense of blameless experience, leaving nostalgia to the locals.

REVIEWED BY STEPHEN A. KLIMENT
From *OCULUS*, vol. 66, no.4 © 2005 The American Institute of Architects, New York Chapter. Reproduced with permission.

Getting Published

Design firms do not feel fulfilled without publication of their projects. The following remarks are not in-depth guidelines for publication so much as brief but realistic tips.

Never approach editors with the attitude that they are simply a vehicle for your work. Treat them as professionals. Their job is to size up their audiences and to publish material that informs these audiences, perhaps uplifts them, maybe even entertains them. Their agenda may differ radically from yours, but respect it. It is their business, and they are calling the shots.

Recognize too that a media decision to publish your work is not a simple one, and hinges on such factors as the publication's backlog in your subject and its editorial calendar, which is commonly made up in the early fall for the following year and available on the magazine's Web site. Although flexible, the calendar rarely accommodates major changes without good reason. Another factor is your celebrity as a designer (lack of celebrity sometimes helps too, as every editor likes to discover new talent).

The following list offers additional dos and don'ts on approaching the media.

Do

Identify the right editor (check the masthead).

Write or e-mail. Phone or fax only if the editor knows you.

State if drawings, details, and professional photography are or will be available.

Show that you are familiar with the journal's editorial calendar.

Eschew hype, by voice or mail.

Exploit direct contact opportunities, such as seminars or conventions.

Don't

Follow up too soon, or more than once in three weeks. If it's obviously a "no-go," give up with grace.

Contact simultaneously more than one publication with the same idea.

Insist on reviewing the edited text.

Submit prewritten articles. Send an idea letter instead.

SCENARIO

Submitted Letter

You have developed skills over the years in designing workplaces that respect the physical and mental needs of the design worker. You wish to share this knowledge with your colleagues through the pages of a respected professional journal. Following is a sample submittal letter.

Andrea Esterhazy
Senior Editor
Architectural Chronicle
1C Clinton Street
Chicago, IL 60600

Dear Andrea [if you know her; otherwise "Dear Ms. Esterhazy"):

I see from your 2006 calendar that *Architectural Chronicle* will feature a design of the new workplace in October. I want to propose an article on the human resources factors that should, but often fail to, influence workplace design.

As associate partner at Harnischfeger and Haas one of my tasks is to research and apply good practices for making office workers happy and productive. Concepts include ideal mixes of open and semi-enclosed offices; issues of privacy and productivity; access to on-line networks; and options for individual controls over comfort, noise, and lighting. In the last five years I have researched and designed six projects totaling 400,000 sq. ft. of state-of-the-art work space—all of it in successful operation.

I can submit a detailed outline within two weeks, and furnish drawings, details, and professional photography to illustrate a range of problems and solutions. I attach three examples, with brief text and picture captions.

I hope the suggestion appeals to you, and I look forward to your response.
Sincerely,
George Lodge
Associate Partner

COMMENT

This letter is brief and to the point, and doesn't presume to send an entire article before getting some encouragement in advance. Give Ms. Esterhazy two or three weeks to reply, then follow up with a phone call or e-mail. You may of couse mail the letter and attachments, but a smart letter sent through the mail carries extra cachet.

Writing On-line 11

Not so many years ago writing by traditional print formats was manifestly different from writing for transmission on-line. Writing for print was formal; text was smooth, flowing, and overburdened with adjectives, adverbs, and other verbal paraphernalia; punctuation was scrupulous; so was use of capital letters (caps) according to grammatical formulas that stretched to antiquity. Correspondence salutations were proper and reserved ("dear"); so were closing phrases such as "Sincerely"—all of this whether or not the recipient was dear or whether your own message was sincere. Dialogue was no swifter than the postal service and could take days.

On-line messages on the other hand are informal; verbal paraphernalia is rare; salutations are minimal or ignored altogether, since the recipient's name is in the "To" box. It is open season on caps and punctuation. Responses and exchanges are instant (see sample, below).

SAMPLE E-MAIL EXCHANGE

From: STEPHEN KLIMENT
Sent: 16 May 2005 3:43 PM
To: Russ_Romme@msn.com
Subject: Wetlands Essay

Hi Russ:
  Please advise status of the Wetlands essay.
Best
Steve

From: Russ Romme
Sent: 16 May 2005 4:59 PM
To: STEPHEN KLIMENT
Subject: RE: Wetlands Essay

  Sorry Steve, I've been busier than a . . .
  I'll try to get to it this weekend. Thanks for the nudge.
Russ

Today these distinctions have become blurred, or said another way, the on-line style is fast replacing the formalities of print. Not that the typed, mailed letter is going out of style; it's just that the briskness, informality, and terseness of electronic messaging now pervades most types of writing by design professionals, except perhaps for specifications and legal contracts. There lawyers still call the shots as they correctly worry about the exact meaning of words and the implications for the future of a project or contract if the wrong word creeps into the document.

Writing E-mail

E-mailspeak. It is common to use hip, current forms and phrases that signal to the sender that you're cool. See the list below for examples of e-mailspeak. Phrases such as "this will get the idea in Joe's face" are simply more at ease in e-mail than in conventional correspondence. When old-time courtesies are used, the result can be droll (see the sample letters opposite). The hectic, dynamic flavor of writing in the age of e-mail is also epitomized by a new kind of wordplay characterized by *New York Times* "On Language" columnist William Safire as "JammedTogether" names (examples: AutoCAD, PowerPoint, HarperCollins, FrontPage). There are also signs that the compressed nature of e-mail is creeping into conventional writing. Some even characterize e-mail as a form of conversation.

Specimens of e-mailspeak	*Plainspeak equivalents*
Webster	One who often browses the Web
Ping	notify
Digerati	Folks who have risen to the elite ranks of those dealing with the on-line world
Pomo	Postmodern
IMHO	In my humble opinion
Charlie in engineering is a cypherpunk [Note: a cypherpunk is a crypto with an attitude. A crypto is one obsessed with codes and cyphers.]	Charlie is too concerned about playing his cards close to the chest, thereby keeping team members out of the picture

For additional examples, see *WIRED Style*, listed in Resources.

Responses. If the original e-mail message leans to the concise and unadorned, the responses can be positively anorexic. Since the mechanics of responding to e-mail are so simple—you click on the "reply to sender" option on the "compose" menu—answers may be short to the point of curtness.

Punctuation. Capital letters, hyphens, and other stylistic staples are sometimes omitted from e-mail messages ("steve, spoke with chuck thursday please send back up info on monday's job meeting asap williejo"). This underscores the utilitarian nature of the medium as well as the nonconformist mindset of many of its champions.

Forwarding. Forwarding e-mail without comment has emerged as the ultimate in zero-effort, zero-writing communication.

Point of no return. E-mail is not a forgiving medium. A leisurely review of a letter typed on paper before you sign it may reveal typos plus thoughts inaccurately stated or inelegantly phrased; you fix it, then mail it. No such luxury is given to e-mail: the hectic ethos of the medium demands instant dispatch. Once the "send" command is pressed, it's too late to fix, unless you undergo an awkward corrective follow-up. A Wall Street trader reportedly e-mailed a love note to a friend, and with one wrong click sent it instead to 1000 coworkers. Some e-mailed back to say they "didn't know he cared." The moral: Check e-mail just as carefully as paper mail.

Attachments. Be sure to check out your recipient's system. Some attached files must be decoded and recoded if crossing certain network and platform lines. Some firms have installed stringent firewalls to ward off junk mail and viruses. If in doubt, paste the entire text of the attachment into your main message, then send as one message. Drawback: You may lose your formatting. Or send all in .pdf format.

Enrichment. Some browser software allows you to embellish your e-mail text with borders and textured backgrounds, colored text, and funky text margins. Just because this is possible is no reason to do it, as it surely runs counter to the no-frills ethic of professionals conversing on-line.

Literacy. The tension between e-mailspeak and old courtesies was never more pointed than in an exchange of letters in *The Times* of London. A letter to the editor (not shown) first raised this issue, and a week later the following two responses appeared in the newspaper under the heading "Sign-off of the Times."

Sir,

Mr. Adrian Dodd-Noble suggests the "your obedient servant" is perhaps an unsatisfactory closing for an e-mail.

Could I be the first to conclude an e-pistle to the editor with a "smiley."
Yours, [smiley face art]
David T. Staples
[street address and e-mail address given]

Reproduced by permission.

Sir,

The march of technology must not be allowed to erode courtesy and civilization. In a civilized society, any written communication should be signed off with a suitably courteous salutation, whatever "netiquette"—or perhaps nerdiquette—may or may not require.
I remain, Sir, yours truly and electronically,
Henry Robinson
[street address and e-mail address given]

Reproduced by permission.

Following are added examples of e-mail messages and responses. Note the concise, sharp style. Sample A shows prime design professional Nunez e-mailing his consultant, and her response.

E-MAIL CORRESPONDENCE SAMPLE A

From: Alvaro Nuñez
To: Gblandings@azu.com
Sent: March 31, 2005 2:20 p.m.
cc: Robert O'Connor
Subject: Furniture for Robison

Georgia: Carpenters and painters are out of the Robison House. Still no word on delivery of first furniture consignment from Milan. If Robisons are to move in June 1 as in contract, we'll need action. Best—Al

From: Georgia Blandings
Sent: March 31, 2005 2:32 p.m.
To: Anuñez@azu.com
cc: Robert O'Connor [intranet converts to on-line address]
Subject: Re: Furniture for Robison

Al: Milan's New York supplier tells me furniture on ship docked in New York harbor. Expect delivery to site in three business days. Thanks for the prod.—Georgia

Sample B is from Mr. Nuñez to David Cheng, the senior landscape designer.

E-MAIL CORRESPONDENCE SAMPLE B

From: Alvaro Nuñez
Sent: April 2, 2005 10:13 a.m.
To: Dcheng@azu.com
cc: Robert O'Connor
Subject: Weekend fiasco

David, this rain-sodden weekend [Cheng was out of town at a project meeting] was chaos on the site of Adams municipal park. Only two members of Citizens Group, which was supposed to unload two truckloads of dirt for the shrub and tree planting later this week, showed. Cats-and-dogs both days. Three trucks arrived, unloaded the dirt, which now sits in one corner, in no shape to be dispersed for the planting. Can you meet 12:30 in conference room B for a working lunch to sort this out?—Al

From: David Cheng
Sent: April 2, 2005 10:18 a.m.
To: Alvaro Nuñez [intranet converts to online address]

cc: Robert O'Connor
Subject: Weekend fiasco
  Yep

From: Robert O'Connor [partner in charge]
Sent: April 2, 2005 10:22 a.m.
To: Alvaro Nuñez
Subject: Weekend fiasco
  al—i'll join you—bob

Writing for print developed its etiquette over centuries. E-mail has had twenty years at most to develop its own. Here are pointers to good e-mail manners:

1. Use clear subject lines. They should be informative, not cryptic. But don't start your message in the subject line—it's tacky. "Reminder" is too cryptic. "Reminder: project meeting Thursday" is better." After all, you want them to open the message.

2. Jazz. Don't jazz up an e-mail message with fancy features (fonts, margins, cute symbols, color). It looks cheap, and may not arrive the way you sent it. If you must, do it in an attachment, but there you risk the attachment being turned away by the recipient's firewall.

3. Group messaging. Restrict names in the cc line to those who need to know. List on the bcc line those who need to know, but unbeknownst to names on the cc line. *"Replying to all" creates a geometric jump in the volume of traffic as each recipient replies to every other. Use this device sparingly.* If you want a gabfest, set up a chat room or blog. The bcc line has an added practical purpose, however. If you're writing to a large list, with their names in the "To" field, the recipient may end up with a list of names six inches deep before getting to the message. To avoid this, place all the names in the bcc field. That way recipients get to see only their own names.

4. Confidentiality. Run-of-the-mill e-mail messages are easily tracked, especially if a firm has a surveillance system in place. Special systems exist to encrypt messages and make them impossible to intercept or to copy, print, or forward them. Lesson: don't write anything you wouldn't want your grandmother to see.

5. Monitoring. Check your business e-mail every hour. If you keep your computer connected on-line, most hardware will audibly signal receipt of a message. If you depend on your Blackberry, a beep will signify a message. Note that at this writing, a Blackberry will not accept attachments.

6. Temper. Do not write or respond in anger. Twenty minutes after you send the message, you'll be sorry.

7. Avoid humor. Chances are two in three recipients will misinterpret the joke.

8. Proofread. Spell-check is fallible. It will only fix wrong spelling; it won't supply the right word. I once misspelled "building." Spell-check corrected it to "bullock." That's how it went out.

9. To write or not to write. If you're not convinced the message will help, don't write it.

10. Time. Keep an electronic address book, sorted by contacts and frequent contacts. This saves finding and typing e-mail addresses, and avoids typos. Develop a signature block with your own name and contact information. Set your computer so that all outgoing messages automatically include this "signature."

11. Edit your inbox and sent folders. Fat inboxes and sent folders burden your firm's storage system. Some design firms automatically cut employees off at, say, 40MB of stored messages, or archive anything older than six months.

12. Send your message when you write it. If you're wired and away from a dataline, as at an airport, or if your Blackberry is in a dead zone, you may think you sent the message, but it may not have gone through.

13. Home and work. Unlike personal phone calls, incoming and outgoing personal e-mail messages are far less disruptive to colleagues. A certain amount is acceptable. How often you use them is a matter for your own work ethic.

14. Avoiding e-mail. There are times when a phone call is worth fifty e-mails. Or, to express old-fashioned formality and when time is not a factor, send a letter on your best stationery. This is especially true when you're writing to invite a speaker or a design award judge, to notify a winner of an award program, or a first-time letter of interest to a prospective client.

If you're not sure what to do, visit www.TE3C.org, the Electronic Communications Compliance Council, which offers and updates best practice advice.

The Web Site

A design firm's Web site typically may include some, many, or all of the following contents, depending on the firm's goals, ambition, and budget (the entries, except for the first, are in no particular order):

• A welcome screen or home page, which also serves as a directory or index to the site's other parts.

• Lists of completed projects, divided, if the list is long, into appropriate categories, such as by building type or type of client. As many projects as feasible should be hyperlinked to, and shown large on, individual screens (see next item).

• Screens showing one or more images of completed projects, augmented by design, technical, and sometimes operating data.

• Staff biographies, with or without faces.

• A list of articles published about the firm's projects, hyperlinked to full texts.

• A list of published articles and books written by principals and staff (articles hyperlinked to full texts).

- A directory of qualification forms on file with government agencies (e.g., SF 330), and hyperlinked to full texts (but you may want to control access to this information).
- The design firm's vision/mission/goals statement. Compose this with care and ingenuity so it comes across as a factual, realistic, believable document, not an array of overblown generalities that could apply to any firm in any profession.
- News about the firm (new projects, promotions, awards). Can also serve as an internal newsletter.
- Office announcements (these are accessed only by office staff supplied with a password and ID).
- Project management status reports (these are accessed by team members and designated others).
- Key contacts, with mailing addresses, key telephone and fax numbers, and e-mail addresses.

For pointers on how to compose your Web-based brochure, see pages 45–47.

An emerging sign of status is for individual designers and students to strut their own Web sites, not necessarily a part of the official school or firm site. It supplements e-mail and affords more personal exchanges with "visitors."

Web Sites Benefits and Challenges

What's in it for your firm? In creating a Web site, the design firm can realize benefits but must also look out for challenges.

Marketing. The Web brochure assumes client prospects are in the habit of browsing for design firms' home pages. It's more dependable to alert the client through some other medium, such as e-mail. Try to get your Web site onto the major search engines, such as Google or Yahoo! for added exposure. So you can monitor and classify the level of your Web site traffic, leave space near the opening screen for a "visitor" to register.

Basis for preparing proposals. Saves time and lessens the chance of error by containing all the firm's databases needed to fabricate a proposal. Helps if the prime professional is linked to the Web sites of frequent consultants. Control access.

Project management. Links members of a project team—in-house and external. Some firms establish independent Web sites for individual projects.

Morale builder. By incorporating chatrooms (and events) and bulletin boards, the Web site helps to interconnect the design firm's community, especially if the firm has branch offices.

Quality. Creating even a simple Web site entails selecting from a huge array of potential content, format design, and visual design options. Choose the best mix and the one most in character with your firm. Nothing hurts more than a dull, uninformative, stale, or out-of-date home page; you lose the browser on the first visit, and the browser may never return. To create traffic, seek to offer something compelling over and above facts about your firm, such as building codes, ADA regulations, building conservation guidelines, access to government Web sites, lists of consultants and contractors. These extras are known as "fish food."

Update. Appoint a Web boss to update the site at intervals. Some parts, such as newly completed projects, can be on a looser schedule (bimonthly, for instance) compared to staff changes or new address, telephone, fax, and e-mail information.

Security. Registration and control of access are critical.

Recruitment tool. Post open positions and provide a submittal template for applicants.

Web Writing

Web Writing has much in common with e-mail writing. Both are required to transmit information to and receive responses from people who are short on time and often short on patience. They are not as grounded in the graceful verbal forms of past generations, and live and work in an age that places a premium on unadorned facts delivered in a hard-hitting style, with little room for embellishments.

But writing for the Web site has demands that go beyond even those of e-mail. Once you are browsing the Web, you face the additional challenge of linking words to other words, other screens, other sites. Directing the visitors so they understand the message, link up to other significant sites, and don't become bored in the process makes the Web site seem not so much a writing challenge as a musical composition.

Questions arise: Which words on each page should serve as links? How should they be dispersed on a page? How many links are too many? Too few? How big a text block is sufficient or too long? How much information should be conveyed by text? How much left to art? Behavioral scientists who analyze subjects' eye movements may have definitive answers. Meanwhile, we are left with a modest track record based on short-term experience that has yielded the following pointers:

• Humanize your Web site. Sites are identified by four fields of up to three numbers each, separated by periods (thus: 256.125.72.88). Selecting and registering a domain name (e.g., http://www.richardmeier.com) injects a more human, informal note. To register or be assigned an address, type InterNIC into your search engine and follow instructions.

• Write short text. Keep sentences short—twelve words average. Users don't read so much as scan. A trained eye can pick up blocks of type around forty words long (or five to eight lines) without strain. Keep the measure (or width of a column of text) narrow, under forty characters. If you go wider, you will need to increase the type size, the space between lines, or both. One expert suggests limiting text and graphics per screen to 100KB (a one-page single-spaced letter takes up about 30KB as text).

• Use simple words. Shun designer-babble and vocabulary that's too high-tech. You never know how versed in design terminology a potential client browsing the Web will be. Even designer-visitors have no time or desire to figure out jargon.

• Graphics only? Give photographs and other graphic items the benefit of some text. Viewers need words to orient themselves; they are uncomfortable without them. Equally, don't overpepper the screen with hyperlinks (except perhaps on the home or index page); it distracts from the page's basic message and makes the screen look like Swiss cheese.

• Consider surfing as an experience. Unlike reading a letter on paper or as e-mail, surfing a Web site for information is an act of exploration, and text must support the experience, not hamper it through complex or clumsy wording.

• Create headlines for the first or "splash" screen and other key screens. Make headlines simple, informative, and prominent in size or color.

• Help guide the reader. Every screen should carry a common navigation bar indicating where you are and what to do to get to the next or previous screen and to the home or index page. Think about visitors negotiating a metropolitan subway system or hiking on a trail—they'll probably choose the most likely path but can always fall back on signs or a trail map. Make important buttons large to avoid inaccurate clicking by a tired navigator.

• Avoid long categories. Stratify long lists into subgroups, each with a heading (for example, divide project lists into building types, long lists of a single building type into building subtypes, linked to more detailed sources—see the listing below). Experts feel six to ten entries is maximum for a list for easy screen reading. For example:

PROJECTS
Healthcare facilities
    Acute care hospitals
    Medical centers
    Special focus facilities (cancer; cardiac; mental; emergency; children; women)
    Long-term facilities (nursing; assisted living)
    Specialty centers (Alzheimer's disease; AIDS)
    Laboratories
    Primary care facilities
    Medical offices
    Fitness facilities

• Eliminate time wasters. Monitor what you post on to the site. Cut text and images ruthlessly. Visual images should convey useful information; cute, strictly feel-good images are distracting and possibly patronizing.

Check out Web sites of other design firms. Addresses, known as URLs, change, as do names of firms, so consult google.com, yahoo.com, or the ProFile directory (see Resources) for the latest data.

For two examples of reader-friendly Web texts, see the following.

EASTLAKE STUDIO PORTFOLIO: LAKESIDE RESIDENCE

LAKESIDE RESIDENCE

In 1993, a Chicago couple retained Eastlake Studio to design a home in Lakeside, Michigan, on a site they owned on the eastern shore of Lake Michigan. They wanted a home that would initially serve as a weekend retreat, and ultimately as a permanent residence. The three-acre site is composed of two contrasting natural settings—an open prairie and a heavily wooded ravine, which empties into Lake Michigan about 200 yards north of the site.

The couple views their new home as a secluded retreat from their urban residence, but also as a place for entertaining weekend guests. While privacy from neighbors and the road was important, bringing the natural environment into their home directed the final solution. They envisioned a home in harmony with its surroundings, made of a scale in proportion to the prairie landscape.

SITE PLAN

Our solution sites the house on the edge of the ravine with an approach along the south edge of the site in order to keep the open prairie to the north clear.

The organizing principle for the structure joins a 4-foot planning module with a stepped circulation path. Four nodes distributed along the circulation path bring light into the center of the residence through large windows and skylights. The path also separates spaces oriented to the two basic site elements—prairie and ravine.

Morning spaces such as the master bath and breakfast area are located on the prairie (east) side, while large windows orient evening spaces such as bedrooms and the main living area to the site's most dramatic views on the ravine (west) side. In elevation, gently sloping curved roofs tie the complex plan together, link the ravine to the prairie, and reduce the scale of the large residence.

LIVING ROOM

The ceiling of the living room rises above as windows open to the ravine outside. A flagstone chimney provides a focus for activities within the room.

For the building's enclosure, we chose materials that reflected the natural landscape of the site and the context of the area. Horizontal cedar siding, limestone fireplaces, and aluminum roofing were combined to provide a subtle, understated image. The 4-foot planning module is expressed in elevation by vertical trim elements that separate segments of horizontal siding. Wood decks located on the private ravine side contrast with the stone patio and walks leading to the primary entrance on the prairie side.

FRONT ENTRANCE

A cedar pergola marks the main entrance. The 4-foot planning module is expressed by the vertical trim elements separating the segments of horizontal siding.

The irregularity of the plan is tied together by the curved aluminum roof.

The Lakeside Residence was also developed into an interactive walk-through for the Chicago Villa competition sponsored by the Chicago Athenaeum.

(www.eastlakestudio.com)

WEB SITE SAMPLE B

PLANNING ISSUES IN THE DIGITAL AGE
Library Design for the Future

Some pundits are predicting the demise of libraries in the electronic age. Nonsense. We believe libraries will not only survive, but prosper. Here's why.

Librarians have always been dedicated to assisting people in the search for information, and with constantly changing software, users will need even more assistance in the retrieval, manipulation, and management of information.

Learning is increasingly understood as a social enterprise. Libraries are even more important as a place where users can interact and share knowledge.

Group learning facilities will increasingly benefit by being clustered together, both by allowing flexibility between media centers, on-line classrooms, and group study rooms, as well as by allowing for shared staff support.

Book collections aren't about to disappear. Given the economics of publishing and the high cost of scanning, centuries' worth of books will still need to be stored, made accessible and, ideally, made easy to browse.

Users want to study in inviting environments. Even though dorm rooms may be wired into the networks, they may not be ideal places for quiet study.

But libraries won't survive as is, and as with all important change, half the trick is figuring out how to get there from here.

Think "Service Oriented Information Center." The evolution of libraries into an expanded instructional role is blurring traditional distinctions between reference and instructional functions. The programming and design process can explore creative ways to help integrate staff as well as technology, and to optimize the delivery of services.

Think in terms of future functions, not today's space models. New types of spaces will be needed. With growing interaction between staff, users, and equipment, planning for noise control will be important. Increasing demands for access to resources on a twenty four-hour basis will require redefinition of the library security envelope.

Be rigorous about wiring distribution and management. In today's tight budget world, your ability to respond is limited not only by equipment, but also by the physical limitations of your existing facility. Developing accessible but concealed paths for data wiring is essential.

Build in flexibility and adaptability. Thoughtful planning can make the difference in creating a building that can change in response to new, unanticipated functions.

At Davis Brody Bond we understand the complex challenges facing you and can assist you in planning to meet them, from the earliest feasibility and programming stages to furnishing and fit-out.

We have a history of innovation in over forty years of practice, involving many different types of buildings. We are comfortable dealing with the ambiguity of change and the challenges of the future.

We are among the nation's leading architectural designers focusing on library projects. Our awards reflect the care we take in the detail of design which not only makes our libraries function well, but also creates spaces people enjoy using.

And most important, we understand that you need a problem solver, not a preconceived solution. We analyze your particular library's needs to come up with a unique approach to your requirements.

(www.davisbrody.com)

Davis Brody Bond, LLP. Reproduced by permission.

Setting Up Your Web Site

This book is about writing, and isn't intended to serve as a primer for setting up your Web site. But these few suggestions will help you.

Option 1. Create a Web site by retaining a Web design consultant. Some are generalists, some specialize in creating Web sites for architects, engineers, and other design professionals. They charge an initial fee, plus a monthly fee for maintenance—a critical function for you or your consultant. These services include Web site design, development, maintenance, hosting, domain registration, Internet marketing, database development, and Flash animation. As you work with consultants, always keep your audience in mind. You don't want your message to sink in a sea of misdirected graphic hoopla. And make sure key words ("facilities management," health care facilities planning) are registered so clients are directed to your Web site.

Option 2. Do it yourself. The main browser software companies offer do-it-yourself software. Microsoft has FrontPage, Adobe has PageMill, Netscape has Communicator, Claris has HomePage, Symantec has VisualPage. These aids are for the general user and are not necessarily geared to the unique demands of the design professional. Special touches must come from you, and the setup software may be able to accommodate your choices. The software is similar to some word-processing software that offers a variety of suggested graphic output formats to make life easier for the graphically timid, but can't spawn works of great uniqueness and originality.

If you choose option 2, the best person to shepherd and maintain the site is, in the experience of many firms, a design professional with a fondness for the Web, not a strictly computer person.

A Web site is not the only electronic path to your markets. For firms that opt for a CD-ROM-based brochure, the CD-ROM has these benefits and limitations:

Used as an alternative to a print or Web-based brochure, the CD-ROM can be targeted more than a Web site, without the Web's temptations to digress.

The CD-ROM is amenable to dramatic multimedia effects, including 3D modeling of sites for clients, virtual reality demonstrations of yet-to-be-finished projects, 3D walkthroughs of completed projects using QuickTimeVR or other software, "talking heads" of principals narrating the firm's vision and accomplishments, live staff biographies, and sound throughout. A free copy of Foster and Partners' CD-ROM was sent to subscribers of *Architectural Review* (see page 107).

There are no bandwidth limitations, as there is no transmission through telephone lines or cable. Special effects consume great bandwidth; when accessed on the Web, they greatly retard downloading.

Any "published" CD-ROM is essentially out of date the day it is burned. (Web sites are updated regularly, some sites every day.) Software such aa Macromedia Director allows the CD-ROM's master disk to be updated in-house when the supply of copies is about to run out.

As noted, QuickTimeVR allows the viewer to capture the action on the CD-ROM. It is typically built into common browsing software such as Netscape's and Microsoft's, and incorporated into the CD-ROM itself.

To sum up, writing for e-mail, Web sites, and CD-ROMs differs from writing on paper largely in a loosening of the traditional rules of grammar and forms of salutation. There is a focus on conciseness of message. In the moving-picture atmosphere of the CD-ROM, the writing of scripted, spoken content vies with written prose (most written prose today could benefit from the livelier language of speech). As the electronic medium dominates the work and lives of new generations of professional design firms, these changing standards are ending up dominating the written language.

12 Writing as a Career

Career writers who write about design are either trained as design professionals, have degrees in English or journalism, or come from the world of art history. No one field of training is best, so long as the resulting work is professional in content and form.

It is critical for career writers to understand the practical side of the design discipline they cover. Even if a topic does not call for the down-and-dirty aspects of construction or plant irrigation or cost control, the knowledge imbues their writing with greater depth and authenticity than one finds in the subjective, aesthetic "facadism" that still pervades much writing about design. "I will allow that the critic who has not a practical knowledge of technique is seldom able to say anything on the subject of real value," wrote W. Somerset Maugham in *The Moon and Sixpence* (London: Collins, 1936, p. 8–9).

Considering a Writing Career

Of the career options open to the design graduate or licensed design professional (see list in chapter 8, Job Prospects), writing has the fewest practitioners. This is because of the slender number of full-time magazine positions and the limited opportunities for freelance contributors. Such a career does, however, offer fulfillment. It provides regular contact with broad reaches of the profession; bracing travel; fellowship, often long-term and cordial, with leading players; and the delight of disseminating useful information and opinions with sometimes lasting impact. There are invitations to judge design and other award contests, to mix with students and faculty at design schools, and, if you reach a top position in the field, a comfortable income.

Full-time editorial careers begin typically at entry levels labeled editorial assistant or assistant editor. These junior positions commonly entail writing up short news and product items—although these two tasks have been known to develop, owing to the zeal of the players, into staff specialties with added authority. As openings occur, junior editors are given more important writing assignments, contacts with eminent sources, and chances to edit the work of others, including contributors.

Top positions, such as managing editor, executive editor, or editor in chief, open up seldom given the limited number of professional and special-interest design journals, but the same can be said about top positions in any industry. Criteria for these top appointments typically include a combination of talent, track record, management and leadership ability, the right balance of assertiveness and diplomacy, and luck of timing.

Correspondents and Contributors

Some publications retain full-time correspondents in key U.S. and international cities. Others employ "stringers", part-time reporters and writers who keep a nose out for news, interview local design celebrities, and review design projects. They are paid by the word or by published length. Stringers are the eyes and ears of a publication outside of its immediate area, and their writing needs to match the style of the publication they service.

Candidates should send resumes, samples, and a hint at the range of their good contacts to the publication's managing editor or, in the case of newspapers, the section editor. These editors, despite rumors to the contrary, are always glad to have a reserve of names even when there are no openings.

Part-time design reporters are typically freelancers, and do this as a sideline to a regular job. Staff writers moonlighting for other design magazines sometimes resort to pseudonyms.

Some freelance design writers make a good living by combining writing with lecturing, teaching, editorial consulting, and writing an occasional book. (Refer also to chapter 10, Writing for the Media.)

Publishers of architectural and engineering books sometimes appoint full-time acquisition editors who have a design professional background.

Writing a Book

Writing a book about design demands more effort than writing articles and criticism, chiefly because of the mental and physical marathon such a project represents. A book has the value of permanence, generating a deeper level of discussion, and influencing trends. Notable examples include Venturi's *Complexity and Contradiction in Architecture,* Siegfried Giedion's *Space, Time, and Architecture,* Reyner Banham's *Theory and Design in the First Machine Age,* Le Corbusier's *When the Cathedrals Were White,* and more recently, the works of Jencks, Frampton, Vidler, Koolhaas, and Kurokawa; the classic works of Vitruvius, Alberti, and Viollet-le-Duc; and, not least, the great pattern books —the generators of most of this country's domestic design and construction.

Before deciding to write a book, consider:

Books take time. It is not a three-days-a-week evening task. You will need to set aside hours every day, or days every week.

Books usually do not generate income through royalties until long after they are published. The book advance will not pay for your bed and board, unless you are a celebrity.

Check out your marketplace. Who besides you cares about the topic? Are those interested necessarily the ones with the cash to buy books?

Is your research done, or will it entail a major search for material? If you already have great expertise in the subject, you save research time.

Is a book the best medium for your topic? Would an article series be better, or an illustrated lecture series followed by a CD-ROM?

Does writing come easily to you? If not, don't underestimate the time you will need to complete the manuscript. If the book is logically organized and clearly written and follows the writing guidelines mentioned throughout this book, it will need little editing and your editor will be happy. If it does not, expect to revise under the guidance of your editor, or have the manuscript heavily edited. Consider these issues up front, and make realistic decisions about your time and the likely financial return.

A book about your firm's design work is a good marketing item, and you may write such a book yourself. More commonly an outside writer is retained to take on the task, typically writing a long introduction to the illustrations, bringing to it a detached point of view more likely to appeal to a publisher and to the marketplace. Much critical comment is unlikely, however, as design firms use such books as powerful marketing tools, which they subsidize by committing to buy a quantity of copies.

Finding a Publisher

To find a book publisher, review the books of houses that publish books in your field. Decide whose publications—in quality of design, writing, and layout—best fit your purpose. Send a one-page outline of your idea to an editor there. This should yield immediate encouragement or a turn-down before you invest more time and effort.

If encouraged, develop a prospectus, an outline, and (if asked) a sample chapter. The prospectus is a two- to four-page description of your topic, why it is important, and who will make up the buying audience. How much of this buying audience is reachable by direct mail—an efficient selling medium for most professional design books? How many words will the book contain, and how many illustrations? The outline lists chapter headings and main subheadings, and proposed artwork. The typical chapter should come from the center of the book—not the introduction or the conclusion. Editors commonly demand it in order to assess your writing style, level of knowledge, and appropriateness to the intended audience.

Approach one publisher at a time, not several at once, and insist on prompt responses. If your proposal is accepted, your editor will give you a contract specifying your rights and obligations and those of the publishing house. The contract covers deadlines; the size, computation, and payment of royalties and advances on royalties; rights and obligations; and more.

Frequent or full-time design writers often engage an agent, who makes the initial overtures and retains a percentage of your earnings.

Career Prospects

Career writers face a new world in the twenty-first century. Internet access to currently elusive data greatly simplifies the research process that still underlies most writing on complex topics such as design. And while I know of no software that will prepare a quality text based merely on inputting key words and linkages, such programs are technically possible. For example, for years design firms have routinely used master specifications on projects: the spec writer's task is to select texts from a range of alternative master texts, and edit these to achieve the intended meaning—no need to invent the text from ground zero.

None of this means an end to writing for publication on paper. Nor does it mean the passing of the book and the magazine; these have a physical convenience that goes back to antiquity. Electronic media, however, offer a vehicle for extending access to information well beyond the printed page, and few can predict the impact of plans by search engines such as Google to disseminate electronically texts of entire books, both in and out of copyright.

13 On Your Feet

This chapter focuses on the challenges of speaking, its organization and delivery. The designer faces these challenges at lectures and interviews.

Queen Victoria used to complain that whenever Prime Minister Gladstone came to brief her on affairs of state, he would address her "as though we were at a public meeting." Speaking is an art and a science, with its own rules, opportunities, and pitfalls. What you say must be immediately intelligible; a listener who misses a word or phrase cannot relisten the way a reader can reread. Nor can you as the speaker retrace your steps and "unsay" a wrong word or thought. If you bore your audience, you will have a short career as a speaker. When preparing a speech, pay attention to these points:

• Be sure content and delivery are simple and direct. Listeners have no time for convoluted phrasing.

• Shun statistics or lists unless you have visual backup.

• Keep sentences short; it takes a practiced performer to deliver long sentences.

• Restate your main points. There's wisdom in the old motto: "tell 'em what you're going to say; say it; then tell 'em what you just said." Restate, but don't repeat. A good example comes from Scripture. Note how the Psalms, written to be recited, not read, repeat each thought within a single verse (Psalm 24, King James Version):

1. The earth is the Lord's, and the fullness thereof; the world, and they that dwell therein.

2. For he hath founded it upon the seas, and established it upon the floods.

3. Who shall ascend into the hill of the Lord? or who shall stand in his holy place?

Gestures count. Just as the graphic format can make or muddy your message, so can your appearance, your gestures, and the physical setting. People find it harder to absorb spoken information than written text. So the listener

190

who wants to retain the content of a speech has to either take notes (distracting for the listener) or run a tape recorder (an obvious duplication of effort since the tape must be played back later or transcribed).

Speaking is a two-way street. Gauge your audience, pick up signals—of excitement, mild interest, or boredom—and adjust your delivery accordingly. Like most speaking activity, the client interview is also a two-way street. It should not be a forum for the prospective client merely to pick up information about your firm; that should already be in your brochure, which the client has presumably at least scanned prior to the interview. The point of the interview is to give the client the chance to evaluate you and your associates—for example, how you deal with questions about the project's potential and limitations. Interviews and presentations have these special considerations:

It is a dialog, not a speech. The interview is a flexible occasion. Your presentation, ranging from simple slides to multimedia showbiz, may be interrupted at any time by a query. Some selection committee members deliberately interrupt presenters to see how they respond under pressure.

Beware the dangers of designer-babble. Designer-babble or jargon is even riskier in a verbal presentation than in writing. Odds are that your audience is composed of laypeople, and dishing out clever verbal ammo is a sure way to calamity. Avoid clunkers such as "the plastic qualities of a facade," or "the controlled clash of volumes."

Consider using audiovisual support. An endless array of aids is available to your firm's presenter. The 35mm slide or overhead projector has been largely supplanted by PowerPoint, computer-generated 3D animations, and Virtual Reality productions convertible to screen projection using specialized equipment. Techniques for preparing such presentations are described in other works, such as Curtis Charles and Karen Brown's *Multimedia Marketing for Design Firms.* Such whiz shows are two-edged swords, however; if overused, they will steal attention away from the presenter. Do not rest your case on too much high-tech razzmatazz. The client is looking you over as a problem solver, not a technical wizard. Control the show yourself (managed best from a laptop) or get a well-rehearsed assistant.

Learn how to take questions. Respond briefly and to the point; no speeches. Avoid being drawn into a detailed discussion of a proposed project whose outlines you don't yet know.

Avoid techno overkill. Steer clear of showing complex engineering diagrams or elaborate computer printouts of project schedules or complex budget breakdowns. Most of the committee cannot follow them. Use brief, simple descriptions—contrary to current wisdom, a word can be worth a thousand pictures.

Lectures and Speeches

A keynote speech at a national conference, an evening lecture to students, a speech to government officials—these contrast with a client presentation mainly in that you are granted a block of uninterrupted time instead of the give-and-take of an interview.

Preparation According to Orvin Larson in *When It's Your Turn to Speak* (see Resources), when asked how long it took Daniel Webster to prepare his famous "Reply to [Senator Robert] Hayne" speech of 1830, Webster said, "twenty years." Always assume that some day you will be asked to speak, whether it's about computer applications in the office, planning the new workplace, innovative landmark legislation, or building on wetlands. Start a speech file, making occasional notes and inserting pieces of information or a chance phrase in the areas of your expertise.

When you are to give a speech, schedule a silent hour and jot down ideas, however remote, on the assigned topic. Review your speech file for nuggets. Record all these on a notepad or, better still, on index cards—one idea per card, or start a Word folder. Arrange the cards in a sequence that allows a build-up. For example, if your theme is "design-build and the design professional's accountability," consider this possible outline:

1. The owner wants construction value for the money.
2. Traditional design-bid-build techniques sometimes suffer because design and construction don't meet until the bid stage.
3. Design-build provides single responsibility, and aids in packaging subcontractor bids and phasing construction.
4. The design professional has the chance to take the initiative, by launching and managing design-build teams.
5. The owner receives more effective control over quality, schedule, and costs, but sometimes forgoes direct access from the designer.
6. Design-build entails risk.

Expand your outline to full length, adding examples. Except for quotes, avoid writing out full sentences that tempt you to read your speech to the audience; you cannot both read and look at the audience—crucial to a good speech. Limit your notes to short phrases. With a large audience (250 or more), you can get by with frequent glances at your cards; not so with a smaller group. Write notes large so they are easy to scan; set your word processor to 14-point type (minimum). If you're lucky, you will be able to use a teleprompter.

Rehearse the speech once or twice, including a dry run if you have visual aids; anything more will kill spontaneity.

Politicians and top executives write out speeches so they can hand them out to the press in advance and avoid embarrassing boners. That's why most such speeches are dull. As a design professional, you should feel comfortable enough in your command of the material to speak from notes. A read speech often sounds as though it was written for publication, not for oral delivery.

Here are some examples of liberties you should consider for greater impact:

Written:

We must consider cost, schedule, and quality control . . .

Spoken:

We have to watch over cost control and schedule control and quality control . . .

Written:

Architects, engineers, and landscape architects had big backlogs of work . . .

Spoken:

Architects were busy, engineers were busy, so were the landscape architects . . .

When preparing a speech, keep several other things in mind:

Speed of delivery. Count on delivering about eighty-five words a minute, or 1275 in a quarter-hour. Radio announcers are trained to deliver 200 words a minute, except when they are reading the "fine print" of a commercial, when the speed seems to double. (I have heard hog callers approach this maximum.) If in doubt, slow down—better to speak too slowly than too quickly. Pause between sections; silence is a great attention-getter.

Sign posting. Consultant and author Antony Jay recommends resetting the scene for the forgetful listener at points during the speech—for example, "So here we are—the new site survey showed a high water table but the foundation had been designed to fit an earlier survey."

Audience size. The larger the audience, the more it reacts as one person, and the easier it is to influence. Large audiences react less to the subject matter, more to your personality. That doesn't mean you should dilute intellectual content, but you need to simplify concepts and work on your delivery.

Attention span. The classic attention span of the fifty-minute lecture is shown in the chart below. Insert your lighter material in the thirty- to forty-minute slot; the heavier stuff at the beginning and the end.

Humor. Jokes are a good way to loosen up a medium-to-large audience. With groups of fewer than ten people, all you will get is embarrassed snickers. If you cannot tell jokes well or deliver a resounding punchline, pass them up. A flat joke is worse than none. Insist on a link between your joke and your topic.

Using PowerPoint

PowerPoint reinforces your speech even if the slides contain only words, not images. Use PowerPoint slides for short (maximum six to eight item) bulleted lists of key points, or to add force to a quote or slogan. You can run the slides manually from a laptop, or set them on automatic. A great benefit of the medium is that you can, if you want, build a list incrementally, rather than show the entire slide at once. Avoid these pitfalls:

Audiences are sharper at the start and finish of a typical 50-minute lecture. Keep the heavy stuff out of the 30- to 40-minute time slot.

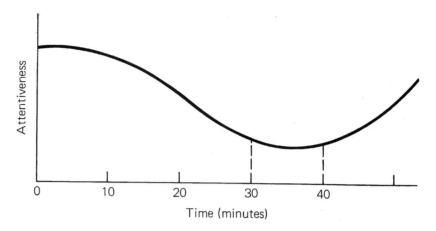

- If the lights are out the audience can't see you; if the lights are on, they cannot see the slides. Therefore don't spread the slides throughout the speech: focus them in one or two time-slots. Remember, the screen draws the listeners' focus away from you.
- PowerPoint comes with bells and whistles—some useful, some annoying. By all means use different color backgrounds—no more than two or three—to mark separate sections. Avoid new slides rolling in from all sides, and disable the raucous noise available to introduce a new slide.

Most office software is equipped with do it yourself PowerPoint, with directions.

The Press Interview

If you are interviewed by a member of the professional press researching a story, develop a few notes on the subject and speak frankly. If you suspect you didn't get all the points right, the editor will welcome a correction by voice- or e-mail.

When speaking with a daily press reporter—who often interviews design professionals for reactions to daily events and, especially, catastrophes such as a terrorist attack, an earthquake, or a windstorm—be prudent. Because of deadlines, chances are you'll not have a chance to correct what you said. To avoid being misquoted, answer all questions with a complete sentence or rephrase the question in your own way before you respond. Never respond merely with a yes or no. For example: Reporter: "Do you agree that changes in the city zoning law will end up driving out low-income families?"

Poor answer:
"No, because of built-in safeguards." (Next morning: "Designer denies that new zoning will displace the poor.")

A better answer:
"The changes in the zoning law are subject to an overall plan. The plan is aimed at encouraging families to live in the city—families of all incomes. Safeguards have been built into the changes. For instance . . ."

The aim is to get a complete answer into the reporter's notebook. Observe how seasoned politicians field questions from the press.

The Broadcast Interview

A radio or television interview has special ground rules. First, you cannot retract a mistake, unless the studio tapes your interview before airing it and allows you to tape over the mistake. Second, instead of addressing an audience in the dozens or hundreds, you are talking to an audience of perhaps two or three, clustered around a family room TV set or sitting in a car with the radio on. You do not have a captive audience; if they lose interest, they flip the channel, and you're history.

For broadcast, therefore, an informal, fireside-chat format is in order. No great oratorical statements or overwrought facial or other gestures. The TV camera exaggerates all. Avoid long sentences; people have been known to start out on one, then not know how to finish it. Your time on camera is likely to be strictly limited: a couple of minutes on the evening news, longer if you're a guest of Charlie Rose. So make your key points first; you won't know how much time you'll have. Look at the interviewer, not the camera.

Radio has its own quirks. (See *The Associated Press Broadcast News Handbook* in the Resources section.) Silences are useful in a live speech and at times on television (you look wise, as though thinking deeply about your next remark). On radio, a silence of more than five seconds signals to your listeners that the transmitter has failed or, worse, that you had a stroke. A kindly interviewer will help you bridge such gaps. A short opening statement written out in advance in colloquial language will get you off on the right foot. Typed-out material works better on radio, as no one can see you. (Just don't rustle the paper.) Gesture all you like when on radio—it may add animation to your voice.

14 Graphics: Medium for the Message

The success of your message is not just in the way it reads; it's also in the way it looks. If the design of a page, sheet, proposal, brochure, portfolio, Web site, or e-mail confuses the reader or is just plain unreadable (dark-brown 6-point sans serif type on a medium-brown background), you are wasting your time writing anything at all.

The following observations and guidelines for good graphics are divided into four factors: readability, appropriateness, image, and fashion.

Readability

The most innovative graphics are useless if the reader cannot make out the message. Therefore, whether you are a firm principal deciding on a new letterhead or a design for a marketing brochure or portfolio; a partner in charge of creating a cover and inside format for an important feasibility or planning report; or a doctoral candidate readying your dissertation, remember this adage. While Marshall McLuhan claims with some truth that the medium is the message, whenever the message is thwarted by the medium, there is no message. These pointers will help to prevent your message from being obscured by the graphic medium:

- Create contrast between type color and background.
- Make type large enough to be read in comfort; don't attempt to pack too much information into a limited space. Even 7-point type is hard to read without a magnifying glass. Line spacing that is too tight (say a point or less), and paragraphs that are too long (over fifteen lines) in relation to column width, are hard to read. Long passages in sans serif type are usually harder to read than serif type.
- Avoid drop-out type (type printed in white or a light color against a dark background). Too much is tiring on the eyes.
- Just because popular pagemaking software allows you to shape columns of text in any shape (such as a milk jug or an hour glass) doesn't mean it's always a good thing to do if it ends up unreadable. For example, the text of an article about seismic distortion could well take on the curved shape of a tall building deflected by lateral pressures. But what's the point if you cannot comfortably read the type.

- Provide adequate borders and margins. The eye needs rest. An inch all around a letter or memo is a minimum for comfort.

Once you have dealt graphically with the basic need to communicate, you face the question of graphic appropriateness.

There is in fact no absolute right or wrong in graphics. What counts is whether the design is right or wrong for its purpose. It's clearly inappropriate to print out a planning report on flimsy paper with a short-lived binding if it is to be widely disseminated among senior corporate or public officials. Even so, some designers believe that public officials dislike ostentatious use of public funds, so a cheaply produced report should spell "economy." A news release printed on heavy-coated paper denies the purpose of the release, which is to be read briefly, the content edited for a news story, then the whole discarded.

Similarly, it makes little tactical sense to clothe a proposal to a cost-conscious inner-city school district in elaborate binding, glossy overlays, and a large range of color, when a straightforward assembly of pages, possibly with simply colored dividers, in a decent off-the-shelf binder, is far more appropriate. On the other hand, when a proposal is for design services to a Hollywood magnate, it is in order for the packaging to reflect a certain richness, as it appears to place proposer and client on the same level.

As Thomas F. McCormick, who was Public Printer of the United States in the late 1970s, told a seminar for graphic designers: "Even some top-grade newsprint looks 'cheap and dirty'—but it's still the most effective paper there is for publishing daily news. But to put the *National Geographic* on the same paper would ruin it."

Appropriateness is also a matter of detail. Take typefaces. A common typeface, such as Times Roman, is good for a news release. An elegant, old-line, serif typeface, such as Cheltenham or Clarendon, works well for a formal report on proposed restoration of a major historical landmark. A more playful typeface—or font, as it is known in the printing trade—is proper for an exhibit panel of your prize-winning design for an amusement park or a paper on fold and blob technology.

Page size is another graphic decision that shapes the impact of the written message. There is no reason to abandon the standard 8½- by 11-inch format (or the A4 size used by many overseas nations) for standard project correspondence. Chances are it will be filed, and odd page sizes aggravate.

On the other hand, if you want something read but not filed, do go to a different page size: it struts the document's difference and demands to be looked at. Any paper supplier will tell you that there are attractive, nonstandard paper sizes cut from the basic 25- by 38-inch sheet that incur no wastage and thus no premium cost.

Unlike appropriateness, which applies to the project, image applies to and expresses your firm. Graphic image is a key ingredient of any firm's communications. Each firm at some stage must determine what the firm is and how to express that through its public contacts and internal behavior. Do you want to convey an informal, convivial image, or one of sobriety and restraint? Of tradition and concern for historic values, or up-to-the-minute cool? Would you rather project a concern for the client's pocketbook, or is your skill in creating innovative, envelope-stretching forms? Do you want to stress youth? vigor? wisdom? experience? Do you go gently into that good market, or practice the hard sell?

Translate your decision into graphic terms. A conservative image may be expressed through dignified type, symmetry, subdued colors, bulk. A brash image shows through bright colors, unorthodox text arrangement, deliberately mixed typefaces. Budget-consciousness comes across by selecting resolutely bargain-basement materials, bindings, and common, popular fonts.

Oddly enough, the impression of economy is not always cheaply come by. A famous graphic designer created a one-inch-thick report from pieces of paper of a dozen different sizes, and bound together by three off-the-shelf bronze marine fittings. The effect, while not cheap, was sensational, as though it had been knocked together in a spare moment, and you can be sure it wasn't ignored.

What if appropriateness conflicts with image? If you are pursuing clients whose general culture matches yours, well and good. But suppose your firm is known for jagged forms and space-age materials, and you decide to compete for a regional bank headquarters against two notable, conservative firms also on the short list. Your choices include:

1. Making the proposal package and other marketing correspondence in a conservative graphic cloak;

2. Figuring that the previous option isn't going to fool anyone, stick with your image, along with a high-tech presentation if required;

3. Developing an inoffensive, bland (neither conservative nor innovative) marketing package that doesn't draw attention to itself.

My choice is the second. What's yours?

Fashion

Over and above other concerns is the power of fashion. Graphic fashion tends to go in cycles—like hems, cuisines, and art—and is influenced not unreasonably by the technology available. The 1970s and 1980s saw formal arrangements of type in clean vertical columns, separated chastely from the artwork, with right angles dominant.

Today, great opportunities lie in computer-aided graphics through programs such as Photoshop and Illustrator, sketching and modeling programs such as 3D Studio Max, Form Z, and SmartSketch, and publishing systems such as QuarkXpress and InDesign, even in free downloadable software. An open, loose quality has captured much graphic design. There is a wealth of new typefaces; they are often mixed together; type is set in any desired shape, from rectangle to half moon to star; type, headlines, and artwork freely mingle.

Thus fashion plays an essential part in the way your written message reaches your selection committee, client, project team member, or design honor award judges. That is as it should be, up to a point. After all, design has always expressed its society. Pitted against fashion, however, especially in firms of long lineage, is the tradition and culture of the firm. How such conflicts are resolved is among the more engaging of life's challenges.

15 Writing by the Product Manufacturer

"How will this product or material or equipment support my design concept?" That's the first question asked by architects, interior and urban designers, and landscape architects, as well as by consultants in the various engineering disciplines, lighting, and acoustics, whenever they read a manufacturer's promotional piece.

The copywriters whom manufacturers retain to inform the nation's design professions about new and existing products, materials, and equipment face peculiar challenges. They need to satisfy the following needs simultaneously:

The designer's need to have information that is accurate, complete, and in a usable form;

The company's need to sell a product;

The company's need not to give away proprietary information to competitors;

Product images that look professional without being boring, and images that evoke emotion without being crass, vulgar, or unconnected with the advertised product;

Dissemination in several formats (print; CD-ROM; on-line) linkable into the designer/specifier's information-seeking and decision-making network.

Here are writing yardsticks that cut across all marketing communication channels:

Do

• Write to press the designer/specifier's hot buttons. These buttons include the facts or product's applications; evidence of superior performance when compared to existing products; appearance; alternate choices; ease of connecting to adjacent installed products; operating life; environmental attributes; price; delivery; manufacturer's support. From these data the designer will judge to what extent the product supports the design.

• Keep sentences short and snappy. You may even break some basic rules of grammar ("every sentence must contain a subject, verb, and predicate") in favor of a looser sentence structure ("There's more to see. More to choose. More to like . . ."—from an advertisement by Weather Shield). Where chapter 1 advocates short sentences—not above twenty words—product copy should aspire to even shorter sentences ("Fine artists aren't limited to just one color. So why should architects be limited to just pine?"—from the same advertisement).

- Shun the abstract and the trivial. Be concrete. Your reader isn't looking for flights of fancy, just the facts. ("New Hi-LR™ Optima RH95™ ceilings are specifically designed for open plan offices. With an NRC of .85–1.00 and Articulation Class (AC) of 190–210, they prevent reflected noise between cubicles. Sounds too good to be true? Listen for yourself."—from an advertisement by Armstrong.)

- Use headlines of strength and meaning. ("817 hits. No errors."—headline for an ad by Pella Windows & Doors accompanying a photograph of a renovated warehouse within hitting distance of Camden Yards, Baltimore's ballpark. The name of the window series also happens to be "817".)

Don't
- Write so much copy that your message loses its selling focus. You seek a single, punchy message. There are exceptions: Rolls Royce and Mercedes Benz disregarded this notion some years ago; the advertising was noted for its long texts describing the cars' mechanical specifications in awesome detail. The idea was to convey to buyers the idea that they were getting their money's worth in quality and performance.

- Neglect the designer/specifier's information needs in favor of superficial verbal brilliance. Always remember that you are an information provider, not a poet.

Direct Mail Copy

It's a safe bet that direct mail is only as good as your mailing list. The best-fashioned direct mail package won't yield a decent return if sent to the wrong destinations. What makes for a good list is part statistical odds, part trial and error, part common sense.

Direct mail from the product manufacturer typically comes in the form of the glossy, four- to eight-page product piece (often a reprint of an advertisement, or a product catalog destined for or taken from Sweet's catalog). The piece is best accompanied by a cover letter from a senior marketing executive. A second format, rare nowadays, is the postcard deck, made up of postcard-sized or double postcard–sized information cards and mailed to prospects three or four times a year.

The regular (8½- by 11-inch) format mailing pieces—whether original, reprints from an advertisement, or a catalog originally created for Sweet's—need to observe the basic laws of promotional copy: attract the designer prospect's attention through some device; then, in the short attention span available, press one or more hot buttons. This will either close the sale then and there (unlikely) or else motivate the prospect to ask for more information by demanding an extended brochure, clicking on the company's Web site, or requesting a sales call.

Cover Letter   The cover letter is a powerful lead-in to the mailed piece. To spur the designer to read on, the letter must get to the point fast and summarize succinctly the benefits to the reader of reading on. The letter should be short—a half page, perhaps. It is not the vehicle for formal courtesies and elaborate product prose.

COVER LETTER FOR MANUFACTURER'S DIRECT MAIL PIECE

Dear Interior Designer:

You can see from the enclosed eight-page illustrated brochure that PDQ Company's furniture system for the new workplace covers a wide range of stylistic choices. What you cannot so easily see from the photographs and drawings are the benefits the system brings to you and your clients. These include:

• Adaptability to frequent staff moves, all done simply by your in-house custodial staff.
• Built-in data, lighting, and comfort-control connections.
• Multiple-file storage at each station that offers security whenever more than one shift of workers is assigned to the work station.
• Top quality by seasoned Maine cabinetmakers and other craftspeople working in our technically advanced manufacturing plant.
• Our own technical staff available to you 24 hours a day.

Read our brochure. If you need more information, consult our Web site (www.pdq.com), call us at 207/555-0000 and ask for David Jones, or e-mail me at djones@pdq.com.
Sincerely,
David Jones
Executive Vice President

(Note that this letter, sent from the mythical company PDQ, focuses on what cannot be readily seen from the photographs, namely, benefits derived by specifying the company's workplace system. The text is brief, and zeroes in on the types of features an interior designer needs to know.)

Avoid using the fax as a transmission medium for new product information. You have no control over the receiver's printer quality. What's more, unsolicited faxes are against the law.

Advertising Copy   Advertising copywriters are known to be attracted more to the glamour of consumer advertising than to the serious material demanded by advertising to the business customer or specifier. Advertising copy often ends up either listless or saddled with a phony consumer tone guaranteed to alienate the design-

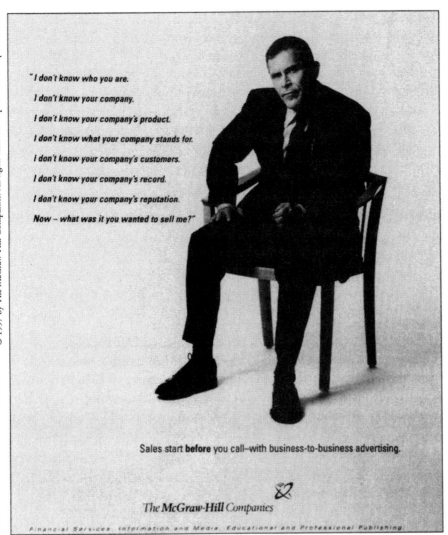

"*I don't know who you are.*

I don't know your company.

I don't know your company's product.

I don't know what your company stands for.

I don't know your company's customers.

I don't know your company's record.

I don't know your company's reputation.

Now – what was it you wanted to sell me?"

Sales start **before** you call–with business-to-business advertising.

The McGraw-Hill Companies

Financial Services   Information and Media   Educational and Professional Publishing

This classic advertisement, with the figure updated every few years, is a superb example of brawny copy-writing, choice of image, smart psychology, and design.

er who is just looking for facts and application information, not jazzy unrelated visuals and glitzy prose.

Designers are human, and respond to the same selling stimuli as other consumers. That, however, cannot justify copy that fails to provide factual information, or hides it under a blanket of showbiz glitz more appropriate to selling deodorant or Alaskan cruises. Advertisers routinely test the impact of their advertisements, copy included, on focus groups of prospective customers to see what sells product and what doesn't. These consistently show the designer's preference for ads that depict a product clearly, simply, with the copy tight, brisk, and focused on applications.

For a classic example of brilliant advertising copywriting, see the ad above. A major publishing company used this ad to appeal to advertisers. It is a superior example of a smart concept, suitable image, and sparkling copy.

Writing Copy for Electronic Marketing

Electronic-based product information systems have now evolved to where designers routinely import product information, including details, into project drawings and specifications.

Writing effective copy for manufacturers' Web sites and CD-ROMs follows the same hot-button tactics that work so well for printed matter. Copywriting must be spartan, focusing on usable facts and removing all surplus words and syllables. Recognize that, with a click of the mouse, the specifier can move easily to the next screen or even to a competitor's Web site.

Buyer's Guides

The term "buyer's guide" embraces a number of publication types, some printed, some electronic, in which the caliber of writing has an impact on the designer's understanding. These works include:

- Directories (cross-referenced listings of products and manufacturers, typically arranged to conform to the 50- (formerly 16-) category Construction Specifications Institute MASTERFORMAT®);
- Annual "buyer's guide" issues of magazines;
- CD-ROMs, such as ARCAT (Arcat, Inc.), quarterly CD-ROMs shipped to subscribers of the publishers' catalog files. The CD-ROMs include drawings and details exportable to the designer's drawing.
- On-line access, such as Sweets Catalog Files containing over 60,000 products and downloadable in .pdf format.

The quality of copy in these guides and directories varies. Product write-ups in magazines are either written by the magazine's editors and qualify as editorial matter or are supplied by the manufacturer and printed in space paid for by that manufacturer as advertising. Magazines' product editors lack the resources to research and assess each product they write up. Consequently, they evaluate manufacturers' claims from a viewpoint of logic and personal knowledge, and avail themselves freely of such qualifying terms as "allegedly," "reportedly," "according to the manufacturer," and "is said to have."

The best descriptive copy is made up of short sentences, a simple structure, and a level of technical terminology compatible with the presumed level of skill of the reader. If you have the space and enough data, divide the copy into logical groupings, such as basic product description, features, benefits, and key performance data.

The following examples show two types of write-up for the same fictional product: first as paid matter, then as editorial matter. Note the difference.

SAMPLE A (ADVERTISING VERSION)

SOUND ABSORPTION

DiCarlo-Smith DECIBEL bronze sound-absorbing panels are suitable for attaching to ceilings and walls. DECIBEL panels offer an exceptionally attractive high-tech look combined with sound-absorption of 2 sabins per square foot at frequencies between 1000 and 2000 cycles per second. DECIBEL panels may also be textured to include corrugations, as well as custom designs. A DECIBEL panel is air-permeable, non-fibrous, and totally resistant to harsh environments. Contact us.

DiCarlo-Smith
213/010-1001
www.dicars.com

SAMPLE B (EDITORIAL VERSION)

SOUND-ABSORPTIVE PANELS

Manufacturer's DECIBEL bronze sound-absorbing panels are suitable for attaching to ceilings and walls. Panels are said to offer a high-tech look, and are rated for sound-absorption at 2 sabins per square foot at frequencies between 1000 and 2000 cycles per second, according to manufacturer. Panels may be textured to include corrugations, and manufacturer offers custom designs. The panels are air-permeable, non-fibrous, and resistant to harsh environments, states the manufacturer.

DiCarlo-Smith
213/010-1001
www.dicars.com

The manufacturer's writer needs to create interest-provoking language without turning off the designer/specifier with flamboyant prose, lack of taste in the visuals, or preoccupation with the trivial.

The best advice to product writers who lack practical design experience (and many of them fall into that category) is to meet and get to know designers and specifiers. Find out what the designer reads professionally, then study it so you can identify with the designer's concerns.

16 International Style

Many design firms have projects overseas. Some firms have even established international offices. More and more firms outsource certain tasks, such as renderings, CAD drafting and design, and construction documents (about 6% send such tasks offshore, according to a 2004 survey by the newsletter *Principal's Report*).

Keeping pace with these trends is the rising demand for functional written communication linking English-speaking design professionals with the flourishing economies, short or long-term, of Asia, Europe, the Middle East, and South America, and the emerging economies of Central and Eastern Europe. Forging solid links with these regions is a crucial test of the writing skills of principals who spearhead marketing or manage projects for design firms eager to establish an overseas presence. For example, Kaplan McLaughlin Diaz, a San Francisco-based architectural firm with a large volume of Asian commissions, has developed Japanese and Chinese versions of key brochure sections listing its qualifications. KMD's three-hole punched fact sheets are assembled in beige binders as needed for developing new business.

It is vital, first of all, to become familiar with the mores and values of nations where you want to do business. To be effective, conversions both from English into the local language and from the local language into English must be checked by a person who knows each language's nuances and colloquialisms. Especially prone to gaffes are texts composed in English by overseas associates for whom English is a second language (see these examples of lax quality control). What counts in the end are not the words, but the meaning.

Swiss wine menu:
"Our wines leave you nothing to hope for."

Ad for a Hong Kong dentist:
"Teeth extracted by the latest methodists."

In a Paris lobby:
"Please leave your values at the front desk."

Taiwan Pepsi ad:
Original: "Come alive with the Pepsi generation."
Translation: "Pepsi will bring your ancestors back from the dead."

Sales pitch from a Copenhagen airline:
"We take your bags and send them in all directions."

Excerpt reproduced with permission from article "Speaking in Tongues" published in *@issue:*, v. 3, no. 1. *@issue:* The Journal of Business & Design is published by Corporate Design Foundation.

When communicating on overseas projects, consider carefully the writing of such items as marketing materials, agreements, contract documents, correspondence, and speeches.

Marketing Materials

Special editions of your brochure need to be prepared if you plan a major sally into overseas markets. They show that you are familiar with local conditions and/or are ready to associate with a local counterpart.

The text must define unfamiliar English technical terms, shun jargon, cite dimensions and other quantities in metric units, and avoid cultural references that could cause offense. You clearly cannot afford to create a package to fit every possible target nation, but basic firm qualification statements stored in your marketing database may be adapted as needed. Most word-processing programs contain symbols that let you write, if needed, in languages using the Latin or Cyrillic alphabets. Some word-processing software extensions include kanji (a system of Japanese writing using Chinese-derived characters). The best rule is to keep text to a minimum; let the photographs and drawings do the talking.

Agreements and Contract Documents

Because business practices vary by region and often by country, written words are open to misinterpretation. Local associates and consultants can advise on particular meanings.

Follow local conventions. Because words are more easily misinterpreted than drawings, firms insert more of the design intent into the drawings and less into the specifications. In the United States it is also common practice for firms to carry an overseas project through design development, then hand document production and contract administration over to the associated local firm. The local firm completes the documents to comply with local standards and regulations. Some firms use a short-form performance specification to accompany the drawings.

Project Correspondence

Project correspondence is especially sensitive to local cultural values and the nuances of words. Many nations have not yet adapted to the more direct American way of writing. Hence greater formality is in order (see the examples of correspondence to two Asian nations on pages 208–210). On the other hand, many who also practice overseas claim that the world is beginning to adopt American forms of writing.

That does not mean you should ignore local etiquette, such as in forms of salutation and endings. Salutations and farewells of course vary from country to country and region to region, and it's not hard to find out the right form in advance. For example, a common error in addressing an individual from a Spanish-speaking nation is to address, say, Agostín Vázquez González, as "Dear Señor González" when that is in fact his mother's maiden name. The correct form is "Dear Señor Vázquez" or, in Spanish, "Estimado Señor Vázquez."

"When corresponding with clients whose native language is other than English, style is not the issue," says Leslie E. Robertson, prominent New York–based structural engineer with a large global practice. Writing style is international, whether you are writing to the United Kingdom, Malaysia, or Japan. "What you do have to worry about is the context of the words you use. Words have multiple meanings, and it's the context that provides the right meaning. Words have to be chosen carefully so they can be construed only one way." Misunderstandings occur when a letter in English is translated, as it often is, into the local language in order to inform non–English speakers about the project. When the recipient is influential, a poorly translated letter can create a lot of static.

Avoid lumping all nations in a region under a single umbrella. Southeast Asia, for example, is not a single culture. As she compares Chinese communication with Japanese, Lena Ning Zheng, long-time director of China projects at Kaplan McLaughlin Diaz, has pointed out that China tends to adopt a subtle, classical, formal outlook in its dealings with foreign consultants, with scholarship honored in written and spoken communications. This at times clashes with the "let's get down to brass tacks" approach of Western or Westernized design firms. Japan, on the other hand, is by and large more welcoming to Western efficiency in verbal and written contacts.

Following are a request for information and a subtle reminder of an overdue fee payment.

LETTER A

Mr. Tetsuo Nagae
Shimizu Corporation Civil Engineering
Midosuji Honmachi Building, 8F
No. 5-7, Honmachi, 3-chome
Chuo-ku, Osaka 541 JAPAN
Via fax/modem: 81 (6) 271-1595
Re: Miho Museum Bridge

Dear Nagae-san:
For another project we are seeking a free-draining material to be used for

an area of paving not all that different from that of the Miho Museum Bridge. The paving being on grade, there is no thought of using the material in conjunction with grating. If possible, we would be very appreciative if you could provide to us the following:

• the name, address, facsimile and the like of the supplier of the material for the Miho Museum Bridge;
  • a copy of the technical specification for the material; and
  • the name and address of any United States supplier of a similar material.

It is our intention to enter the design of the bridge in one or more competitions. We will send to you copies of the entries as they are prepared.

We were told that Shimizu had entered the bridge in one or more competitions. If so, could you provide to us a copy of the submitted material?

Much to our surprise, ENR has honored LERA for the design of the bridge. With the written copy of this letter we will enclose copies of that material.

Best regards,
Leslie E. Robertson Associates

SCENARIO

Your firm has completed 75% contract documents for a new hotel in Djakarta, Indonesia. The client is long overdue in paying the latest installment of your fee, in an amount of $125,000. You have invoiced the client's lower echelon staff three times with no result. You now decide to contact the Indonesia-based hotel chain's president, Mr. Kim Juarto (name and project are fictitious) to get action. Your relationship with the client has been friendly, and while you do not want to spoil this, you also want to be paid, perhaps in a lump sum, perhaps in installments. Here's a letter presenting your case.

LETTER B

Mr. Kim Juarto
President
Imperial Hotels International
2345 Bali Drive
4404 Djakarta
Indonesia

Dear Mr. Juarto:

I am pleased to report that contract documents for Imperial's new hotel in Djakarta are now seventy-five percent complete. This puts us two weeks ahead of schedule.

I write, however, not just to keep you aware of progress but also to ask for your support in a matter we are having trouble resolving. At this point in the project, in line with our contractual agreement, we have invoiced your project management staff for $125,000 for services completed. We issued the original request for payment on 12 January 2005. To this day there was no response. We re-sent the invoice on 12 April, 12 June, and 12 October, but to no avail.

I would greatly appreciate your attention to this matter. Timely compensation is essential for our firm to operate. We are flexible within reason, and if necessary we can renegotiate a payment schedule that better suits you.

I look forward to hearing from you or your staff.

Sincerely yours

Ian Hansen

Principal

Adapted from a letter submitted by Mr. Hansen in an assignment the author gave to his class at the City College of New York

Speeches

Once established in an overseas nation, with a project well in hand, visiting principals are sometimes asked to speak at business, governmental, or professional functions. Contrary to the more informal delivery based on a few notes, as recommended in chapter 13, here it is prudent to write out your remarks beforehand and have them checked by a local colleague.

Other Qualifying Factors

The design and construction team on large overseas projects is typically composed of individuals and firms from all over the globe. Coordinating the process, with its array of different time zones, languages, and work methods, demands meticulous management. Hence communications, whether in writing or by voice, are a critical component of success. Follow these pointers:

• Recruit the ideal employee—a local design professional trained in the United States or other English-speaking nation;
• Vet all written material for potential misinterpretation of words, phrases, and usage;
• Become familiar with the host nation's culture and values;
• Keep written material simple: eliminate pages, sections, paragraphs, sentences, or words that don't contribute to the message and that could raise the odds on a gaffe finding its way into text,
• Say it through drawing if possible.

For style guidelines in expressing currencies, measurements, time zones, and phone numbers in overseas correspondence, including e-mail, refer to Hale, *WIRED Style* (see Resources).

How to Measure Impact 17

Ernest Hemingway would never have condoned using formulas to measure the quality of writing. But that doesn't reduce the value of monitoring and measuring writing quality. It serves everyone—design firms, public and corporate facility staffs, the professional and general design media, the building product manufacturing and advertising community, design students and faculty, and, above all, the reader.

Managers in each of these groups should commit regularly—once a year at least—to monitoring their communication program. Do this by gathering representative samples of your entire printed and on-line output. Then subject each item to rigorous evaluation of content and format. Include in the review a marketing principal, a project manager, a cooperative client, and, if possible, an impartial expert. This process alone will help principals and staff realize that quality standards apply as much to communication as to design.

For evaluating text and graphics, consider the set of editorial and graphic judging criteria developed some years ago by New York–based designer Ivan Chermayeff and myself. The criteria are flexible; you should modify them to fit the printed, CD-ROM, or Web product you are judging. Here is an updated, abridged excerpt of these criteria:

- *Planning, organizational logic*
  Are the contents logically organized?
  Is the organization clearly expressed through graphics?
- *Reader's wayfinding*
  Are charts, tables, and matrices easily understood by the layperson?
  Are titles and headlines clearly worded?
  Are visual devices (pull-quotes, decks, subheads) used as aids to readers?
  Are illustrations clearly captioned?
  Are paragraphs limited to comfortable reading length (twelve to fifteen lines)? On the Web site, is there a logical progression of content from the home or "splash" page? Are navigation bars provided? Do the links work?
- *Style*
  Are words and sentences short and devoid of jargon (see the eight principles of good writing in chapter 1)

Are spelling, punctuation, and abbreviation consistent?

Is the writing geared to the level of understanding of the audience's least informed reader?

Is the message intent clear?

- **Illustrations**

Are photographs of the appropriate quality for the medium (print, on-line, video)?

Are floor plans and other line drawings sharp, uncluttered, properly labeled, and equipped with scales and orientation indicators?

- **Production quality**

Is the paper stock appropriate to the purpose of the item? (Brochures can lose points for a design firm because they may be seen as too lavishly produced for a modestly financed client. Others suffer, by contrast, because they might seem stingily produced for a patron with luxury tastes.)

Is the printing good, not blurred or smudged?

Are the four process colors printed in good register, with no individual colors showing at the edges?

On a promotional CD-ROM or Web site, are images clear? Was the content formatted to the typical user's probable bandwidth?

- **Sparkle**

Is the overall impact one of freshness, imagination, and originality?

We also devised a scoring method for judging editorial and graphic quality. Each item is rated on a scale from -3 to +3. Best is +3. Each of the columns—one for editorial, one for graphic quality—is then added up, and overall averages computed. (In the example below, numbers are imaginary, not based on an actual item.) Clearly, there's much room for improvement.

SUBJECT	EDITORIAL	GRAPHIC
Planning, organizational logic	+2	+1
Reader's wayfinding	+2	0
Style	0	0
Illustrations	NA	-1
Production quality	NA	+3
Sparkle	+2	+2
Averages (rounded off)	6 ÷ 4 = 1.5	5 ÷ 6 = 1.0

Measuring Written Text

Among ways to measure a text without graphics, best known is the Fog Index, devised by the late Robert Gunning. It rewards clarity by penalizing you for using words that run to too many syllables. You are also penalized for overly long sentences. The index is tied to the presumed level of comprehension of the audience; this is measured by years of schooling. Thus a Fog Index of 17 presumes 17 years of schooling. The Fog Index works as follows:

1. Select a 100-word passage.
2. Count the number of words of three syllables or more.
3. Count the average number of words per sentence.
4. Add items 2 and 3, then multiply the result by 0.4.
5. The result is your Fog Index.

Typical Fog Indexes of professional magazines recently scanned are *Metropolis:* 15; *Architecture:* 15; *Architectural Record:* 13, some four points lower on average than when measured in 1998. Mass circulation magazines such as *People* and *Reader's Digest* typically clock in at less than 10. For more information on the subject, see *How to Take the Fog Out of Business Writing* in the Resources section.

Consider the following scenario. You manage marketing communications in your firm. You have recently come across examples of correspondence, proposals, and other marketing materials that, in your view, are dense and confusing. To make your point, you decide to begin by computing a Fog Index on a sample passage, then, edit the sample to improve its rating.

Applying the Fog Index

Sample passage (before editing):

> "The undersigned and her collaborating team members undertake to implement the necessary contract documents for your secondary level educational facility in the requested time frame of thirty-five work-weeks, with the understanding that in the eventuality of your adding programmatic elements to the scope of work, the completion date will be subject to postponement commensurate with the extent of the aforementioned scope increase. Nevertheless our firm has achieved an excellent level of accomplishment in its confrontations with difficult schedule requirements, and we feel to the highest degree confident that should this eventuality occur we will satisfy the demands of your committee to its satisfaction." [103 words]

Same passage, with words of three syllables or more shown underlined:

> "The <u>undersigned</u> and her <u>collaborating</u> team members <u>undertake</u> to <u>implement</u> the <u>necessary</u> contract <u>documents</u> for your <u>secondary</u> level <u>educational facility</u> in the <u>requested</u> timeframe of thirty-five workweeks, with the <u>understanding</u> that in the <u>eventuality</u> of your adding <u>programmatic elements</u> to the scope of work, the <u>completion</u> date will be subject to <u>postponement commensurate</u> with the extent of the <u>aforementioned</u> scope increase. <u>Nevertheless</u> our firm has achieved an <u>excellent</u> level of <u>accomplishment</u> in its <u>confrontations</u> with <u>difficult</u> schedule <u>requirements</u>, and we feel to the highest degree <u>confident</u> that should this <u>eventuality</u> occur we will <u>satisfy</u> the demands of your <u>committee</u> to its <u>satisfaction</u>."

Note that the long-word count is 29. The sentence count is 2, making the average sentence length 103 ÷ 2 = 51.5. Using Robert Gunning's formula:

1. Length of sample: 103 words
2. Number of long words: 29
3. Average sentence length: 51.5 words
4. (29 + 51.5) x 0.4 = 32.2

The passage yields a daunting Fog Index of 32.2.

Sample passage after editing:

> "Our project team commits to completing required contract documents for your high school within the stipulated thirty-five workweeks. Please realize that should you choose to add elements to the scope of work, the completion date may be delayed. The more modest the changes, the shorter the delay. Despite this risk, our firm has an excellent track record of meeting tough schedule demands. Thus we feel most confident that should you choose to enlarge your scope, we will still meet the time demands of your committee." [85 words]

After editing, the Fog Index drops sharply. A swift scan reveals a long-word count of 9, and an average sentence length of 85 ÷ 5 = 17 words. Thus 9 + 17 = 26, and when multiplied by 0.4 yields a score of 10.4. Note that in the editing process the length of the original passage dropped from 103 to 85, which itself helped to reduce the Index.

To help raise the writing quality in your firm, plan to select a half-dozen samples from your arsenal of communications products. Consider an item of e-mail correspondence, the executive summary from a recent report or proposal, the text from a design award submittal, a memo to your staff, a Web-posted vision statement, a midproject letter to a client. Identify one or more 100-word passages in each item and compute the Fog Indexes. Next, take those same passages, edit them to replace avoidable long words, shorten the sentences, then recompute the Fog Index. The aim is to share the findings with your staff and improve the firm's overall writing level.

Editing a Text

The act of editing covers several levels of effort. It can begin and end with simple editing for punctuation, spelling, and factual accuracy. It can build up to major surgery by replacing words, cutting sentences, and even rearranging entire paragraphs.

Supervisors in many professions are required to edit subordinates' writing, including those in design firms; public, institutional, or corporate facilities agencies; design schools; and magazines. Newcomers to editing should heed the following editing pointers:

- Identify the text's precise intent.
- Read the text through once; avoid getting bogged down in detail.
- Reread the text and make any major changes of structure, such as moving paragraphs or cutting out chunks of text that detract from the desired effect.
- Edit in detail, changing the order of sentences, replacing needlessly long words, and clarifying jargon. Check for spelling and correct usage (every firm or organization should have a style guide on hand; see the Resources). Verify factual accuracy.
- Reread what you have, and make final corrections. Check especially the opening paragraph (does it sing?) and the closing paragraph (does the text take its leave on the right note?).
- Note that tinkering with someone else's text can ruffle their ego. Be gentle with the author, but not with the text.

For an example, see the pre- and post-edited sample text below. If you edit directly on screen (and some editors find it easier), click on Tools, then on Track Changes. Changes show in red; this allows you to share pre- and post-edited versions with your staff (see page 216, top):

If you prefer to edit on paper, use traditional proofing marks (page 216 bottom and page 217).

Before
"The undersigned and her collaborating team members undertake to implement the necessary contract documents for your secondary level educational facility in the requested time frame of 35 workweeks, with the understanding that in the eventuality of your adding programmatic elements to the scope of work, the completion date will be subject to postponement commensurate with the extent of the aforementioned scope increase. Nevertheless our firm has achieved an excellent level of accomplishment in its confrontations with difficult schedule requirements, and we feel to the highest degree confident that should this eventuality occur we will satisfy the demands of your committee to its satisfaction."

After
"Our project team commits to completing required contract documents for your high school within the stipulated 35 workweeks. Please realize that should you choose to add elements to the scope of work, the completion date may be delayed. The more modest the changes, the shorter the delay. Despite this risk, our firm has an excellent track record of meeting tough schedule demands. Thus we feel most confident that should you choose to enlarge your scope, we will still meet the time demands of your committee."

~~The undersigned and her collaborating~~ Our project team commits to completing required contract documents ~~members undertake to implement the necessary~~ for your high school~~secondary level educational facility~~ within the stipulated ~~in the requested time frame of~~ 35 workweeks. Please realize that ~~;~~ should you ~~with the understanding that in the eventuality of your~~ choose to ~~adding programmatic~~ elements to the scope of work, the completion date may ~~will~~ be delayed. The more modest the changes, the shorter the delay. ~~subject to postponement commensurate with the extent of the aforementioned scope increase.~~ Despite that risk, our firm has ~~Nevertheless our firm has achieved~~ an excellent track record of meeting tough schedule demands. ~~level of accomplishment in its confrontations with difficult schedule requirements, and~~ Thus we feel ~~to the highest degree~~ confident that should you choose to enlarge your scope, ~~this eventuality occur~~ we will meet ~~satisfy~~ the time demands of your committee. ~~to its satisfaction.~~"

The edited copy showing tracked changes.

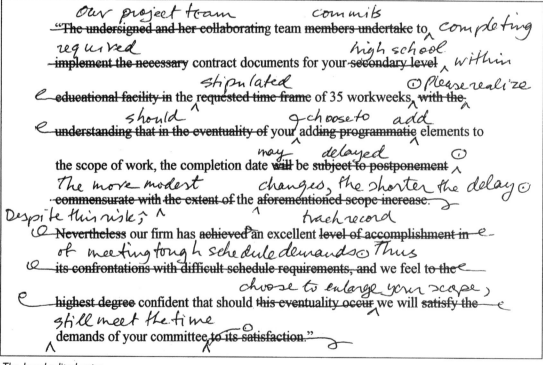

The hand-edited copy.

Cho͡ose paper with imagination.	ℓ	take out
Cho͡ose paper with imagination.	͡	close up
Cho‿se paper with imagination.	͡o	insert letter
Choose paper‿with imagination.	#	insert space
Choose paper wit‿ imagination.	h	change letter
Choose paper with imagination.	STET	keep as is
Choose p‿per with imagination.	∿	reverse letters
Choose‿with paper imagination.	⌒	transpose word
]Choose paper with imagination.	]	move in, align
[Choose paper with imagination.	[	move out, align
¶Choose paper with imagination.	¶	start paragraph
Choose paper ∕ith imagination.	/l.c.	lower case
choose paper with imagination.	≡u.c.	upper case
Choose paper with imagination.	ITAL	italicize
Choose paper with imagination.	══	set in small capitals
Choose paper with imagination.	═══	set all in capitals
Choose paper with imagination.	∿∿∿	set all in bold
Choose ▭ with imagination. paper	⌐⌐	align, raise and lower
Choose paper ∧ with imagination.	⋏	use a ∧ to add a ,
Choose paper with imagination⊙	⊙	use a O to add a .
Choose paper with imagination⊙	⊙	use a O to add a ; or :
Choose paper with imagination!∕	!∕	use a / to add a ! or ?
Choose paper‿with imagination.	-∕	use a / to add a -
Choose paper (with imagination.)	(∕)	use a / to add ( )
Choose paper [with imagination.]	[∕]	use a / to add [ ]
Choose paper⌄with imagination.⌄	⌄	use a ∨ to add ' and ""
▢Choose paper with imagination.	▢	Em quad space or indent

Common proofreading marks.

Conclusions   Good writing has become more critical than ever because the on-line medium demands a higher focus on economy of words and the arrangement of words for maximum impact. You see in some ways a throwback to the age of the telegram—whenever you use more words than you need, the long-term cost is on you.

Resources

WRITING

Branwyn, Gareth. *Jargon Watch: A Pocket Dictionary for the Jitterati.* San Francisco: HardWired, 1997. A 5- by 3½-inch nano-lexicon of cool jargon. My favorites are *domainism* ("Internet prejudice. Judging others on the basis of how cool/uncool their email address is. See also Domain Dropping."), and *cobweb,* a Web site that hasn't been updated for a long time; a dead Web page.

Brereton, John C. and Mansfield, Margaret A. *Writing on the Job.* New York: W. W. Norton, 1997. Practical writing guide in publisher's "pocket guide" series (actually fits in pocket) for all occupations. Generous with examples that cover format and content. Includes useful chapter on editing a text.

Capelin, Joan. *Communication by Design: Marketing Professional Services.* Atlanta: The Ostberg Press, 2005. Twenty-nine principles designed to create successful marketing communications, including press releases, presentations, and PR.

Frankfurt, Harry G. *On Bullshit.* Princeton, NJ: Princeton University Press, 2005. Separates the true from the—well, read the title. Defines the term and compares to such competing terms as *lie, humbug, claptrap, balderdash, hokum, drivel, imposture, quackery*, and *buncombe.* $9.95 worth of dynamite in sixty-eight pages. By September 2005, had been on the *New York Times* Sunday book review best-seller list for twenty-three weeks, ranking as high as sixth.

Gunning, R. and Kallan, R. A. *How to Take the Fog Out of Business Writing.* Chicago: Dartnell Corp., 1994. Includes a simple formula for determining the amount of "fog" in your firm's written output.

Hale, Constance, ed. *WIRED Style: Principles of English Usage in the Digital Age.* San Francisco: HardWired, 1996. Nimbly navigates the shifting verbal currents of the post-Gutenberg era. Covers new words, new meanings, new acronyms that come with onset of the Web. Coolly designed boxed book—prevailing colors are salmon, lime green, and black—shows how style is being shaped by modern digital custom. Includes listings of digital jargon.

Interstate Transportation Trainers. *Truck Divers Dictionary.* Jamaica, NY: Interstate Transportation Trainers, Inc., P.O. Box 229, Jamaica, NY 11431, no date. How truck drivers talk among themselves.

Kliment, Stephen A. "But What Do You *Mean?*" *Architecture*, November 1996. The uphill struggle for clarity in contemporary writing.

——. "Eschewing Obfuscation: Ideas for Cleaning Up Our Language Act." *Architectural Record,* April 1992.

Koren, David. *Architect's Essentials of Marketing.* Hoboken, NJ: John Wiley & Sons, 2005. Covers marketing strategy, business development (a.k.a. getting the job), and marketing tools and resources.

"Make Your Newsletter a Powerful Marketing Tool," *Design Firm Management and Administration Report,* February 2003. New York: IOMA, 2003. Setting objectives, content, and format. The five steps in preparing a good newsletter.

Minto, Barbara. *The Pyramid Principle: Logic in Writing and Thinking, 2nd ed.* London: Minto International Inc., 1996. How to organize your thoughts to build up a clear, logical message. A global classic.

Peña, William M. and Parshall, Steven A. *Problem Seeking: An Architectural Programming Primer, 4th ed.* Hoboken, NJ: John Wiley & Sons, 2001. Classic work describing the ideal procedure for defining a design problem—or any other problem, for that matter. The five steps are: establish goals; collect and analyze facts; uncover and test concepts; determine needs; state the problem.

Safford, Dan. *How to Write Winning Proposals: An Expert Guide to Planning, Writing and Managing Proposals That Win.* Seattle, WA: PS Associates, Inc., 2005. A detailed guide to effective tactics. http://www.psassociates.com.

Strunk, W. Jr. and White, E. B. *The Elements of Style, 4th ed.* Boston: Allyn and Bacon, 2000. Classic, no-nonsense 105-page book has revealed the principles of good writing to generations of American college students (first edition, 1935). Focus is on good usage of the English language, the best fast-track to clear writing. Celebrated rules include: "write in a way that comes naturally;" "write with nouns and verbs;" "do not overstate;" "do not explain too much;" "avoid fancy words." A higher-priced 2005 edition adds little beyond a series of arcane illustrations.

The Associated Press. *The Associated Press Stylebook and Libel Manual.* New York: The Associated Press, 2004. Complete guide to newspaper journalism.

——. *The Word: An Associated Press Guide to Good News Writing.* New York: The Associated Press, 2000.

The Chicago Manual of Style: The Essential Guide for Writers, Editors, and Publishers, 15th ed. Chicago: University of Chicago Press, 2003. This bible of writers and editors guarantees consistency.

Truss, Lynne. *Eats, Shoots & Leaves: The Zero Tolerance Approach to Punctuation.* New York: Gotham Books, 2003. Hilarious accounts of how sloppy punctuation leads to verbal disasters.

Welsh, Judith. *How to Write Powerful Press Releases.* Knoxville, TN: Eastern Media Network, 2004. When and how often to write a release, creating an angle, mastering the three most effective words ("free," "best," and "new"), and writing attention-gabbing heads. For use by all professions and crafts.

Wienbroer, D. R., Hughes, E., and Silverman, J. *Rules of Thumb for Business Writers, 2nd ed.* New York: McGraw-Hill, 2005. Any way you look at it, design professionals, when they write, are business writers, and must observe the same rules of thumb as reporters who write for the nation's business press. Helpful firing line advice is divided into six sections, including the writing process, correct usage and punctuation, and "writing with power."

Zinsser, William. *On Writing Well.* New York: HarperPerennial, 1998. Makes the point that good thinking must precede good writing. Author practices what he preaches.

SPEAKING

Larson, Orvin P. *When It's Your Turn to Speak.* New York: Harper & Row, 1971. A classic guide. Out of print but used copies available from on-line booksellers.

On Public Speaking. "No-brainer" series videocassette, with printed outline. Falls Church, VA: Cerebellum Corp., 1998. Cheerful guide to the challenges, errors, and pointers in preparing and delivering a good speech.

Stern, Robert A. M. *Final presentation by Robert Stern and two associates for the City of Jacksonville (FL) main library competition.* Videocassette. Miami, FL: SunCam Inc., 2001. Useful example of a successful presentation to a large—over twenty member—selection committee. Demonstrates effective use of words, sentences, voice tone, visual props, pauses, and responses to questions.

GRAPHICS

Linton, Harold. *Portfolio Design, 3rd ed.* New York: W. W. Norton, 2004. Practical handbook on the design of portfolios and its underlying self-marketing objectives. Covers graphic concept, page layout, and image selection.

Wurman, Richard Saul. *Information Architects.* New York: Graphis, Inc./ Watson Guptill Publications, 1997. High-style graphics illustrate architect Wurman's view that a disciplined process of logic and common sense underlie any good explanation. Includes one hundred examples of information design, using examples of graphic design by the world's top graphic designers, with lucid commentary by Wurman. Urges Wurman: "it's more important to get your point across than to be beautiful; edit drastically—don't include more information than the situation requires; gear new information to information the reader already has."

ON-LINE

Doherty, Paul. *Cyberplaces: The Internet Guide for Architects, Engineers, and Contractors, 2nd ed.* Kingston, MA.: R. S. Means Co., 2000. Accompanied by CD-ROM and Web access. Guide to training, applications, sites.

Krotz, Joanna L. *Got E-mail Manners? See These Dos and Don'ts.* One of several guides to creating and managing e-mail, posted by Microsoft on 19 May 2005, http://go.microsoft.com/?linkid=3063398. Solid advice on writing, managing e-mail communication.

SELECTED WEB SITES

www.architectureweek.com. News of design and building. Updated daily. Hyperlinked to news story sources.

www.archnewsnow.com. Daily compendium of news stories and articles on architecture and design from the world's media. Bulletins linked to sources, some of which require registration for access.

BROADCAST

Kalbfeld, Brad. *The Associated Press Broadcast News Handbook*. New York: McGraw-Hill, 2000. Speaks for itself.

PUBLICITY

AIA *archiwire*. Washington, DC: American Institute of Architects. Design professionals may post news about their firms as well as photos on this AIA-managed wire service, which distributes your news to main media. Cost: $150 per news release ($75 for AIA members). http://archiwire.aia.org.

Newsletters in Print. Farmington Hills, MI: Thomson Gale. Annual directory includes information on editorial focus and contact data.

2006 Awards Directory. Oakland, CA: Kenney and Associates. Lists over 650 award programs geared to architects, engineers, contractors, and related disciplines. www.kenneyassociates.com.

The Publicity Directory for the A/E/C Industry, 14th ed. Boston, MA: The Fuessler Group, Inc. Annual by subscription, includes quarterly updates. Available in hard copy and on CD. Lists over 200 professional magazines and webzines, with contact info. Includes all major national and regional architectural, engineering, interiors and landscape design, and construction magazines, as well as trade magazines serving clients' own markets, organized by key markets. Also posts latest editorial calendars, and tips on contacting the editors. www.fuessler.com/pub.html.

FIRM DIRECTORY

ProFile *The Architects Sourcebook, 20th ed*. Norcross, GA: Reed Construction Data, 2005. Listings include arrangement by firms, specialties, and key individuals. Excellent source for tracking and browsing individual firms' Web sites.

Credits

Color artwork photographed by Patricia Lambert.

PAGE 101: *Top left:* By permission of Butler Rogers Baskett Architects. Designed by Greg Simpson of Ephemera Design, Inc. *Top right:* By permission of the Architectural League. Design by Pentagram. *Bottom:* DS-8 Interior Rendering, 2000. Image by John Cirka for Zeidler Partnership Architects. From 2005 calendar by Autodessys. Inc.

PAGE 102: *Top left and right:* By permission of Platt Bayard Dovell White Architects, LLP. *Middle:* By permission of Holt Hinshaw. *Bottom:* By permission of H³ Hardy Collaboration Architecture, LLC. Photograph © Peter Mauss/ESTO. All rights reserved.

PAGE 103: *Top left and right:* By permission of Ann Beha Architects and Kohn Pedersen Fox. *Bottom left and right:* Courtesy Leslie E. Robertson Associates, RLLP.

PAGE 104: *Top left and right:* By permission of 3D/I. *Bottom:* Courtesy of F+K. Photo by Benny Chan.

PAGE 105: *Top left:* © 1974 Cahners Books, a division of Cahners Publishing Co., Inc. *Top center:* The Arup Journal © Arup 2005. Image: David Griffiths Photography. *Top right:* The Arup Journal © Arup 2005. Image: Christian Richters. *Center:* The Arup Journal © Arup 2005. Images: Dennis Gilbert/VIEW & Lesley Graham. *Bottom:* By permission of URS Corporation.

PAGE 106: *Top left:* Reproduced with permission from *@issue: The Journal of Business and Design*, V7N2, published by Corporate Design Foundation. Cover photo by Gerald Bybee. *Top right:* Reproduced by permission. © 2005 The American Institute of Architects New York Chapter. *Left:* Reprinted from *Engineering News-Record*, © The McGraw-Hill Companies, Inc. May 30, 2005. All rights reserved. *Center and bottom right:* Used with permission from *Architectural Record*, a division of The McGraw-Hill Companies, Inc. © 2005 McGraw-Hill. Center photo by Steve Hall © 2005 Hedrich Blessing.

PAGE 107: © Emap Construct 1998.

PAGE 108: *Top left and right:* Design by Pentagram. Reproduced by permission. Photos by Laboratorio de Creación Maldeojo. Introduction by Alex Marashian. *Bottom:* By permission of Pasanella + Klein Stolzman + Berg Architects. Design by Memo Productions. Photography by Paul Warchol.

Index